LITERATURE
Uses of the Imagination

Wish and Nightmare

Circle of Stories: One

Circle of Stories: Two

The Garden and the Wilderness

The Temple and the Ruin

Man the Myth-Maker

The Perilous Journey

A World Elsewhere: Romance

A World Enclosed: Tragedy

The Ways of the World: Satire and Irony

A World Remade: Comedy

The suggestions of reviewers have aided us in our final preparation of materials for this book. We gratefully acknowledge the critical assistance of:

Margaret Hamilton
La Cañada High School
La Cañada, California

Anne Hunter McMichael
Nova High School
Fort Lauderdale, Florida

Araminta Seal
John H. Reagan High School
Austin, Texas

Dana Wall
Sioux City Community Schools
Sioux City, Iowa

W. T. JEWKES

Professor of English
The Pennsylvania State University

Supervisory Editor
NORTHROP FRYE

University Professor
University of Toronto

A World Remade:
Comedy

HARCOURT BRACE JOVANOVICH, INC.

New York   Chicago   San Francisco   Atlanta   Dallas

Printed in the United States of America

ISBN 0-15-333540-8

ACKNOWLEDGMENTS: *For permission to reprint copyrighted material, grateful acknowledgment is made to the following sources:*

Delacorte Press: "Report on the Barnhouse Effect," copyright 1950 by Kurt Vonnegut, Jr. from *Welcome to the Monkey House* by Kurt Vonnegut, Jr. A Seymour Lawrence Book/Delacorte Press. Originally appeared in *Collier's.*

The Devin-Adair Company: "All the Sweet Buttermilk . . ." by Donagh MacDonagh from *44 Irish Short Stories,* copyright 1955 by The Devin-Adair Company.

Dodd, Mead & Company, Inc.: "Gertrude the Governess; or Simple Seventeen" from *Laugh With Leacock* by Stephen Leacock, copyright 1930 by Dodd, Mead & Company, Inc.; copyright renewed 1958 by George Leacock.

Doubleday & Company, Inc.: "Ballad of the Clairvoyant Widow," copyright 1941, 1951 by Theodore Roethke from *The Collected Poems of Theodore Roethke.*

Farrar, Straus & Giroux, Inc.: "The Key" from *A Friend of Kafka and Other Stories* by Isaac Bashevis Singer, copyright © 1969, 1970 by Isaac Bashevis Singer. Originally published in *The New Yorker* Magazine, December 6, 1969.

Raoul Lionel Felder, Executor of the Estate of Damon Runyon, Jr.: "Madame La Gimp" by Damon Runyon.

Grove Press, Inc.: Chapter Seventeen "Mecca" from *The Autobiography of Malcolm X* with the assistance of Alex Haley, copyright © 1964 by Alex Haley & Malcolm X; copyright © 1965 by Alex Haley and Betty Shabazz. From *Black Skin, White Masks* by Frantz Fanon, copyright © 1955 by Grove Press, Inc. Excerpts titled "The Umbrella Oracle" and "Busu" from *Anthology of Japanese Literature* by Donald Keene, copyright © 1955 by Grove Press, Inc.

Harcourt Brace Jovanovich, Inc.: "since feeling is first" and "nobody loses all the time" by E. E. Cummings, copyright, 1926, by Horace Liveright; renewed, 1954, by E. E. Cummings, from his volume *Poems 1923–1954.* "The People Will Live On" from *The People, Yes* by Carl Sandburg, copyright, 1936, by Harcourt Brace Jovanovich, Inc.; renewed, 1964, by Carl Sandburg. "The Beautiful Changes" from *The Beautiful Changes and Other Poems* by Richard Wilbur, copyright, 1947, by Richard Wilbur.

Harper & Row, Publishers, Inc.: "Just One More Time" from *The Brigadier and the Golf Widow* by John Cheever, copyright © 1955 by John Cheever.

Houghton Mifflin Company: An abridgment of "Mutsmag" from *Grandfather Tales,* collected and retold by Richard Chase, copyright 1948 by Richard Chase.

Alfred A. Knopf, Inc.: "My Father Enters the Church," copyright 1931, 1932 by Clarence Day; renewed 1960 by Mrs. Katharine B. Day, from *The Best of Clarence Day.*

The illustrations on pages xvi-1, 54-55, 112-13, 164-65, 210-11, and 260-61 are by Jeannine Guertin.

COVER: photograph by Allan Philiba

Contents

Introduction   xiii

1   The Way of the World

The Greatest Man in the World   JAMES THURBER   2
Catch-22   *from the novel by* JOSEPH HELLER   9
The John B. Sails   *a West Indian folk song*   12
Making the Right Connections   *from* The Importance of Being
    Earnest   OSCAR WILDE   14
Goodbye to All Cats   P. G. WODEHOUSE   27
My Father Enters the Church   CLARENCE DAY   44

2   The World's Way Undone

nobody loses all the time   E. E. CUMMINGS   56
Mutsmag   *an Appalachian folk tale retold by* RICHARD CHASE
    58
The Umbrella Oracle   IHARA SAIKAKU *translated by* RICHARD
    LANE   65
The Body in the Window-seat   *from* Arsenic and Old Lace
    JOSEPH KESSELRING   68
The Catbird Seat   JAMES THURBER   82
Busu   *a Japanese Nō play translated by* DONALD KEENE   92
"All for a lady fair"   *a medieval lyric translated by* BRIAN STONE
    99
"All the Sweet Buttermilk . . ."   DONAGH MAC DONAGH   101

3 Love Conquers All

Song WILLIAM BLAKE 114

Cupid and Psyche *a Greek myth retold by* JAY MACPHERSON
115

The Boor ANTON CHEKHOV *translated by* AVRAHM YARMOLIN-
SKY 126

Aucassin and Nicolette *a French legend retold by* BARBARA
LEONIE PICARD 140

Gertrude the Governess; or Simple Seventeen STEPHEN LEA-
COCK 147

There Goes the Bride *from* The Graduate CHARLES WEBB
156

4 The Beautiful Changes

Putting Winter to Bed E. J. PRATT 166

Madame La Gimp DAMON RUNYON 171

The Beautiful Changes RICHARD WILBUR 184

Pygmalion and Galatea *a Greek myth retold by* EDITH HAMILTON
189

A Blessing JAMES WRIGHT 192

The Key ISAAC BASHEVIS SINGER 193

A New Race *from* Childhood's End ARTHUR C. CLARKE
203

5 From the Mountain Top

New Life at Kyerefaso EUFA THEODORA SUTHERLAND 212

The Vision of Odin *a Scandinavian myth retold by* A. *and*
E. KEARY 218

"And I saw a new heaven and a new earth . . ." REVELATION
21: 1–5 220

The Rose-Beetle Man *from* My Family and Other Animals
  GERALD DURRELL 221

"The wolf also shall dwell with the lamb . . ." ISAIAH 11: 6–9
  231

Happiness *from the* Dhammapada, *a Buddhist scripture translated by* F. MAX MULLER 232

Changes IV *words and music by* CAT STEVENS 233

Mecca *from* The Autobiography of Malcolm X MALCOLM X
  237

The Steeple-Jack MARIANNE MOORE 252

A Human World *from* Black Skins, White Masks FRANTZ FANON
  255

6 The People Will Live On

Carry On STEPHEN STILLS 262

Just One More Time JOHN CHEEVER 263

Holiday Memory DYLAN THOMAS 268

The First Jasmines RABINDRANATH TAGORE 275

A Refusal to Mourn the Death, by Fire, of a Child in London
  DYLAN THOMAS 276

Report on the Barnhouse Effect KURT VONNEGUT, JR. 277

since feeling is first E. E. CUMMINGS 294

Ballad of a Clairvoyant Widow THEODORE ROETHKE 295

The People Will Live On CARL SANDBURG 297

Index 303

Introduction

Without a sense of pattern in life, man would feel like a lonely child lost in a vast dark forest. But because of his powers of observation, man is able to perceive patterns in the world around him: the daily cycle of day and night; the seasonal cycle of spring, summer, autumn, and winter; the life cycle of birth, maturity, death, and rebirth through succeeding generations. In addition to these outer, physical patterns, man is also conscious of patterns in his inner world. He fears the harshness of winter, disease, and death. He longs for the warmth of summer, health, and life.

Just as patterns recur in our outer and inner worlds, they also recur in our imaginative expressions—that is, in our literature. In fact the recurring imaginative patterns of the whole human race are reflected in literature. Just as we see in nature the cycle of the seasons, so we can see a cycle of related narrative patterns in literature: Romance, Tragedy, Irony, and Comedy. Romance tells us how strong and beautiful heroes and heroines set out in search of the kind of world that we would all ideally like to live in—a green and golden world of eternal summer. Tragedy tells the story of how man, though he is capable of great and noble things, must at last come to terms with the limits of his power to change the world, and how he must inevitably fall toward death, just as autumn leaves must fall. Irony presents us with experience in the wintry world, the opposite of sunny Romance. In Irony, happy dreams of brave new worlds vanish in the harsh light of experience, and man's principal challenge is to find a way of surviving in an alien universe. Finally, Comedy tells the story of how new societies emerge to take the place of old, dying ones. In Comedy new life springs up through the barriers that try to hold it back, much as new shoots in spring break forth from the barren winter earth.

Each of these four basic story patterns—Romance, Tragedy, Irony, and Comedy—is presented in the books in this series. Like each season, each story form is unique in itself. But just as the four seasons together make up the story of the year's natural cycle, so too these four story patterns make up the story of the human race. This larger story tells us how man is born into a great inheritance, how he somehow loses it and must wander far in lonely desert places, and how he at last, by his own creative efforts, is able to regain what he lost.

W. T. J.

A World Remade: Comedy

1

THE WAY OF THE WORLD

Jeannine Guertin

The Greatest Man
in the World

JAMES THURBER

Looking back on it now, from the vantage point of 1940, one can only marvel that it hadn't happened long before it did. The United States of America had been, ever since Kitty Hawk, blindly constructing the elaborate petard by which, sooner or later, it must be hoist. It was inevitable that some day there would come roaring out of the skies a national hero of insufficient intelligence, background, and character successfully to endure the mounting orgies of glory prepared for aviators who stayed up a long time or flew a great distance. Both Lindbergh and Byrd, fortunately for national decorum and international amity, had been gentlemen; so had our other famous aviators. They wore their laurels gracefully, withstood the awful weather of publicity, married excellent women, usually of fine family, and quietly retired to private life and the enjoyment of their varying fortunes. No untoward incidents, on a worldwide scale, marred the perfection of their conduct on the perilous heights of fame. The exception to the rule was, however, bound to occur, and it did, in July 1937, when Jack ("Pal") Smurch, erstwhile mechanic's helper in a small garage in Westfield, Iowa, flew a secondhand, single-motored Bresthaven Dragon-Fly III monoplane all the way around the world, without stopping.

Never before in the history of aviation had such a flight as Smurch's ever been dreamed of. No one had even taken seriously the weird floating auxiliary gas tanks, invention of the mad New Hampshire professor of astronomy, Dr. Charles Lewis Gresham, upon which Smurch placed full reliance. When the garage worker, a slightly built, surly, unprepossessing young man of twenty-two, appeared at Roosevelt Field in early July 1937, slowly chewing a great quid of scrap tobacco, and announced, "Nobody ain't seen no flyin' yet," the newspapers touched briefly and satirically upon his projected twenty-five-thousand-mile flight. Aeronautical and automotive experts dismissed the idea curtly, implying that it was a hoax, a publicity stunt. The rusty, battered, secondhand plane wouldn't go. The Gresham auxiliary tanks wouldn't work. It was simply a cheap joke.

Smurch, however, after calling on a girl in Brooklyn who worked in the flap-folding department of a large paper-box factory, a girl whom he later described as his "swect patootie," climbed nonchalantly into his ridiculous plane at dawn of the memorable seventh of July, 1937, spit a curve of tobacco juice into the still air, and took off, carrying with him only a gallon of bootleg gin and six pounds of salami.

When the garage boy thundered out over the ocean, the papers were forced to record, in all seriousness, that a mad, unknown young man—his name was variously misspelled—had actually set out upon a preposterous attempt to span the world in a rickety, one-engined contraption, trusting to the long-distance refueling device of a crazy schoolmaster. When, nine days later, without having stopped once, the tiny plane appeared above San Francisco Bay, headed for New York, spluttering and choking, to be sure, but still magnificently and miraculously aloft, the headlines, which long since had crowded everything else off the front page—even the shooting of the Governor of Illinois by the Vileti gang—swelled to unprecedented size, and the news stories began to run to twenty-five and thirty columns. It was noticeable, however, that the accounts of the epoch-making flight touched rather lightly upon the aviator himself. This was not because facts about the hero as a man were too meager but because they were too complete.

Reporters, who had been rushed out to Iowa when Smurch's plane was first sighted over the little French coast town of Serly-le-Mer, to dig up the story of the great man's life, had promptly discovered that the story of his life could not be printed. His mother, a sullen short-order cook in a shack restaurant on the edge of a tourists' camping ground near Westfield, met all inquiries as to her son with an angry "Ah, I hope he drowns." His father appeared to be in jail somewhere for stealing spotlights and lap robes from tourists' automobiles; his younger brother, a weak-minded lad, had but recently escaped from the Preston, Iowa Reformatory and was already wanted in several western towns for the theft of money-order blanks from post offices. These alarming discoveries were still piling up at the very time that Pal Smurch, the greatest hero of the twentieth century, blear-eyed, dead for sleep, half-starved, was piloting his crazy junkheap high above the region in which the lamentable story of his private life was being unearthed, headed for New York and a greater glory than any man of his time had ever known.

The necessity for printing some account in the papers of the young man's career and personality had led to a remarkable predicament. It was of course impossible to reveal the facts, for a tremendous popular feeling in favor of the young hero had sprung up, like a grass fire, when he was halfway across Europe on his flight around the globe. He was, therefore, described as a modest chap, taciturn, blond, popular with his friends, popular with girls. The only available snapshot of Smurch, taken at the wheel of a phony automobile in a cheap photo studio at an amusement park, was touched up so that the little vulgarian looked quite handsome. His twisted leer was smoothed into a pleasant smile. The truth was, in this way, kept from the youth's ecstatic compatriots; they did not dream that the Smurch family was despised and feared by its neighbors in the obscure Iowa town, nor that the hero himself, because of numerous unsavory exploits, had come to be regarded in Westfield as a nuisance and a menace. He had, the reporters discovered, once knifed the principal of his high school—not mortally, to be sure, but he had knifed him; and on another occasion, surprised in the act of stealing an altar cloth from a church, he had bashed the sacristan over the head with a pot of Easter lilies; for each of these offenses he had served a sentence in the reformatory.

Inwardly, the authorities, both in New York and in Washington, prayed that an understanding Providence might, however awful such a thing seemed, bring disaster to the rusty, battered plane and its illustrious pilot, whose unheard-of flight had aroused the civilized world to hosannas of hysterical praise. The authorities were convinced that the character of the renowned aviator was such that the limelight of adulation was bound to reveal him, to all the world, as a congenital hooligan, mentally and morally unequipped to cope with his own prodigious fame. "I trust," said the Secretary of State, at one of many secret Cabinet meetings called to consider the national dilemma, "I trust that his mother's prayer will be answered," by which he referred to Mrs. Emma Smurch's wish that her son might be drowned. It was, however, too late for that—Smurch had leaped the Atlantic and then the Pacific as if they were millponds. At three minutes after two o'clock on the afternoon of July 17, 1937, the garage boy brought his idiotic plane into Roosevelt Field for a perfect three-point landing.

It had, of course, been out of the question to arrange a modest little reception for the greatest flier in the history of the world. He was received at Roosevelt Field with such elaborate and pretentious ceremonies as rocked the world. Fortunately, however, the worn and spent hero promptly swooned, had to be removed bodily from his plane, and was spirited from the field without having opened his mouth once. Thus he did not jeopardize the dignity of this first reception illumined by the presence of the Secretaries of War and the Navy, Mayor Michael J. Moriarity of New York, the Premier of Canada, Governors Fanniman, Groves, McFeely, and Critchfield, and a brilliant array of European diplomats. Smurch did not, in fact, come to in time to take part in the gigantic hullabaloo arranged at City Hall for the next day. He was rushed to a secluded nursing home and confined in bed. It was nine days before he was able to get up or, to be more exact, before he was permitted to get up. Meanwhile the greatest minds in the country, in solemn assembly, had arranged a secret conference of city, state, and government officials, which Smurch was to attend for the purpose of being instructed in the ethics and behavior of heroism.

On the day that the little mechanic was finally allowed to get up and dress and, for the first time in two weeks, took a great chew of tobacco, he was permitted to receive the newspapermen—this by way of testing him out. Smurch did not wait for questions. "Youse guys," he said—and the *Times* man winced—"youse guys can tell the cock-eyed world dat I put it over on Lindbergh, see? Yeh—an' made fools o' them two frogs." The "two frogs" was a reference to a pair of gallant French fliers who, in attempting a flight only halfway round the world, had, two weeks before, unhappily been lost at sea. The *Times* man was bold enough, at this point, to sketch out for Smurch the accepted formula for interviews in cases of this kind; he explained that there should be no arrogant statements belittling the achievements of other heroes, particularly heroes of foreign nations. "Ah, enough of that," said Smurch. "I did it, see? I did it, an' I'm talkin' about it." And he did talk about it.

None of this extraordinary interview was, of course, printed. On the contrary, the newspapers, already under the disciplined direction of a secret directorate created for the occasion and composed of statesmen and editors, gave out to a panting and restless world that "Jacky," as he had been arbitrarily nicknamed, would consent to say only that he was very happy and that anyone could have done what he did. "My achievement has been, I fear, slightly exaggerated," the *Times* man's article had him protest, with a modest smile. These newspaper stories were kept from the hero, a restriction which did not serve to abate the rising malevolence of his temper. The situation was, indeed, extremely grave, for Pal Smurch was, as he kept insisting, "rarin' to go." He could not much longer be kept from a nation clamorous to lionize him. It was the most desperate crisis the United States of America had faced since the sinking of the *Lusitania*.

On the afternoon of the twenty-seventh of July, Smurch was spirited away to a conference room in which were gathered mayors, governors, government officials, behaviorist psychologists, and editors. He gave them each a limp, moist paw and a brief, unlovely grin. "Hah ya?" he said. When Smurch was seated, the Mayor of New York arose and, with obvious pessimism, attempted to explain what he must say and how he must act when presented to the world, ending his talk with a high tribute to the hero's courage and integrity. The Mayor was followed by Governor Fanniman of New York, who, after a touching declaration of faith, introduced Cameron Spottiswood, Second Secretary of the American Embassy in Paris, the gentleman selected to coach Smurch in the amenities of public ceremonies. Sitting in a chair, with a soiled yellow tie in his hand and his shirt open at the throat, unshaved, smoking a rolled cigarette, Jack Smurch listened with a leer on his lips. "I get ya, I get ya," he cut in nastily. "Ya want me to ack like a softy, huh? Ya want me to ack like that—— baby-faced Lindbergh, huh? Well, nuts to that, see?" Everyone took in his breath sharply; it was a sigh and a hiss. "Mr. Lindbergh," began a United States Senator, purple with rage, "and Mr. Byrd—" Smurch, who was paring his nails with a jackknife, cut in again. "Byrd!" he exclaimed. "Aw, *dat* big—" Somebody shut off his blasphemies with a sharp word. A newcomer had entered the room. Everyone stood up, except Smurch, who, still busy with his nails, did not even glance up. "Mr. Smurch," said someone sternly, "the President of the United States!" It had been thought that the presence of the Chief Executive might have a chastening effect upon the young hero, and the former had been, thanks to the remarkable cooperation of the press, secretly brought to the obscure conference room.

A great, painful silence fell, Smurch looked up, waved a hand at the President. "How ya comin'?" he asked, and began rolling a fresh cigarette. The silence deepened. Someone coughed in a strained way. "Geez, it's hot, ain't it?" said Smurch. He loosened two more shirt buttons, revealing a hairy chest and the tattooed word "Sadie" enclosed in a stenciled heart. The great and important men in the room, faced by the most serious crisis in recent American history, exchanged worried frowns. Nobody seemed to know how to proceed. "Come awn, come awn," said Smurch. "Let's get out of here! When do I start cuttin' in on de parties, huh? And what's they goin' to be *in* it?" He rubbed a thumb and forefinger together meaningly. "Money!" exclaimed a state senator, shocked, pale. "Yeh, money," said Pal, flipping his cigarette out of a window. "An' big money." He began rolling a fresh cigarette. "Big money," he repeated, frowning over the rice paper. He tilted back in his chair and leered at each gentleman, separately, the leer of an animal that knows its power, the leer of a leopard loose in a bird-and-dog shop. "Aw, let's get some place where it's cooler," he said. "I been cooped up plenty for three weeks!"

Smurch stood up and walked over to an open window, where he stood staring down into the street, nine floors below. The faint shouting of newsboys floated up to him. He made out his name. "Hot dog!" he cried, grinning, ecstatic. He leaned out over the sill. "You tell 'em, babies!" he shouted down. "Hot diggity dog!" In the tense little knot of men standing behind him, a quick, mad impulse flared up. An unspoken word of appeal, of command, seemed to ring through the room. Yet it was deadly silent. Charles K. L. Brand, secretary to the Mayor of New York City, happened to be standing nearest Smurch; he looked inquiringly at the President of the United States. The President, pale, grim, nodded shortly. Brand, a tall, powerfully built man, once a tackle at Rutgers, stepped forward, seized the greatest man in the world by his left shoulder and the seat of his pants, and pushed him out the window.

"He's fallen out the window!" cried a quick-witted editor.

"Get me out of here!" cried the President. Several men sprang to his side, and he was hurriedly escorted out of a door toward a side entrance of the building. The editor of the Associated Press took charge, being used to such things. Crisply he ordered certain men to leave, others to stay; quickly he outlined a story which all the papers were to agree on, sent two men to the street to handle that end of the tragedy, commanded a Senator to sob and two Congressmen to go to pieces nervously. In a word, he skillfully set the stage for the gigantic task that was to follow, the task of breaking to a grief-stricken world the sad story of the untimely, accidental death of its most illustrious and spectacular figure.

The funeral was, as you know, the most elaborate, the finest, the solemnest, and the saddest ever held in the United States of America. The monument in Arlington Cemetery, with its clean white shaft of marble and the simple device of a tiny plane carved on its base, is a place for pilgrims, in deep reverence, to visit. The nations of the world paid lofty tributes to little Jacky Smurch, America's greatest hero. At a given hour there were two minutes of silence throughout the nation. Even the inhabitants of the small, bewildered town of Westfield, Iowa, observed this touching ceremony; agents of the Department of Justice saw to that. One of them was especially assigned to stand grimly in the doorway of a little shack restaurant on the edge of the tourists' camping ground just outside the town. There, under his stern scrutiny, Mrs. Emma Smurch bowed her head above two hamburger steaks sizzling on her grill—bowed her head and turned away, so that the Secret Service man could not see the twisted, strangely familiar, leer on her lips.

How do the government authorities want Smurch to behave? What does Smurch want to do?

Why is the society in this story not a free and open one? Why do you think a society or a group might fear odd or non-conforming behavior?

Why do the government officials succeed in preventing Smurch from doing what he wants? Do you think Smurch should have been allowed to be himself? Why or why not?

Can you think of current examples of this conflict between the less-than-perfect individual being himself and the public or official expectations of a national figure?

Catch-22

From the novel by
JOSEPH HELLER

"You're wasting your time," Doc Daneeka was forced to tell him.

"Can't you ground someone who's crazy?"

"Oh, sure. I have to. There's a rule saying I have to ground anyone who's crazy."

"Then why don't you ground me? I'm crazy. Ask Clevinger."

"Clevinger? Where is Clevinger? You find Clevinger and I'll ask
him."

"Then ask any of the others. They'll tell you how crazy I am."

"They're crazy."

"Then why don't you ground them?"

"Why don't they ask me to ground them?"

"Because they're crazy, that's why."

"Of course they're crazy," Doc Daneeka replied. "I just told you
they're crazy, didn't I? And you can't let crazy people decide whether
you're crazy or not, can you?"

Yossarian looked at him soberly and tried another approach. "Is
Orr crazy?"

"He sure is," Doc Daneeka said.

"Can you ground him?"

"I sure can. But first he has to ask me to. That's part of the rule."

"Then why doesn't he ask you to?"

"Because he's crazy," Doc Daneeka said. "He has to be crazy to keep
flying combat missions after all the close calls he's had. Sure, I can
ground Orr. But first he has to ask me to."

"That's all he has to do to be grounded?"

"That's all. Let him ask me."

"And then you can ground him?" Yossarian asked.

"No. Then I can't ground him."

"You mean there's a catch?"

"Sure there's a catch," Doc Daneeka replied. "Catch-22. Anyone who wants to get out of combat duty isn't really crazy."

There was only one catch and that was Catch-22, which specified that a concern for one's own safety in the face of dangers that were real and immediate was the process of a rational mind. Orr was crazy and could be grounded. All he had to do was ask; and as soon as he did, he would no longer be crazy and would have to fly more missions. Orr would be crazy to fly more missions and sane if he didn't, but if he was sane he had to fly them. If he flew them he was crazy and didn't have to; but if he didn't want to he was sane and had to. Yossarian was moved very deeply by the absolute simplicity of this clause of Catch-22 and let out a respectful whistle.

"That's some catch, that Catch-22," he observed.

"It's the best there is," Doc Daneeka agreed.

Yossarian saw it clearly in all its spinning reasonableness. There was an elliptical precision about its perfect pairs of parts that was graceful and shocking, like good modern art, and at times Yossarian wasn't quite sure that he saw it all, just the way he was never quite sure about good modern art or about the flies Orr saw in Appleby's eyes. He had Orr's word to take for the flies in Appleby's eyes.

"Oh, they're there, all right," Orr had assured him about the flies in Appleby's eyes after Yossarian's fist fight with Appleby in the officers' club, "although he probably doesn't even know it. That's why he can't see things as they really are."

"How come he doesn't know it?" inquired Yossarian.

"Because he's got flies in his eyes," Orr explained with exaggerated patience. "How can he see he's got flies in his eyes if he's got flies in his eyes?"

It made as much sense as anything else, and Yossarian was willing to give Orr the benefit of the doubt because Orr was from the wilderness outside New York City and knew so much more about wildlife than Yossarian did, and because Orr, unlike Yossarian's mother, father, sister, brother, aunt, uncle, in-law, teacher, spiritual leader, legislator, neighbor and newspaper, had never lied to him about anything crucial before. Yossarian had mulled his newfound knowledge about Appleby over in private for a day or two and then decided, as a good deed, to pass the word along to Appleby himself.

"Appleby, you've got flies in your eyes," he whispered helpfully as they passed by each other in the doorway of the parachute tent on the day of the weekly milk run to Parma.

"What?" Appleby responded sharply, thrown into confusion by the fact that Yossarian had spoken to him at all.

"You've got flies in your eyes," Yossarian repeated. "That's probably why you can't see them."

Appleby retreated from Yossarian with a look of loathing bewilderment and sulked in silence until he was in the jeep with Havermeyer riding down the long, straight road to the briefing room, where Major Danby, the fidgeting group operations officer, was waiting to conduct the preliminary briefing with all the lead pilots, bombardiers and navigators. Appleby spoke in a soft voice so that he would not be heard by the driver or by Captain Black, who was stretched out with his eyes closed in the front seat of the jeep.

"Havermeyer," he asked hesitantly. "Have I got flies in my eyes?"

Havermeyer blinked quizzically, "Sties?" he asked.

"No, flies," he was told.

Havermeyer blinked again. "Flies?"

"In my eyes."

"You must be crazy," Havermeyer said.

"No, I'm not crazy. Yossarian's crazy. Just tell me if I've got flies in my eyes or not. Go ahead. I can take it."

Havermeyer popped another piece of peanut brittle into his mouth and peered very closely into Appleby's eyes.

"I don't see any," he announced.

Appleby heaved an immense sigh of relief. Havermeyer had tiny bits of peanut brittle adhering to his lips, chin and cheeks.

"You've got peanut brittle crumbs on your face," Appleby remarked to him.

"I'd rather have peanut brittle crumbs on my face than flies in my eyes," Havermeyer retorted.

If Catch-22 is an example, what kind of rules do these military authorities set down?

How is Yossarian's position in relation to authority similar to Pal Smurch's?

The John B. Sails

A West Indian folk song

Oh, we come on the sloop *John B.*, My gran'-fad-der an' me.

Round Nas - sau Town we did roam, Drink - ing all

night, we got in a fight, I feel so break - up I want to go

REFRAIN

home! So hoist up the *John B.* sails, See how de main - s'l set,

Send for de Capt'n a - shore, Lem - me go home! Lem - me go

home! .... Lem - me go home! I

feel so break - up I want to go home! ....

2. De first mate he got drunk,
   Break up de people's trunk.
   Constable come aboard an' take him away.
   Mr. Johnstone, please let me alone.
   I feel so break-up I want to go home! REFRAIN

3. De poor cook he got fits,
   Tro' 'way all de grits,
   Den he took an' eat up all o' my corn!
   Lemme go home, I want to go home!
   Dis is de worst trip since I been born! REFRAIN

How are the experiences of the young man in this song similar to those of
Yossarian and Pal Smurch?

Making the Right Connections

From The Importance of Being Earnest
OSCAR WILDE

Characters

JOHN (JACK) WORTHING, *alias Ernest Worthing*

ALGERNON MONCRIEFF, *friend of Jack*

LADY BRACKNELL, *Algernon's aunt*

GWENDOLEN FAIRFAX, *Lady Bracknell's daughter*

LANE, *Algernon's butler*

Morning room in Algernon's flat in Half-Moon Street [London]. The room is luxuriously and artistically furnished.

(Enter LANE.)

LANE.   Lady Bracknell and Miss Fairfax.

(ALGERNON goes forward to meet them. Enter LADY BRACKNELL and GWENDOLEN.)

LADY BRACKNELL.   Good afternoon, dear Algernon, I hope you are behaving very well.

ALGERNON.   I'm feeling very well, Aunt Augusta.

LADY BRACKNELL.   That's not quite the same thing. In fact the two things rarely go together. *(Sees JACK and bows to him with icy coldness.)*

ALGERNON *(to GWENDOLEN)*.   Dear me, you are smart!

GWENDOLEN.   I am always smart! Am I not, Mr. Worthing?

JACK.   You're quite perfect, Miss Fairfax.

GWENDOLEN.   Oh! I hope I am not that. It would leave no room for developments, and I intend to develop in many directions. *(GWENDOLEN and JACK sit down together in the corner.)*

LADY BRACKNELL.   I'm sorry if we are a little late, Algernon, but I was obliged to call on dear Lady Harbury. I hadn't been there since her poor husband's death. I never saw a woman so altered; she looks quite twenty years younger. And now I'll have a cup of tea and one of those nice cucumber sandwiches you promised me.

ALGERNON.   Certainly, Aunt Augusta. (*Goes over to tea table.*)

LADY BRACKNELL.   Won't you come and sit here, Gwendolen?

GWENDOLEN.   Thanks, Mama, I'm quite comfortable where I am.

ALGERNON (*picking up empty plate in horror*).   Good heavens! Lane! Why are there no cucumber sandwiches? I ordered them specially.

LANE (*gravely*).   There were no cucumbers in the market this morning, sir. I went down twice.

ALGERNON.   No cucumbers!

LANE.   No, sir. Not even for ready money.

ALGERNON.   That will do, Lane, thank you.

LANE.   Thank you, sir. (*Goes out.*)

ALGERNON.   I am greatly distressed, Aunt Augusta, about there being no cucumbers, not even for ready money.

LADY BRACKNELL.   It really makes no matter, Algernon. I had some crumpets with Lady Harbury, who seems to me to be living entirely for pleasure now.

ALGERNON.   I hear her hair has turned quite gold from grief.

LADY BRACKNELL.   It certainly has changed its color. From what cause I, of course, cannot say. (ALGERNON *crosses and hands tea.*) Thank you. I've quite a treat for you tonight, Algernon. I am going to send you down with Mary Farquhar. She is such a nice woman, and so attentive to her husband. It's delightful to watch them.

ALGERNON.   I am afraid, Aunt Augusta, I shall have to give up the pleasure of dining with you tonight after all.

LADY BRACKNELL (*frowning*).   I hope not, Algernon. It would put my table completely out. Your uncle would have to dine upstairs. Fortunately he is accustomed to that.

ALGERNON.   It is a great bore, and, I need hardly say, a terrible disappointment to me, but the fact is I have just had a telegram to say that my poor friend Bunbury is very ill again. (*Exchanges glances with* JACK.) They seem to think I should be with him.

LADY BRACKNELL.   It is very strange. This Mr. Bunbury seems to suffer from curiously bad health.

ALGERNON.   Yes, poor Bunbury is a dreadful invalid.

LADY BRACKNELL.   Well, I must say, Algernon, that I think it is high

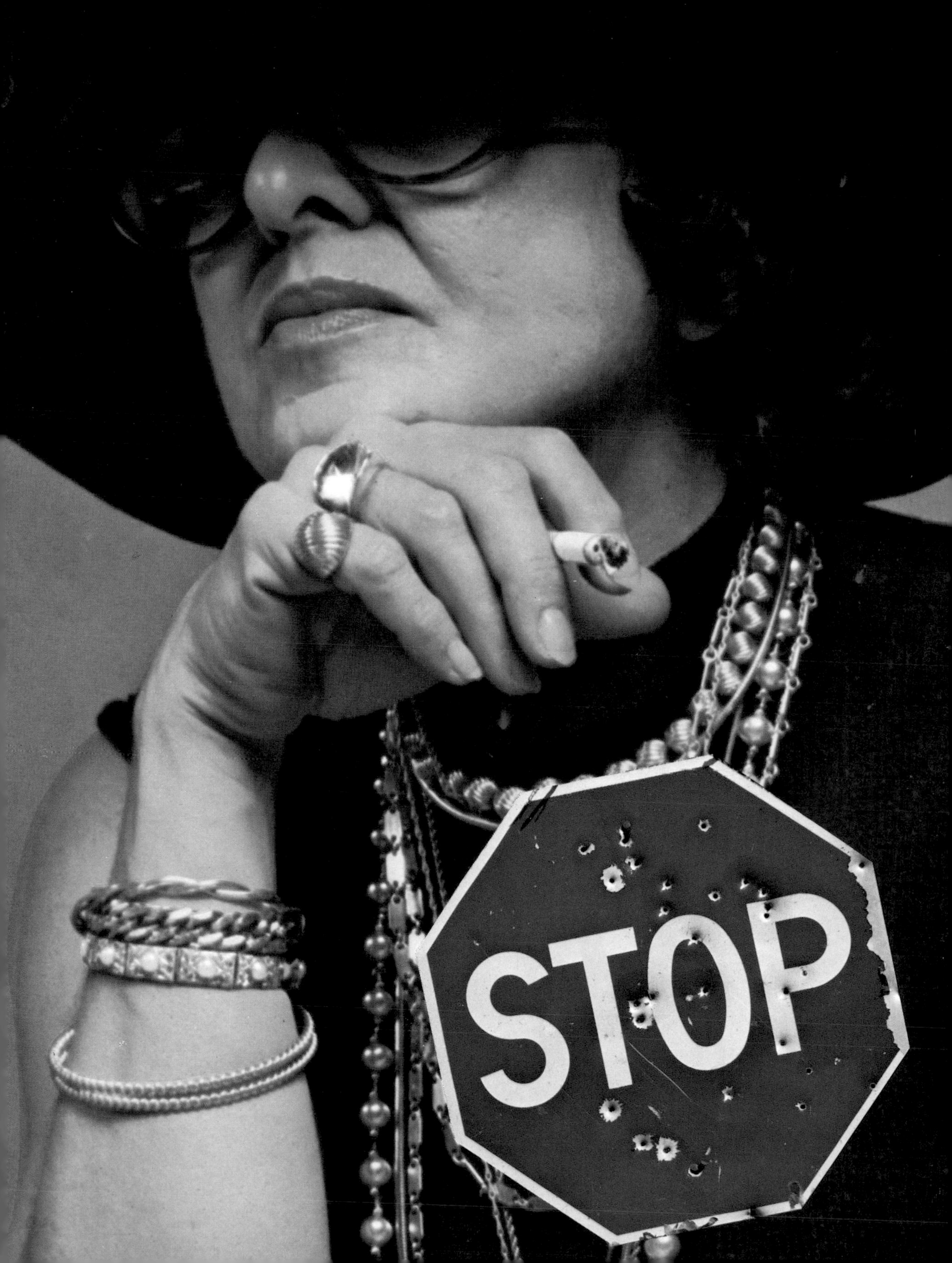
STOP

Hans Moser

© 1970 Hans Moser

coming back suddenly into a roo
her about.

JACK (*nervously*).   Miss Fair
you more than any g

GWENDOLEN.   Yes, I an
in public, at any rate, y
have always had an irre
I was far from indifferent
We live, as I hope you know,
fact is constantly mentioned in
zines, and has reached the provinc
has always been to love someone
something in that name that inspires
ment Algernon first mentioned to me
Ernest, I knew I was destined to love you.

JACK.   You really love me, Gwendolen?

GWENDOLEN.   Passionately!

JACK.   Darling! You don't know how happy you've m

GWENDOLEN.   My own Ernest!

JACK.   But you don't really mean to say that you couldn
my name wasn't Ernest?

GWENDOLEN.   But your name is Ernest.

JACK.   Yes, I know it is. But supposing it was something else? L
mean to say you couldn't love me then?

GWENDOLEN (*glibly*).   Ah! That is clearly a metaphysical speculatio,
and like most metaphysical speculations has very little reference at
all to the actual facts of real life, as we know them.

JACK.   Personally, darling, to speak quite candidly, I don't much care
about the name of Ernest. . . . I don't think the name suits me at all.

GWENDOLEN.   It suits you perfectly. It is a divine name. It has a music
of its own. It produces vibrations.

JACK.   Well, really, Gwendolen, I must say that I think there are lots
of other much nicer names. I think Jack, for instance, a charming
name.

GWENDOLEN.   Jack? . . . No, there is very little music in the name Jack,
if any at all, indeed. It does not thrill. It produces absolutely no vibrations. . . . I have known several Jacks, and they all, without exception, were more than usually plain. Besides, Jack is a notorious
domesticity for John! And I pity any woman who is married to a
man called John. She would probably never be allowed to know the

ng pleasure of a single moment's solitude. The only really
me is Ernest.

wendolen, I must get christened at once—I mean we must get
ed at once. There is no time to be lost.

OLEN.   Married, Mr. Worthing?

stounded).   Well . . . surely. You know that I love you, and you
me to believe, Miss Fairfax, that you were not absolutely indif-
erent to me.

NDOLEN.   I adore you. But you haven't proposed to me yet. Nothing has been said at all about marriage. The subject has not even
been touched on.

ACK.   Well . . . may I propose to you now?

GWENDOLEN.   I think it would be an admirable opportunity. And to
spare you any possible disappointment, Mr. Worthing, I think it
only fair to tell you quite frankly beforehand that I am fully determined to accept you.

JACK.   Gwendolen!

GWENDOLEN.   Yes, Mr. Worthing, what have you got to say to me?

JACK.   You know what I have got to say to you.

GWENDOLEN   Yes, but you don't say it.

JACK (goes on his knees).   Gwendolen, will you marry me?

GWENDOLEN.   Of course I will, darling. How long you have been about
it! I am afraid you have had very little experience in how to propose.

JACK.   My own one, I have never loved anyone in the world but you.

GWENDOLEN.   Yes, but men often propose for practice. I know my
brother Gerald does. All my girl-friends tell me so. What wonder-
fully blue eyes you have, Ernest! They are quite, quite blue. I hope
you will always look at me just like that, especially when there are
other people present.

(Enter LADY BRACKNELL.)

LADY BRACKNELL.   Mr. Worthing! Rise, sir, from this semirecumbent
posture. It is most indecorous.

GWENDOLEN.   Mama! (He tries to rise; she restrains him.) I must beg you
to retire. This is no place for you. Besides, Mr. Worthing has not
quite finished yet.

LADY BRACKNELL.   Finished what, may I ask?

GWENDOLEN.   I am engaged to Mr. Worthing, Mama. (They rise together.)

LADY BRACKNELL.   Pardon me, you are not engaged to anyone. When

you do become engaged to someone, I, or your father, should his health permit him, will inform you of the fact. An engagement should come on a young girl as a surprise, pleasant or unpleasant, as the case may be. It is hardly a matter that she could be allowed to arrange for herself. . . . And now I have a few questions to put to you, Mr. Worthing. While I am making these inquiries, you, Gwendolen, will wait for me below in the carriage.

GWENDOLEN (*reproachfully*).   Mama!

LADY BRACKNELL.   In the carriage, Gwendolen! (GWENDOLEN *goes to the door. She and* JACK *blow kisses to each other behind* LADY BRACKNELL'S *back.* LADY BRACKNELL *looks vaguely about as if she could not understand what the noise was. Finally turns round.*) Gwendolen, the carriage!

GWENDOLEN.   Yes, Mama. (*Goes out, looking back at* JACK.)

LADY BRACKNELL (*sitting down*).   You can take a seat, Mr. Worthing. (*Looks in her pocket for notebook and pencil.*)

JACK.   Thank you, Lady Bracknell, I prefer standing.

LADY BRACKNELL (*pencil and notebook in hand*).   I feel bound to tell you that you are not down on my list of eligible young men, although I have the same list as the dear Duchess of Bolten has. We work together, in fact. However, I am quite ready to enter your name, should your answers be what a really affectionate mother requires. Do you smoke?

JACK.   Well, yes, I must admit I smoke.

LADY BRACKNELL.   I am glad to hear it. A man should always have an occupation of some kind. There are far too many idle men in London as it is. How old are you?

JACK.   Twenty-nine.

LADY BRACKNELL.   A very good age to be married at. I have always been of opinion that a man who desires to get married should know either everything or nothing. Which do you know?

JACK (*after some hesitation*).   I know nothing, Lady Bracknell.

LADY BRACKNELL.   I am pleased to hear it. I do not approve of anything that tampers with natural ignorance. Ignorance is like a delicate exotic fruit; touch it and the bloom is gone. The whole theory of modern education is radically unsound. Fortunately in England, at any rate, education produces no effect whatsoever. If it did, it would prove a serious danger to the upper classes, and probably lead to acts of violence in Grosvenor Square. What is your income?

JACK.   Between seven and eight thousand a year.

LADY BRACKNELL (*makes a note in her book*).   In land or in investments?

JACK.   In investments, chiefly.

LADY BRACKNELL.   That is satisfactory. What between the duties expected of one during one's lifetime, and the duties exacted from one after one's death, land has ceased to be either a profit or a pleasure. It gives one position and prevents one from keeping it up. That's all that can be said about land.

JACK.   I have a country house with some land, of course, attached to it, about fifteen hundred acres, I believe; but I don't depend on that for my real income. In fact, as far as I can make out, the poachers are the only people who make anything out of it.

LADY BRACKNELL.   A country house! How many bedrooms? Well, that point can be cleared up afterward. You have a town house, I hope? A girl with a simple, unspoiled nature, like Gwendolen, could hardly be expected to reside in the country.

JACK.   Well, I own a house in Belgrave Square, but it is let by the year to Lady Bloxham. Of course, I can get it back whenever I like, at six months' notice.

LADY BRACKNELL.   Lady Bloxham? I don't know her.

JACK.   Oh, she goes about very little. She is a lady considerably advanced in years.

LADY BRACKNELL.   Ah, nowadays that is no guarantee of respectability of character. What number in Belgrave Square?

JACK.   One hundred and forty-nine.

LADY BRACKNELL (*shaking her head*).   The unfashionable side. I thought there was something. However, that could easily be altered.

JACK.   Do you mean the fashion, or the side?

LADY BRACKNELL (*sternly*).   Both, if necessary, I presume. What are your politics?

JACK.   Well, I am afraid I really have none. I am a Liberal Unionist.

LADY BRACKNELL.   Oh, they count as Tories. They dine with us. Or come in the evening, at any rate. Now to minor matters. Are your parents living?

JACK.   I have lost both my parents.

LADY BRACKNELL.   To lose one parent, Mr. Worthing, may be regarded as a misfortune; to lose both looks like carelessness. Who was your father? He was evidently a man of some wealth. Was he born in what the Radical papers call the purple of commerce, or did he rise from the ranks of the aristocracy?

JACK.   I am afraid I really don't know. The fact is, Lady Bracknell, I said

I had lost my parents. It would be nearer the truth to say that my parents seem to have lost me. . . . I don't actually know who I am by birth. I was . . . well, I was found.

LADY BRACKNELL. Found!

JACK. The late Mr. Thomas Cardew, an old gentleman of a very charitable and kindly disposition, found me and gave me the name of Worthing, because he happened to have a first-class ticket for Worthing in his pocket at the time. Worthing is a place in Sussex. It is a seaside resort.

LADY BRACKNELL. Where did the charitable gentleman who had a first-class ticket for this seaside resort find you?

JACK (*gravely*). In a handbag.

LADY BRACKNELL. A handbag?

JACK (*very seriously*). Yes, Lady Bracknell. I was in a handbag—a somewhat large, black leather handbag, with handles to it—an ordinary handbag in fact.

LADY BRACKNELL. In what locality did this Mr. James, or Thomas, Cardew come across this ordinary handbag?

JACK. In the cloakroom at Victoria Station. It was given to him in mistake for his own.

LADY BRACKNELL. The cloakroom at Victoria Station?

JACK. Yes. The Brighton line.

LADY BRACKNELL. The line is immaterial. Mr. Worthing, I confess I feel somewhat bewildered by what you have just told me. To be born, or at any rate bred, in a handbag, whether it had handles or not, seems to me to display a contempt for the ordinary decencies of family life that reminds one of the worst excesses of the French Revolution. And I presume you know what that unfortunate movement led to? As for the particular locality in which the handbag was found, a cloakroom at a railway station might serve to conceal a social indiscretion—has probably, indeed, been used for that purpose before now—but it could hardly be regarded as an assured basis for a recognized position in good society.

JACK. May I ask you then what you would advise me to do? I need hardly say I would do anything in the world to insure Gwendolen's happiness.

LADY BRACKNELL. I would strongly advise you, Mr. Worthing, to try and acquire some relations as soon as possible, and to make a definite effort to produce at any rate one parent, of either sex, before the season is quite over.

JACK. Well, I don't see how I could possibly manage to do that. I can produce the handbag at any moment. It is in my dressing room at home. I really think that should satisfy you, Lady Bracknell.

LADY BRACKNELL. Me, sir! What has it to do with me? You can hardly imagine that I and Lord Bracknell would dream of allowing our only daughter—a girl brought up with the utmost care—to marry into a cloakroom, and form an alliance with a parcel. Good morning, Mr. Worthing!

(LADY BRACKNELL *sweeps out in majestic indignation.*)

Lady Bracknell, as a member of established society, has the power to include or exclude Jack. What kinds of qualifications for marriage to her daughter does Lady Bracknell demand of Jack? What do they tell us about her?

How does Lady Bracknell resemble the other authority figures in this unit?

Why do you think our sympathies are usually with the social underdog, like Jack, rather than with the socially powerful?

If you can get a complete copy of *The Importance of Being Earnest,* read the rest of the play. Find out if, in the end, Jack finds his parents and qualifies to marry Gwendolen.

Goodbye to All Cats

P. G. WODEHOUSE

As the club kitten sauntered into the smoking room of the Drones Club and greeted those present with a friendly miaow, Freddie Widgeon, who had been sitting in a corner with his head between his hands, rose stiffly.

"I had supposed," he said, in a cold, level voice, "that this was a quiet retreat for gentlemen. As I perceive that it is a blasted zoo, I will withdraw."

And he left the room in a marked manner.

There was a good deal of surprise, mixed with consternation.

"What's the trouble?" asked an Egg, concerned. Such exhibitions of the naked emotions are rare at the Drones. "Have they had a row?"

A Crumpet, always well informed, shook his head.

"Freddie has had no personal breach with this particular kitten," he said. "It is simply that since that weekend at Matcham Scratchings he can't stand the sight of a cat."

"Matcham what?"

"Scratchings. The ancestral home of Dahlia Prenderby in Oxfordshire."

"I met Dahlia Prenderby once," said the Egg. "I thought she seemed a nice girl."

"Freddie thought so, too. He loved her madly."

"And lost her, of course?"

"Absolutely."

"Do you know," said a thoughtful Bean, "I'll bet that if all the girls Freddie Widgeon has loved and lost were placed end to end—not that I suppose one could do it—they would reach halfway down Piccadilly."

"Farther than that," said the Egg. "Some of them were pretty tall. What beats me is why he ever bothers to love them. They always turn him down in the end. He might just as well never begin. Better, in fact, because in the time saved he could be reading some good book."

"I think the trouble with Freddie," said the Crumpet, "is that he always gets off to a flying start. He's a good-looking sort of chap who dances well and can wiggle his ears, and the girl is dazzled for the moment, and this encourages him. From what he tells me, he appears to have gone very big with this Prenderby girl at the outset. So much so, indeed, that when she invited him down to Matcham Scratchings he had already bought his copy of *What Every Young Bridegroom Ought to Know*."

"Rummy, these old country-house names," mused the Bean. "Why Scratchings, I wonder?"

"Freddie wondered, too, till he got to the place. Then he tells me he felt it was absolutely the *mot juste*. This girl Dahlia's family, you see, was one of those animal-loving families, and the house, he tells me, was just a frothing maelstrom of dumb chums. As far as the eye could reach, there were dogs scratching themselves and cats scratching the furniture. I believe, though he never met it socially, there was even a tame chimpanzee somewhere on the premises, no doubt scratching away as assiduously as the rest of them. You get these conditions here and there in the depths of the country, and this Matcham place was well away from the center of things, being about six miles from the nearest station.

"It was at this station that Dahlia Prenderby met Freddie in her two-seater, and on the way to the house there occurred a conversation which I consider significant—showing, as it does, the cordial relations existing between the young couple at that point in the proceedings. I mean, it was only later that the bitter awakening and all that sort of thing popped up.

" 'I do want you to be a success, Freddie,' said the girl, after talking a while of this and that. 'Some of the men I've asked down here have been such awful flops. The great thing is to make a good impression on Father.'

" 'I will,' said Freddie.

" 'He can be a little difficult at times.'

" 'Lead me to him,' said Freddie. 'That's all I ask. Lead me to him.'

" 'The trouble is, he doesn't much like young men.'

" 'He'll like me.'

" 'He will, will he?'

" 'Rather!'

" 'What makes you think that?'

" 'I'm a dashed fascinating chap.'

" 'Oh, you are?'

" 'Yes, I am.'

" 'You are, are you?'

" 'Rather!'

"Upon which, she gave him a sort of push and he gave her a sort of push, and she giggled and he laughed like a paper bag bursting, and she gave him a kind of shove and he gave her a kind of shove, and she said 'You *are* a silly *ass!*' and he said 'What ho!' All of which shows you, I mean to say, the stage they had got to by this time. Nothing definitely settled, of course, but Love obviously beginning to burgeon in the girl's heart."

Well, naturally, Freddie gave a good deal of thought during the drive to this father of whom the girl had spoken so feelingly, and he resolved that he would not fail her. The way he would make up to the old dad would be nobody's business. He proposed to exert upon him the full force of his magnetic personality, and looked forward to registering a very substantial hit.

Which being so, I need scarcely tell you, knowing Freddie as you do, that his first act on entering Sir Mortimer Prenderby's orbit was to make the scaliest kind of floater, hitting him on the back of the neck with a tortoise-shell cat not ten minutes after his arrival.

His train having been a bit late, there was no time on reaching the house for any stately receptions or any of that "Welcome to Meadowsweet Hall" stuff. The girl simply shot him up to his room and told him to dress like a streak, because dinner was in a quarter of an hour, and then buzzed off to don the soup and fish herself. And Freddie was just going well when, looking round for his shirt, which he had left on the bed, he saw a large tortoise-shell cat standing on it, kneading it with its paws.

Well, you know how a fellow feels about his shirt front. For an instant, Freddie stood spellbound. Then with a hoarse cry he bounded forward, scooped up the animal, and, carrying it out onto the balcony, flung it into the void. And an elderly gentleman, coming round the corner at this moment, received a direct hit on the back of his neck.

"Hell!" cried the elderly gentleman.

A head popped out of a window.

"Whatever is the matter, Mortimer?"

"It's raining cats."

"Nonsense. It's a lovely evening," said the head and disappeared.

Freddie thought an apology would be in order.

"I say," he said.

The old gentleman looked in every direction of the compass, and finally located Freddie on his balcony.

"I say," said Freddie, "I'm awfully sorry you got that nasty buffet. It was me."

"It was not you. It was a cat."

"I know. I threw the cat."

"Why?"

"Well . . ."

"Dam' fool."

"I'm sorry," said Freddie.

"Go to blazes," said the old gentleman.

Freddie backed into the room and the incident closed.

Freddie is a pretty slippy dresser, as a rule, but this episode had shaken him, and he not only lost a collar stud but made a mess of the first two ties. The result was that the gong went while he was still in his shirtsleeves; and on emerging from his boudoir he was informed by a footman that the gang were already nuzzling their bouillon in the dining room. He pushed straight on there, accordingly, and sank into a chair beside his hostess just in time to dead-heat with the final spoonful.

Awkward, of course, but he was feeling in pretty good form owing to the pleasantness of the thought that he was shoving his knees under the same board as the girl Dahlia; so, having nodded to his host, who was glaring at him from the head of the table, as much as to say that all would be explained in God's good time, he shot his cuffs and started to make sparkling conversation to Lady Prenderby.

"Charming place you have here, what?"

Lady Prenderby said that the local scenery was generally admired. She was one of those tall, rangy, Queen Elizabeth sort of women, with tight lips and cold, *blanc mange-y* eyes. Freddie didn't like her looks much, but he was feeling, as I say, fairly fizzy, so he carried on with a bright zip.

"Pretty good hunting country, I should think?"

"I believe there is a good deal of hunting near here, yes."

"I thought as much," said Freddie. "Ah, that's the stuff, is it not? A cracking gallop across good country with a jolly fine kill at the end of it, what, what? Hark for'ard, yoicks, tallyho, I mean to say, and all that sort of thing."

Lady Prenderby shivered austerely.

"I fear I cannot share your enthusiasm," she said. "I have the strongest possible objection to hunting. I have always set my face against it, as against all similar brutalizing blood sports."

This was a nasty jar for poor old Freddie, who had been relying on the topic to carry him nicely through at least a couple of courses. It silenced him for the nonce. And as he paused to collect his faculties, his host, who had now been glowering for six and a half minutes practically without cessation, put a hand in front of his mouth and addressed the girl Dahlia across the table. Freddie thinks he was under the impression that he was speaking in a guarded whisper, but, as a matter of fact, the words boomed through the air as if he had been a costermonger calling attention to his Brussels sprouts.

"Dahlia!"

"Yes, Father?"

"Who's that ugly feller?"

"Hush!"

"What do you mean, hush? Who is he?"

"Mr. Widgeon."

"Mr. Who?"

"Widgeon."

"I wish you would articulate clearly and not mumble," said Sir Mortimer fretfully. "It sounds to me just like 'Widgeon.' Who asked him here?"

"I did."

"Why?"

"He's a friend of mine."

"Well, he looks a pretty frightful young slab of damnation to me. What I'd call a criminal face."

"Hush!"

"Why do you keep saying 'Hush'? Must be a lunatic, too. Throws cats at people."

"Please, Father!"

"Don't say 'Please, Father!' No sense in it. I tell you he does throw cats at people. He threw one at me. Half-witted, I'd call him—if that. Besides being the most offensive-looking young toad I've ever seen on the premises. How long's he staying?"

"Till Monday."

"My God! And today's only Friday!" bellowed Sir Mortimer Prenderby.

It was an unpleasant situation for Freddie, of course, and I'm bound to admit he didn't carry it off particularly well. What he ought to have done, obviously, was to have plunged into an easy flow of small talk; but all he could think of was to ask Lady Prenderby if she was fond of shooting. Lady Prenderby having replied that, owing to being deficient in the savage instincts and wanton blood lust that went to make up a callous and coldhearted murderess, she was not, he relapsed into silence with his lower jaw hanging down.

All in all, he wasn't so dashed sorry when dinner came to an end.

As he and Sir Mortimer were the only men at the table, most of the seats having been filled by a covey of mildewed females whom he had classified under the general heading of Aunts, it seemed to Freddie that the moment had now arrived when they would be able to get together once more, under happier conditions than those of their last meeting, and start to learn to appreciate one another's true worth. He looked forward to a cozy *tête-à-tête* over the port, in the course of which he would smooth over that cat incident and generally do all that lay within his power to revise the unfavorable opinion of him which the other must have formed.

But apparently Sir Mortimer had his own idea of the duties and obligations of a host. Instead of clustering round Freddie with decanters, he simply gave him a long, lingering look of distaste and shot out of the French window into the garden. A moment later, his head reappeared and he uttered the words: "You and your dam' cats!" Then the night swallowed him again.

Freddie was a good deal perplexed. All this was new stuff to him. He had been in and out of a number of country houses in his time, but this was the first occasion on which he had ever been left flat at the conclusion of the evening meal, and he wasn't quite sure how to handle the situation. He was still wondering, when Sir Mortimer's head came into view again and its owner, after giving him another of those long, lingering looks, said: "Cats, forsooth!" and disappeared once more.

Freddie was now definitely piqued. It was all very well, he felt, Dahlia Prenderby telling him to make himself solid with her father, but

how can you make yourself solid with a fellow who doesn't stay put for a couple of consecutive seconds? If it was Sir Mortimer's intention to spend the remainder of the night flashing past like a merry-go-round, there seemed little hope of anything amounting to a genuine *rapprochement*. It was a relief to his feelings when there suddenly appeared from nowhere his old acquaintance the tortoise-shell cat. It seemed to offer to him a means of working off his spleen.

Taking from Lady Prenderby's plate, accordingly, the remains of a banana, he plugged the animal at a range of two yards. It yowled and withdrew. And a moment later, there was Sir Mortimer again.

"Did you kick that cat?" said Sir Mortimer.

Freddie had half a mind to ask this old disease if he thought he was a man or a jack-in-the-box, but the breeding of the Widgeons restrained him.

"No," he said, "I did not kick that cat."

"You must have done something to it to make it come charging out at forty miles an hour."

"I merely offered the animal a piece of fruit."

"Do it again and see what happens to you."

"Lovely evening," said Freddie, changing the subject.

"No, it's not, you silly ass," said Sir Mortimer. Freddie rose. His nerve, I fancy, was a little shaken.

"I shall join the ladies," he said, with dignity.

"God help them!" replied Sir Mortimer Prenderby in a voice instinct with the deepest feeling, and vanished once more.

Freddie's mood, as he made for the drawing room, was thoughtful. I don't say he has much sense, but he's got enough to know when he is and when he isn't going with a bang. Tonight, he realized, he had been very far from going in such a manner. It was not, that is to say, as the Idol of Matcham Scratchings that he would enter the drawing room, but rather as a young fellow who had made an unfortunate first impression and would have to do a lot of heavy ingratiating before he could regard himself as really popular in the home.

He must bustle about, he felt, and make up leeway. And, knowing that what counts with these old-style females who have lived in the country all their lives is the exhibition of those little politenesses and attentions which were all the go in Queen Victoria's time, his first action, on entering, was to make a dive for one of the aunts who seemed to be trying to find a place to put her coffee cup.

"Permit me," said Freddie, suave to the eyebrows.

And bounding forward with the feeling that this was the stuff to give them, he barged right into a cat.

"Oh, sorry," he said, backing and bringing down his heel on another cat.

"I say, most frightfully sorry," he said.

And, tottering to a chair, he sank heavily onto a third cat.

Well, he was up and about again in a jiffy, of course, but it was too late. There was the usual not-at-all-ing and don't-mention-it-ing, but he could read between the lines. Lady Prenderby's eyes had rested on his for only a brief instant, but it had been enough. His standing with her, he perceived, was now approximately what King Herod's would have been at an Israelite Mothers Social Saturday Afternoon.

The girl Dahlia during these exchanges had been sitting on a sofa at the end of the room, turning the pages of a weekly paper, and the sight of her drew Freddie like a magnet. Her womanly sympathy was just what he felt he could do with at this juncture. Treading with infinite caution, he crossed to where she sat; and, having scanned the terrain narrowly for cats, sank down on the sofa at her side. And conceive his agony of spirit when he discovered that womanly sympathy had been turned off at the main. The girl was like a chunk of ice cream with spikes all over it.

"Please do not trouble to explain," she said coldly, in answer to his opening words. "I quite understand that there are people who have this odd dislike of animals."

"But, dash it . . ." cried Freddie, waving his arm in a frenzied sort of way. "Oh, I say, sorry," he added, as his fist sloshed another of the menagerie in the short ribs.

Dahlia caught the animal as it flew through the air.

"I think perhaps you had better take Augustus, Mother," she said. "He seems to be annoying Mr. Widgeon."

"Quite," said Lady Prenderby. "He will be safer with me."

"But, dash it . . ." bleated Freddie.

Dahlia Prenderby drew in her breath sharply.

"How true it is," she said, "that one never really knows a man till after one has seen him in one's own home."

"What do you mean by that?"

"Oh, nothing," said Dahlia Prenderby.

She rose and moved to the piano, where she proceeded to sing old Breton folk songs in a distant manner, leaving Freddie to make out as best he could with a family album containing faded photographs with

"Aunt Emmy bathing at Llandudno, 1893," and "This is Cousin George at the fancy-dress ball" written under them.

And so the long, quiet, peaceful home evening wore on, till eventually Lady Prenderby mercifully blew the whistle and he was at liberty to sneak off to his bedroom.

You might have supposed that Freddie's thoughts, as he toddled upstairs with his candle, would have dwelt exclusively on the girl Dahlia. This, however, was not so. He did give her obvious shirtiness a certain measure of attention, of course, but what really filled his mind was the soothing reflection that at long last his patch and that of the animal kingdom of Matcham Scratchings had now divided. He, so to speak, was taking the high road while they, as it were, would take the low road. For whatever might be the conditions prevailing in the dining room, the drawing room, and the rest of the house, his bedroom, he felt, must surely be a haven totally free from cats of all descriptions.

Remembering, however, that unfortunate episode before dinner, he went down on all fours and subjected the various nooks and crannies to a close examination. His eye could detect no cats. Relieved, he rose to his feet with a gay song on his lips; and he hadn't got much beyond the first couple of bars when a voice behind him suddenly started taking the bass; and, turning, he perceived on the bed a fine Alsatian dog.

Freddie looked at the dog. The dog looked at Freddie. The situation was one fraught with embarrassment. A glance at the animal was enough to convince him that it had got an entirely wrong angle on the position of affairs and was regarding him purely in the light of an intrusive stranger who had muscled in on its private sleeping quarters. Its manner was plainly resentful. It fixed Freddie with a cold, yellow eye and curled its upper lip slightly, the better to display a long, white tooth. It also twitched its nose and gave a *sotto-voce* imitation of distant thunder.

Freddie did not know quite what avenue to explore. It was impossible to climb between the sheets with a thing like that on the counterpane. To spend the night in a chair, on the other hand, would have been foreign to his policy. He did what I consider the most statesmanlike thing by sidling out onto the balcony and squinting along the wall of the house to see if there wasn't a lighted window hard by, behind which might lurk somebody who would rally round with aid and comfort.

There was a lighted window only a short distance away, so he shoved his head out as far as it would stretch and said:

"I say!"

There being no response, he repeated:

"I say!"

And, finally, to drive his point home, he added:

"I say! I say! I say!"

This time he got results. The head of Lady Prenderby suddenly protruded from the window.

"Who," she inquired, "is making that abominable noise?"

It was not precisely the attitude Freddie had hoped for, but he could take the rough with the smooth.

"It's me. Widgeon, Frederick."

"Must you sing on your balcony, Mr. Widgeon?"

"I wasn't singing. I was saying 'I say'."

"What were you saying?"

" 'I say'."

"You say what?"

"I say I was saying 'I say.' Kind of a heart cry, if you know what I mean. The fact is, there's a dog in my room."

"What sort of dog?"

"A whacking great Alsatian."

"Ah, that would be Wilhelm. Good night, Mr. Widgeon."

The window closed. Freddie let out a heart-stricken yip.

"But I say!"

The window reopened.

"Really, Mr. Widgeon!"

"But what am I to do?"

"Do?"

"About this whacking great Alsatian!"

Lady Prenderby seemed to consider.

"No sweet biscuits," she said. "And when the maid brings you your tea in the morning please do not give him sugar. Simply a little milk in the saucer. He is on a diet. Good night, Mr. Widgeon."

Freddie was now pretty well nonplused. No matter what his hostess might say about this beastly dog being on a diet, he was convinced from its manner that its medical adviser had not forbidden it Widgeons, and once more he bent his brain to the task of ascertaining what to do next.

There were several possible methods of procedure. His balcony being not so very far from the ground, he could, if he pleased, jump down and pass a health-giving night in the nasturtium bed. Or he might curl up on the floor. Or he might get out of the room and doss downstairs somewhere.

This last scheme seemed about the best. The only obstacle in the way of its fulfillment was the fact that, when he started for the door his roommate would probably think he was a burglar about to loot the silver of a lonely country house and pin him. Still, it had to be risked and a moment later he might have been observed tiptoeing across the carpet with all the caution of a slack-wire artist who isn't any too sure he remembers the correct steps.

Well, it was a near thing. At the instant when he started, the dog seemed occupied with something that looked like a cushion on the bed. It was licking this object in a thoughtful way, and paid no attention to Freddie till he was halfway across No Man's Land. Then it suddenly did a sort of sitting high jump in his direction, and two seconds later, Freddie, with a drafty feeling about the seat of his trouserings, was on top of a wardrobe, with the dog underneath looking up. He tells me that if he ever moved quicker in his life it was only on the occasion when, a lad of fourteen he was discovered by his uncle, Lord Blicester, smoking one of the latter's cigars in the library; and he rather thinks he must have clipped at least a fifth of a second off the record then set up.

It looked to him now as if his sleeping arrangements for the night had been settled for him. And the thought of having to roost on top of a wardrobe at the whim of a dog was pretty dashed offensive to his proud spirit, as you may well imagine. However, as you cannot reason with Alsatians, it seemed the only thing to be done; and he was trying to make himself as comfortable as a sharp piece of wood sticking into the fleshy part of his leg would permit, when there was a snuffling noise in the passage and through the door came an object which in the dim light he was at first not able to identify. It looked something like a pen-wiper and something like a piece of a hearth-rug. A second and keener inspection revealed it as a Pekingese puppy.

The uncertainty which Freddie had felt as to the newcomer's status was shared, it appeared, by the Alsatian, for after raising its eyebrows in a puzzled manner it rose and advanced inquiringly. In a tentative way it put out a paw and rolled the intruder over. Then, advancing again, it lowered its nose and sniffed.

It was a course of action against which its best friends would have advised it. These Pekes are tough eggs, especially when, as in this case, female. They look the world in the eye, and are swift to resent familiarity. There was a sort of explosion, and the next moment the Alsatian was shooting out of the room with its tail between its legs, hotly pursued. Freddie could hear the noise of battle rolling away along the passage, and it was music to his ears. Something on these lines was precisely what that Alsatian had been asking for, and now it had got it.

Presently, the Peke returned, dashing the beads of perspiration from its forehead, and came and sat down under the wardrobe, wagging a stumpy tail. And Freddie, feeling that the All Clear had been blown and that he was now at liberty to descend, did so.

His first move was to shut the door, his second to fraternize with his preserver. Freddie is a chap who believes in giving credit where credit is due, and it seemed to him that this Peke had shown itself an ornament of its species. He spared no effort, accordingly, to entertain it. He lay down on the floor and let it lick his face two hundred and thirty-three times. He tickled it under the left ear, the right ear, and at the base of the tail, in the order named. He also scratched its stomach.

All these attentions the animal received with cordiality and marked gratification; and as it seemed still in pleasure-seeking mood and had plainly come to look upon him as the official Master of the Revels, Freddie, feeling that he could not disappoint it but must play the host no matter what the cost to himself, took off his tie and handed it over. He would not have done it for everybody, he says, but where this life-saving Peke was concerned the sky was the limit.

Well, the tie went like a breeze. It was a success from the start. The Peke chewed it and chased it and got entangled in it and dragged it about the room, and was just starting to shake it from side to side when an unfortunate thing happened. Misjudging its distance, it banged its head a nasty wallop against the leg of the bed.

There is nothing of the Red Indian at the stake about a puppy in circumstances like this. A moment later, Freddie's blood was chilled by a series of fearful shrieks that seemed to ring through the night like the dying cries of the party of the second part to a first-class murder. It amazed him that a mere Peke, and a juvenile Peke at that, should have been capable of producing such an uproar. He says that a baronet, stabbed in the back with a paper knife in his library, could not have made half such a row.

Eventually, the agony seemed to abate. Quite suddenly, as if nothing had happened, the Peke stopped yelling and with an amused smile started to play with the tie again. And at the same moment there was a sound of whispering outside, and then a knock at the door.

"Hullo?" said Freddie.

"It is I, sir. Biggleswade."

"Who's Biggleswade?"

"The butler, sir."

"What do you want?"

"Her ladyship wishes me to remove the dog which you are torturing."

There was more whispering.

"Her ladyship also desires me to say that she will be reporting the affair in the morning to the Society for the Prevention of Cruelty to Animals."

There was another spot of whispering.

"Her ladyship further instructs me to add that, should you prove recalcitrant, I am to strike you over the head with the poker."

Well, you can't say this was pleasant for poor old Freddie, and he didn't think so himself. He opened the door, to perceive, without, a group consisting of Lady Prenderby, her daughter Dahlia, a few assorted aunts, and the butler, with poker. And he says he met Dahlia's eyes and they went through him like a knife.

"Let me explain . . ." he began.

"Spare us the details," said Lady Prenderby with a shiver. She scooped up the Peke and felt it for broken bones.

"But listen . . ."

"Good night, Mr. Widgeon."

The aunts said good night, too, and so did the butler. The girl Dahlia preserved a revolted silence.

"But, honestly, it was nothing, really. It banged its head against the bed . . ."

"What did he say?" asked one of the aunts, who was a little hard of hearing.

"He says he banged the poor creature's head against the bed," said Lady Prenderby.

"Dreadful!" said the aunt.

"Hideous!" said a second aunt.

A third aunt opened up another line of thought. She said that with men like Freddie in the house, was anyone safe? She mooted the possibility of them all being murdered in their beds. And though Freddie offered to give her a written guarantee that he hadn't the slightest intention of going anywhere near her bed, the idea seemed to make a deep impression.

"Biggleswade," said Lady Prenderby.

"M'lady?"

"You will remain in this passage for the remainder of the night with your poker."

"Very good, m'lady."

"Should this man attempt to leave his room, you will strike him smartly over the head."

"Just so, m'lady."

"But, listen . . ." said Freddie.

"Good night, Mr. Widgeon."

The mob scene broke up. Soon the passage was empty save for Biggleswade the butler, who had begun to pace up and down, halting every now and then to flick the air with his poker as if testing the lissomeness of his wrist muscles and satisfying himself that they were in a condition to insure the right amount of follow-through.

The spectacle he presented was so unpleasant that Freddie withdrew into his room and shut the door. His bosom, as you may imagine, was surging with distressing emotions. That look which Dahlia Prenderby had given him had churned him up to no little extent. He realized that he had a lot of tense thinking to do, and to assist thought he sat down on the bed.

Or, rather, to be accurate, on the dead cat which was lying on the bed. It was this cat which the Alsatian had been licking just before the final breach in his relations with Freddie—the object, if you remember, which the latter had supposed to be a cushion.

He leaped up as if the corpse, instead of being cold, had been piping hot. He stared down, hoping against hope that the animal was merely in some sort of coma. But a glance told him that it had made the great change. He had never seen a deader cat. After life's fitful fever it slept well.

You wouldn't be far out in saying that poor old Freddie was now appalled. Already his reputation in this house was at zero, his name mud. On all sides he was looked upon as Widgeon the Amateur Vivisectionist. This final disaster could not but put the tin hat on it. Before, he had had a faint hope that in the morning, when calmer moods would prevail, he might be able to explain that matter of the Peke. But who was going to listen to him if he were discovered with a dead cat on his person?

And then the thought came to him that it might be possible not to be discovered with it on his person. He had only to nip downstairs and deposit the remains in the drawing room or somewhere and suspicion might not fall upon him. After all, in a super-catted house like this, cats must always be dying like flies all over the place. A housemaid would find the animal in the morning and report to G.H.Q. that the cat strength of the establishment had been reduced by one, and there would be a bit of tut-tutting and perhaps a silent tear or two, and then the thing would be forgotten.

The thought gave him new life. All briskness and efficiency, he picked up the body by the tail and was just about to dash out of the room when, with a silent groan, he remembered Biggleswade.

He peeped out. It might be that the butler, once the eye of authority had been removed, had departed to get the remainder of his beauty sleep. But no. Service and Fidelity were evidently the watchwords at Matcham Scratchings. There the fellow was, still practicing half-arm shots with the poker. Freddie closed the door.

And, as he did so, he suddenly thought of the window. There lay the solution. Here he had been, fooling about with doors and thinking in terms of drawing rooms, and all the while there was the balcony staring him in the face. All he had to do was to shoot the body out into the silent night, and let gardeners, not housemaids, discover it.

He hurried out. It was a moment for swift action. He raised his burden. He swung it to and fro, working up steam. Then he let it go, and from the dark garden there came suddenly the cry of a strong man in his anger.

"Who threw that cat?"

It was the voice of his host, Sir Mortimer Prenderby.

"Show me the man who threw that cat!" he thundered.

Windows flew up. Heads came out. Freddie sank to the floor of the balcony and rolled against the wall.

"Whatever is the matter, Mortimer?"

"Let me get at the man who hit me in the eye with a cat."

"A cat?" Lady Prenderby's voice sounded perplexed. "Are you sure?"

"Sure? What do you mean sure? Of course I'm sure. I was just dropping off to sleep in my hammock, when suddenly a great beastly cat came whizzing through the air and caught me properly in the eyeball. It's a nice thing. A man can't sleep in hammocks in his own garden without people pelting him with cats. I insist on the blood of the man who threw that cat."

"Where did it come from?"

"Must have come from that balcony there."

"Mr. Widgeon's balcony," said Lady Prenderby in an acid voice. "As I might have guessed."

Sir Mortimer uttered a cry.

"So might I have guessed! Widgeon, of course! That ugly feller. He's been throwing cats all the evening. I've got a nasty sore place on the back of my neck where he hit me with one before dinner. Somebody come and open the front door. I want my heavy cane, the one with the carved ivory handle. Or a horsewhip will do."

"Wait, Mortimer," said Lady Prenderby. "Do nothing rash. The man is evidently a very dangerous lunatic. I will send Biggleswade to overpower him. He has the kitchen poker."

Little (said the Crumpet) remains to be told. At two-fifteen that morning a somber figure in dress clothes without a tie limped into the little railway station of Lower Smattering on the Wissel, some six miles from Matcham Scratchings. At three-forty-seven it departed Londonwards on the up milk train. It was Frederick Widgeon. He had a broken heart and blisters on both heels. And in that broken heart was that loathing for all cats of which you recently saw so signal a manifestation. I am revealing no secrets when I tell you that Freddie Widgeon is permanently through with cats. From now on, they cross his path at their peril.

How is Freddie Widgeon's situation similar to Jack Worthing's in "Making the Right Connections"?

What do the Prenderbys demand of Freddie in order for him to be accepted by the family? How would you describe such a demand?

What similarities do you find among all the blocking characters in this unit?

My Father Enters the Church

CLARENCE DAY

The way it ended was simple. Mother's family had lived at one time in a pretty little two-storied house, called "The Cottage," in East Twenty-ninth Street; it had casement windows, set with diamond-shaped panes of leaded glass, and a grass plot in front. On the other side of the street, at Fifth Avenue, stood the church that is now known as the Little Church Around the Corner. The first Dr. Houghton was the rector in those times, and Mother was fond of him. One day Mother heard that a young relative of his, the Reverend Mr. Morley, had taken a far-away parish near what was then Audubon Park, a mile or two north of where in later years they erected Grant's Tomb. This part of the city was so thinly settled that it was like a remote country suburb. There were dirt roads and lanes instead of streets, and thick, quiet old woods. Mother suddenly got the idea that perhaps this would suit Father, since he seemed bent on "confessing God before men" only where no one was looking. Besides, Mother knew young Mr. Morley, and she felt that here was someone she could go to with her curious problem. She asked him to come down and see her. He was sympathetic. He agreed to make everything as easy for Father as possible.

I don't know just why it was, but somehow that was all there was to it. Father still got in a very bad humor whenever the subject was mentioned; but at least Mother wasn't, any longer, asking the impossible of him. It was thoroughly distasteful and he hated it, but he supposed he could go through it sometime. Perhaps he even got to the point of wishing to get the thing over with.

So the day came on which Father had agreed he would enter the church. The only person who had to be reminded of it was Father himself. I remember excitedly looking out of the window at breakfast, and seeing a hired brougham from Ryerson & Brown's in the street. The coachman had on a blue coat with a double row of bright buttons, and on his legs were faded green trousers from some other man's livery. He was looking up at our front door. His horse was as weather-beaten as the horse on the plains of Siberia, in the picture in my Geography; and he too seemed to be looking up at our house and wondering what would come out of it.

I stood out on our front stoop staring down at them, and listening to the sounds in our hallway. Father had come down to breakfast in a good temper that morning, and the bacon and eggs had suited him for once, and the coffee too had found favor. Mother gave a happy, tender look at this soul she was saving. The dining room seemed full of sunshine, and the whole world light-hearted. But when Mother said it was nearly eight o'clock and the cab would soon be here, Father had demanded what cab. He listened to her answer in horror, and sprang up with a roar.

It was as though an elephant which had been tied up with infinite pains had trumpeted and burst every fetter, after the labor of months. It was all to do over again. Father not only had to be convinced that a day had been set, and that this was the day, but the whole question of baptism had to be reopened and proved. All the religious instruction that had been slowly inscribed on his mind had apparently utterly vanished—the slate was wiped clean. He was back at his original starting point, that this thing was all folderol—it was nothing but a wild idea of Mother's with which he had no concern.

A woman of less determination would have given up, Father was so indignant. But Mother, though frightened and discouraged and tearful, was angry. She wasn't going to let Father off, after all she had done. At first I thought she surely had lost. He was completely intractable. She stood up to him, armed with God's word and the laws of the church, and also, as she despairingly reminded him, with his own "Sacred Promise," and again she learned that not a one of them was any good. But she had one other weapon: Ryerson & Brown's waiting cab.

There were some things that were unheard of in our family: they simply weren't done. One was wasting money on cabs. When we went to the length of ordering a cab, we did not keep it waiting. And the sight of this cab at the door seemed to hypnotize Father. It stood there like a link in some inevitable chain of events. At first he declared it could go to the devil, he didn't care if there were fifty cabs waiting. But he was by habit and instinct a methodical man. When he helped himself to a portion of anything at the table, for instance, he did his best to finish that portion, whether he liked it or not. He got all the more angry if it didn't taste right, but his code made him eat it. If he began a book he was bound to go on with it, no matter how much it bored him. He went through with any and every program to which he once felt committed. The fact that this cab had been ordered, and now stood at the door, prevailed in those depths of his spirit which God couldn't reach. Where I sat on the steps I could hear him upstairs in his room, banging doors and putting on his overcoat and cursing at fate.

Mother darted out and told the coachman where he was to take us; and then she got in, bonneted and cloaked, to wait for Father to come. The coachman looked puzzled when he found we were going to church. He could see we weren't dressed for a funeral, yet it was hardly a wedding. Perhaps he thought we were a very devout family, seeking for some extra worship.

Then Father came down the steps, blackly. He got in the cab. And the horse and the coachman both jumped as Father slammed the door shut.

The cab bumped along over the cobblestones, with its ironshod wheels. The steady-going rattle and jolting made me dreamy. It was soothing to see the landscape slide by, at five or six miles an hour. Milkmen, ladling milk out of tall cans. Chambermaids polishing doorbells. Ladies, with the tops of their sleeves built up high at each shoulder. Horses straining at streetcars. Flocks of sparrows hopping about, pecking at refuse and dung, and waiting until a horse almost stepped on them before flying off.

We drove up Madison Avenue to the Park, and out at West Seventy-second Street. Then under the Elevated, with its coal dust sifting down and stray cinders, blackening the pools in the street; and its little locomotives chuff-chuffing along overhead. At the Boulevard, as upper Broadway was then named, we turned northward. Over toward the river were rocky wastelands, old shanties and goats. The skyline along the Boulevard was one of telegraph poles, along bare blocks and rail fences. I liked the looks of this ungraded district; it was all up-and-down and had ponds in it. And it ought to have comforted Father. No members of the club or the stock exchange could be sighted for miles; they probably never set foot in such regions. What more could Father ask?

But Father was glaring about, looking like a caged lion. Apparently he had confidently believed up to this very moment that Heaven would intervene somehow, and spare him this dose. He had never done Heaven any harm; why should it be malignant? His disappointment was increasingly bitter as he saw he was trapped. Another sort of man would have opened the cab door and bolted. But Father was drinking his hemlock. He also was freely expressing his feelings about it. The hardships of marriage had never before impressed him so sharply. A woman's demands on her husband were simply beyond human reckoning. He felt, and he said plainly to Mother, as the cab rattled on, that if he did this thing for her, it must be understood that it was his supreme contribution. No diamond necklace. No other sacrifices of any kind. He must never be asked to do anything more all his life.

Mother tried to point out that he wasn't doing it for her but for God, but Father said: "Pshaw! I won't hear of it." He had never had any trouble with God till Mother appeared on the scene.

Mother quoted Dr. Garden again to him, but Father said "Pish!"

"Oh Clare, you mustn't," said Mother.

"Bah!" Father roared. "Bah! What do you suppose I care for that fellow!"

"But it's in the Bible."

"Pooh! Damn!"

Mother shuddered at this. Here was a man who defied even the Bible. She half-expected God to come bursting right out of the sky, and bang his fist down on the Ryerson & Brown cab and all in it.

"Damnation!" Father repeated, consumed by his wrongs.

Mother said, oh how could he talk so, on his way to the font! She drew away from him, and then looked back with awe at this being, whose sense of his powers was so great that he would stand up to Anyone.

We had now come in sight of the church. It stood halfway up a steep hill, which the horse climbed at a walk, although Father said if the cab didn't hurry he wouldn't have time to be baptized—he'd be late at the office.

"What is the name of this confounded place?" he said, as we got out, making a jab at the little House of God with his cane.

"Oh Clare dear! Please don't. It's the Church of the Epiphany, I told you."

"Epiphany! Humph," Father grunted. "More gibberish."

Inside it was cold and bare, and it smelled of varnish. The pews were of new yellow pine, and the stained-glass looked cheap. There was nobody present. The sexton had hurried away to fetch the minister, after letting us in.

Father glowered around like a bull in some Plaza del Toro, waiting to charge the reverend toreador and trample upon him. He stood there, boxed up in surroundings where he didn't belong, hurt and outraged and lonely. His whole private life had been pried into, even his babyhood. He had kept decently aloof from the depths of religion, as a gentleman should—he was no emotional tinker like that fellow, John Bunyan—yet here he was, dragged into this damned evangelist orgy, far from his own proper world, in the hands of his wife and a parson.

A footstep was heard.

"Oh, good morning, Mr. Morley," said Mother. "This is Mr. Day."

Mr. Morley was a young man, shy but friendly, with a new-looking beard. He approached our little group trustingly, to shake Father's hand, but he got such a look that he turned to me instead and patted me on the head several times. There was a rich smell of something about him. It wasn't bay-rum, such as Father sometimes used after shaving. It was far more delicious to me than any cologne or sachet scent. And besides, it had much more body to it; more satisfaction. But I couldn't identify it. I only know that it was a magnificent fragrance, and seemed to come from his beard. He led us up to the front of the chuch and the service began.

It says in the prayer book that when a person of riper years is to be baptized, he shall be exhorted to prepare himself, with prayers and with fasting. And if he shall be found fit, "then the Godfathers and Godmothers (the People being assembled upon the Sunday or Prayer Day appointed) shall be ready to present him at the font." I suppose that was why I was taken along, so that there would be enough people there for a congregation: Mother and the sexton and me. The sexton, who seemed a nervous man, was skulking in a rear pew; but Mother and I stood just behind Father, to bolster him up. It was a curious situation for a small boy to be in, as I look back on it.

Mr. Morley presently read an address to the three of us, as we stood there before him. (I condense this and the following quotations, from the service in my old prayer book.) "Dearly beloved," he said to us, "forasmuch as all men are conceived and born in sin, and they who are in the flesh cannot please God, but live in sin; and our Saviour Christ saith, none can enter into the kingdom of God, except he be regenerate and born anew; I beseech you to call upon God that of his bounteous goodness he will grant to this person that which by nature he cannot have; that he may be baptized with Water and the Holy Ghost, and received into Christ's holy Church, and be made a lively member of the same."

Next came a prayer in which Mr. Morley went back to the ark, and spoke of how God saved Noah and his family from perishing by water; and of how God also led the children of Israel safely through the Red Sea; and of how Jesus was baptized in the Jordan. These three incidents were cited as proof that God had sanctified "the element of Water to the mystical washing away of sin."

"We beseech thee," Mr. Morley continued, "that thou wilt mercifully look upon this thy Servant; wash him and sanctify him with the Holy Ghost; that he, being delivered from thy wrath, may be received into the ark of Christ's Church; and being steadfast in faith, joyful through hope, and rooted in charity, may come to the land of everlasting life."

Father was getting restive by this time, but Mr. Morley kept on. He read us a part of the Gospel of John, and a long exhortation and prayer; and after this he bravely turned and spoke as follows to Father:

"Well-beloved, who are come hither desiring to receive holy Baptism, you have heard how the congregation hath prayed that our Lord Jesus Christ would release you of your sins, to give you the kingdom of Heaven, and everlasting life. You have heard also that our Lord hath promised to grant all those things that we have prayed for. Wherefore you must also faithfully, in the presence of these your Witnesses and this whole congregation, promise and answer to the following questions:

"Dost thou renounce the devil and all his works, the vain pomp and glory of the world, with all covetous desires of the same, and the sinful desires of the flesh?"

The answer to this was rather long, and Father of course had not learned it; but Mother whispered the words in his ear, and he repeated some of them impatiently, in a harsh, stony voice. He looked as though he might have been an annoyed Roman general, participating much against his will in a low and barbaric rite.

There were only three more questions, however, and the answers were short.

"O Merciful God," said Mr. Morley, when these were finished, "grant that the old Adam in this person may be so buried, that the new man may be raised up in him. Amen." He had to say this, because it was in the prayer book; but Father's eyes were on fire, and there was a great deal of the old Adam in him, and it didn't look buried.

Four more little prayers followed, and then came the great moment, when Mr. Morley tried to pour water on Father. Owing to Father's being no longer an infant, the prayer book didn't require Mr. Morley to take him into his arms for this purpose, and hold him over the font; but he did have to wet him a little. I don't know how he managed it. I remember how Father stood, grim and erect, in his tailed morning-coat; but when I saw Mr. Morley make a pass at Father's forehead, I am sorry to say I shut my eyes tightly at his frightful sacrilege, and whether he actually landed or not I never knew. But he did go on to say, "I baptize thee," and all the rest of it, to Father. "We receive this person into the congregation of Christ's flock," he added; "and do sign him with the sign of the Cross, in token that hereafter he shall not be ashamed to confess the faith of Christ crucified, and manfully to fight under his banner, against sin, the world, and the devil; and to continue Christ's faithful soldier and servant unto his life's end. Amen."

The baptism part was now over. Father started to leave, but we managed somehow to detain him while we knelt and gave thanks. And, to end with, Mr. Morley urged Father to "mortify all his evil affections," and exhorted Mother and me to remember that it was our part and duty to put Father in mind what a solemn vow he had now made, that so he might grow in grace and the knowledge of Christ, "and live godly, righteously, and soberly, in this present world."

We stood awkwardly still for a moment, but there was nothing else. Mr. Morley started in being chatty, in a more everyday voice. He stood next to me as he talked, and I remember how absorbed I was, again, by his mellow aroma. The odor was so grateful to my senses that it seemed almost nourishing. I sniffed and I sniffed—till all of a sudden I knew what it was. It was cocoa. We seldom had cocoa at our house. It made me feel hungry. I greedily inhaled the last bits of it while Mr. Morley talked on. He said he hoped we'd attend services in this new church of his, sometimes. He began to describe how the bishop had come there to consecrate it.

But Father broke in, saying abruptly, "I shall be late at the office," and strode down the aisle. Mother and I hurried after him. He was muttering such blasphemous things that I heard Mother whisper: "Oh, please, Clare, please; please don't. This poor little church! It'll have to be consecrated all over again."

As we drove off, Mother sank back into her corner of the cab, quite worn out. Father was still seething away, as though his very soul was boiling over. If he could only have known it, long quiet days were ahead, when he and God could go back in peace to their comfortable old ways together; for he was never confirmed, or troubled in any way again by religious demands. But all he could think of, for the moment, were his recent indignities.

He got out at the nearest Elevated station, to take a train for the office, with the air of a man who had thoroughly wasted the morning. He slammed the cab door on us, leaving us to drive home alone. But before he turned away to climb the stairs, he thrust his red face in the window, and with a burning look at Mother said, "I hope to God you are satisfied." Then this new son of the church took out his watch, gave a start, and Mother and I heard him shout "Hell!" as he raced up the steps.

Who is the rebel against established authority in this story? Who is the champion of traditional values? Does either one get their way completely? Why or why not?

In what ways are Mr. and Mrs. Day similar to other fathers and mothers in the stories in this unit?

Why do you think the heroes of the selections in this unit are unsuccessful in breaking down the powerful systems which oppose them?

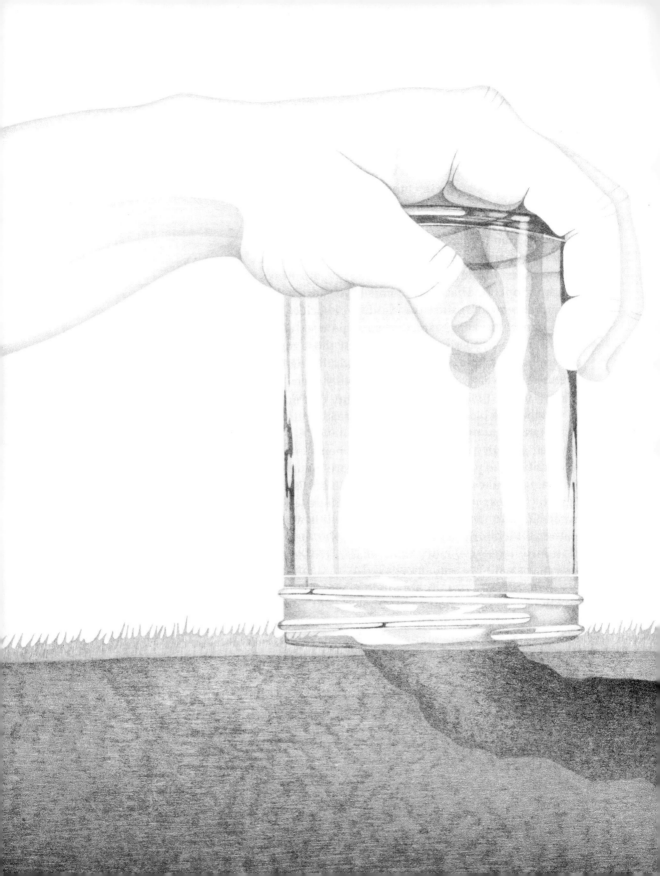

2

THE WORLD'S WAY UNDONE

nobody loses all the time

nobody loses all the time

i had an uncle named
Sol who was a born failure and
nearly everybody said he should have gone
into vaudeville perhaps because my Uncle Sol could
sing McCann He Was A Diver on Xmas Eve like Hell Itself which
may or may not account for the fact that my Uncle

Sol indulged in that possibly most inexcusable
of all to use a highfalootin phrase
luxuries that is or to
wit farming and be
it needlessly
added

my Uncle Sol's farm
failed because the chickens
ate the vegetables so
my Uncle Sol had a
chicken farm till the
skunks ate the chickens when

my Uncle Sol
had a skunk farm but
the skunks caught cold and
died and so
my Uncle Sol imitated the
skunks in a subtle manner

or by drowning himself in the watertank
but somebody who'd given my Uncle Sol a Victor
Victrola and records while he lived presented to
him upon the auspicious occasion of his decease a
scrumptious not to mention splendiferous funeral with
tall boys in black gloves and flowers and everything and

i remember we all cried like the Missouri
when my Uncle Sol's coffin lurched because
somebody pressed a button
(and down went
my Uncle
Sol

and started a worm farm)

E. E. CUMMINGS

Do you think the poet sees Uncle Sol as a total failure? Explain.

Mutsmag

An Appalachian folk tale
Retold by RICHARD CHASE

One time there was an old woman had three girls, Poll and Betts and
Mutsmag. Mutsmag she was the youngest, and Poll and Betts they
treated her awful mean, made her do all the work while they'd lie in
the bed of a mornin', didn't give her nothin' to eat but leftovers.

Well, the old woman died and all she had was a cabbage patch and
an old case-knife. She left the patch of cabbage to Poll and Betts, and
she didn't leave Mutsmag nothin' but that old knife. Poll and Betts
started in eatin' that cabbage, didn't let Mutsmag have a bite of it.
And directly they eat it all up. So then Poll and Betts they decided
they'd go a great journey and seek their fortune, so they borryed some
meal to make journey cakes. Mutsmag begged and begged couldn't she
please go too, and they told her no, she couldn't, but she begged and
begged till fin'lly they told her, said, "All right, you crazy thing, but
you'll have to fix your own journey cakes. Here, go get you some water
in this."

And they handed her a riddel. So Mutsmag took the riddel and ran
down to the spring. Tried to dip her up some water, it 'uld run out.
Dip it up, it 'uld all run out. Then a little bluebird lit on a limb, tilted
over and watched her; and directly it started in singin', says:

> *"Stop it with moss and stick it with clay,*
> *then you can pack your water away!*
> *Stop it with moss and stick it with clay,*
> *then you can pack your water away!"*

"Much obliged," says Mutsmag. "I'll try that." So she smeared clay
inside the riddel and pulled some moss and daubed hit over the clay

and stopped ever' hole. Packed her riddel back to the house plumb full of water. So then her sisters *had* to let her go.

They got down the road a piece, and Poll and Betts started in whisperin'—turned around all at onct, grabbed Mutsmag and tied her to a laurel grub. Snatched her journey cakes and off they run. Mutsmag pulled at the rope and pulled at it; and fin'lly she thought of her old knife and give the rope a rip and aloose it come. So she took out after Poll and Betts.

They looked back directly and there come Mutsmag. "Law! There's that crazy thing again! What'll we do with her this time?" Well, there was an old shop-house right there 'side the road. So they grabbed her and shoved her in that old shop-house. The door-latch was on the outside, so when Poll and Betts slammed the door on Mutsmag there wasn't no way for her to get out. She tried and tried but she couldn't. So finally she set in to hollerin'. Old fox heard her and come to the door.

"Who's in there?"

"Hit's me—Mutsmag."

"What ye want?"

"I want out."

"Unlatch the latch."

"Ain't none. Hit's out there. See can't you push it up."

"What'll ye give me?"

"I'll take ye to the fat of a goose's neck."

So the fox he reached for the latch and pushed it up, and Mutsmag took him where the fat goose was at, and then she put out and caught up with Poll and Betts again.

"Law! Yonder comes that crazy thing! What in the world will we do with her now?"

"Let's make out she's our servin' girl and make her do all the work when we stay the night somewhere."

So they let Mutsmag alone. And about dark they come to a house and hollered and an old woman come out. They asked her could they stay the night. Says, "We got us a servin' girl. She'll do up all the work for ye."

The old woman said yes, they could stay, so Poll and Betts went on in and sat by the fire and Mutsmag went to scourin' the pots.

Now the old woman had three girls about the size of Poll and Betts and Mutsmag, and she sent 'em all up in the loft to sleep. So they cloomb up the ladder and laid down in the straw, went right to sleep

—all but Mutsmag. She stayed awake and listened. Heard somebody come in directly, stompin' around and fussin' at the old woman about supper not bein' ready. Mutsmag looked down quick through the cracks and knotholes, seen it was a giant.

"Hush! Hush!" the old woman told him. "You'll wake up them three fine fat pullets I got for ye up in the loft." Says, "You can get 'em down now and I'll cook 'em for ye."

"HOW'LL I KNOW 'EM FROM YOUR GIRLS?"

"My girls got nightcaps on."

Mutsmag reached right quick and jerked the nightcaps off them three girls, put 'em on her and Poll and Betts, laid back down and went to snorin'. The old giant reached up through the scuttlehole and felt around for the girls that didn't have no nightcaps on. Pulled 'em down out the loft, wrung their necks and throwed 'em over to the old woman. She went to put 'em in the cook-pot, and when she seen what the old giant had done she lit into him with the pot-ladle and nearly beat him to death.

"You ugly old coot!" she hollered at him. "You've gone and got the wrong ones!" And she hit him over the head again. Well, she went to battlin' the old giant with that ladle and the shovel and the poker and whatever she could grab up to beat him with and he went to dodgin' around; and while all that was goin' on, Mutsmag took her old knife and ripped the bedclothes and tied knots and made her a rope. Then she knocked a big hole in the shingles, tied the rope to a rafter and throwed it out, and Poll and Betts and her got away.

Well, they traveled on and traveled on, and the next evenin' they come to the King's house, and he invited 'em in to stay the night. Poll and Betts went to braggin' about what'n-all they done at the old giant's place, make like they was the ones done it. Mutsmag never said a word.

And directly the King said to Poll and Betts, says, "All right. You girls ought to be sharp enough to go back over there and get shet of both of 'em. That old woman's a witch and she's worse than her old man, even if he is a giant. Reckon you can do that for me?"

Of course Poll and Betts couldn't back out then, so they said sure, they could do that. Left there the next mornin', but instead of goin' anywhere close to that giant's place they took out in another direction and that was the last anybody ever seen of 'em.

Well, Mutsmag she never said nothin'. Stayed on there and worked for the King. Then one evenin' she put out and went on down to the giant's house. Had a half-bushel poke of salt with her. So she cloomb up on the old giant's house, got up there next to the chimney, and ever-when the old woman raised the pot-lid Mutsmag sprinkled salt down in the pot of meat she had cookin'. So directly the old giant started in eatin'.

"OLD WOMAN, THE MEAT'S TOO SALTY!"

"Why, I never put in but one pinch!"

"YOU MUST A' PUT IN A HALF-BUSHEL, OLD WOMAN! FETCH ME SOME WATER HERE!"

"There hain't a bit of water up."

"GO TO THE SPRING AND GET SOME! HURRY NOW! I'M JEST ABOUT DEAD FOR WATER!"

"Hit's too dark."

"THROW OUT YOUR LIGHT-BALL!"

So the old woman throwed her light-ball out toward the spring, but Mutsmag was standin' there and caught it on the point of her old knife; and when the old woman came runnin' with the water bucket, Mutsmag squinched the light-ball in the spring and the old woman stumped her toe and fell and broke her neck. So Mutsmag cut off her head with that old knife, took it on back to the King.

He gave her a bushel of gold, says, "I declare, Mutsmag! You're pretty sharp." Says, "That old giant now, he's got a fine white horse he stole from me. Hit's a ten-mile-stepper, and I been tryin' ever' way in the world to get that horse back. You get it for me and I'll pay ye another bushel of gold."

So Mutsmag she went on back about the time it was gettin' dark. Had her apron pocket full of barley. Went in the stable and there was the fine white horse. Hit had bells on its halter, and the rope where it was tied was awful thick and had more knots in it than you could count. Well, Mutsmag, she took her old knife and went to cuttin' on them knots and the horse throwed up his head—

"Dingle! Dingle!"

The old giant come a-runnin' and Mutsmag hid under the trough. The giant he opened the stable door, looked around, went on back. So Mutsmag threw some barley in the trough. The horse went for it and them bells didn't dingle so loud. Mutsmag she started in on them knots again. But the horse eat up all that barley, throwed up his head—

"Dingle! Dingle!"

And here come the old giant! Mutsmag hid by the door. The giant he shoved the door back on Mutsmag, came right on in the stable, looked around, looked around, went on back.

Mutsmag throwed a double-handful of barley in the trough and worked at them knots just as hard as she could tear, but the fine white horse got the barley eat up, throwed his head around—

"Dingle! Dingle!"

And the old giant come so fast Mutsmag just did have time to jump and hide under the bresh of the fine white horse's tail. Giant came on in, had a lantern with him, looked around, looked under the trough, jerked the door back and looked there, looked in all the corners, up in the rafters. Then he got to feelin' around under the horse's belly, stooped down, shined his lantern, looked, says, "HOLD ON NOW, MY FINE WHITE HORSE! YE GOT TOO MANY LEGS BACK HERE!"

And just about that time the fine white horse switched his tail and there was Mutsmag. She made for the door but the old giant grabbed her, says, "NOW I GOT YE!"

"What you goin' to do with me?"

"DON'T KNOW YET. HAIN'T MADE UP MY MIND!"

"Please don't feed me on honey and butter, I just can't stand the taste of honey and butter."

"THAT'S THE VERY THING I'M GOIN' TO DO! HONEY AND BUTTER IS ALL YOU'LL GIT!"

So he locked her up in the chicken house, gave her all the honey and butter she could hold. Mutsmag jest loved honey and butter. She got fat in a hurry. He come to get her fin'lly, reached in and grabbed her by the leg, toted her on to the house, says, "NOW I'M GOIN' TO KEEL YE!"

"How you goin' to kill me?" Mutsmag asked him.

"DON'T KNOW. HAIN'T MADE UP MY MIND!"

"Please don't put me in a sack and beat me to death, 'cause I'd howl like a dog, and I'd squall like cats, and my bones 'uld crack and pop like dishes breakin', and my blood 'uld run and drip like honey."

"THAT'S THE VERY WAY I'M GOIN' TO KEEL YE!"

So he got a big sack and tied Mutsmag in it. Went on out to cut him a club. Time he got good and gone Mutsmag took her old knife and give that sack a rip and a-loose it come. Then she sewed it back right quick and put the giant's old dog in there and as many cats as she could catch and all the old giant's dishes, and she went and got the biggest pot of honey he had and put hit in, too. Then she went and hid.

The old giant come in directly with a big club—looked like he'd pulled him up a good-sized white oak. Drawed back and lammed into that sack. The dog howled and them cats set in to squallin'. The old giant went to grinnin'.

"O YES! I'LL MAKE YE HOWL LIKE DOGS AND SQUALL LIKE CATS!"

Hit it a few more licks and all them cups and saucers and plates and bowls and pitchers started crackin' and poppin'.

"O YES! I'LL MAKE YOUR BONES POP AND CRACK LIKE DISHES!"

Beat right on, and directly the honey started dribblin' out.

"O YES! I'LL MAKE YOUR BLOOD RUN AND DRIP LIKE HONEY!"

So he hit the sack several more licks and then he untied it and went to dump Mutsmag out, and there on the floor was his dog killed, and his cats; and ever' dish he had in the house all broke up, and honey jest runnin' all over everything. He was so mad he nearly busted wide open. Throwed down his club and broke and run. Headed right straight for the stable.

But while he was a flailin' that sack, Mutsmag she'd fin'lly got the rope cut, and had left there a-straddle of that fine white horse and him a-hittin' ten miles ever' step. So the old giant looked to see which-a-way they had headed, seen a streak of dust a way off, and he put out. Came to a deep wide river directly, looked across and there was Mutsmag sittin' on a millrock with a rope through the hole and one end tied around her neck.

"HOW'D YOU GIT OVER THAR?"

"I picked a hole in a rock and tied it around my neck and skeeted the rock across."

So the old giant hunted him up a great big flat rock, picked a hole in it and put a length of rope through, and tied it to his neck, and when he tried to skip the rock across hit jerked him in, and that was the last anybody ever saw of him.

So Mutsmag went and got back on the horse where she had him hid in the bresh, rode on back to the King and he paid her two more bushels of gold—one for gettin' his horse and one for gettin' shet of that old giant.

An impostor is a character who tries to take what is not his or to be what he is not. In what ways were Mutsmag's sisters frauds or impostors?

How is Mutsmag like Cinderella? In what important ways is she different from the traditional character of Cinderella?

Why does Mutsmag triumph over her sisters, the witch, and the giant?

The Umbrella Oracle

A Japanese legend
IHARA SAIKAKU
Translated by RICHARD LANE

Commendable indeed is the spirit of philanthropy in this world of ours!

To the famous "Hanging Temple of Kwannon" in the Province of Kii, someone had once presented twenty oil-paper umbrellas which, repaired every year, were hung beside the temple for the use of any and all who might be caught in the rain or snow. They were always conscientiously returned when the weather improved—not a single one had ever been lost.

One day in the spring of 1649, however, a certain villager borrowed one of the umbrellas and, while he was returning home, had it blown out of his hands by a violent "divine wind" that blew up suddenly from the direction of the shrine on Tamazu Isle. The umbrella was blown completely out of sight, and though the villager bemoaned its loss there was not a thing he could do.

Borne aloft by the wind, the umbrella landed finally in the little hamlet of Anazato, far in the mountains of the island of Kyushu. The people of this village had from ancient times been completely cut off from the world and—uncultured folk that they were—had never even seen an umbrella! All of the learned men and elders of the village gathered around to discuss the curious object before them—reaching agreement, however, only upon the fact that none of them had ever before seen anything like it.

Finally one local wiseman stepped forth and proclaimed, "Upon counting the radiating bamboo ribs, there are exactly forty. The paper too is round and luminous, and not of the ordinary kind. Though I hesitate to utter that August Name, this is without a doubt the God of the Sun, whose name we have so often heard, and is assuredly his divine attribute from the Inner Sanctuary of the Great Shrine of Ise, which has deigned to fly to us here!"

All present were filled with awe. Hurriedly the salt water of purification was scattered about the ground and the divinity installed upon a clean reed mat; and the whole population of the village went up into the mountains and, gathering wood and rushes, built a shrine that the diety's spirit might be transferred hence from Ise. When they had paid reverence to it, the divine spirit did indeed enter the umbrella.

At the time of the summer rains the site upon which the shrine was situated became greatly agitated, and the commotion did not cease. When the umbrella was consulted, the following oracle was delivered: "All this summer the sacred hearth has been simply filthy, with cockroaches boiled in the holy vessels and the contamination reaching even to my Inner Shrine! Henceforth, in this entire province, let there not be a single cockroach left alive! I also have one other request. I desire you to select a beautiful young maiden as a consolation offering for me. If this is not done within seven days, without fail, I will cause the rain to fall in great torrents; I will rain you all to death, so that the seed of man remains no more upon the earth!"

Thus spake the oracle.

The villagers were frightened out of their wits. They held a meeting, and summoned all the maidens of the village to decide which one should serve the deity. But the young maidens, weeping and wailing, strongly protested the umbrella-god's cruel demand. When asked the reason for their excess of grief, they cried, "How could we survive even one night with such a god?"—for they had come to attach a peculiar significance to the odd shape which the deity had assumed.

At this juncture a young and beautiful widow from the village stepped forward, saying, "Since it is for the god, I will offer myself in place of the young maidens."

All night long the beautiful widow waited in the shrine, but she did not get a bit of affection. Enraged, she charged into the inner sanctum, grasped the divine umbrella firmly in her hands and screaming, "Worthless deceiver!" she tore it apart, and threw the pieces as far as she could!

Is there an impostor in this story? Who is it? Who exposes it?

How does the young widow differ from the other villagers? How is she like Mutsmag? Is her attitude toward established religion similar to Mr. Day's in "My Father Enters the Church"? Explain.

The Body in the Window-seat

From Arsenic and Old Lace

JOSEPH KESSELRING

Characters

MORTIMER BREWSTER, *young writer and drama critic*

ABBY and MARTHA BREWSTER, *maiden aunts of Mortimer*

ELAINE HARPER, *Mortimer's fiancée*

MR. GIBBS, *man looking for a room to rent*

TEDDY BREWSTER, *Mortimer's brother, who believes he is Teddy Roosevelt*

Afternoon in the living room of the Brewster home in Brooklyn.

MORTIMER. By the way, I left a large envelope around here last week. It was one of the chapters of my book on Thoreau. Have you seen it?

MARTHA (*pushing armchair into table*). Well, if you left it here it must be here somewhere.

ABBY (*crossing to downstage left of* MORTIMER). When are you going to be married? What are your plans? There must be something more you can tell us about Elaine.

MORTIMER. Elaine? Oh, yes, Elaine thought it was brilliant. (*He crosses to sideboard, looks through cupboards and drawers.*)

MARTHA. What was, dear?

MORTIMER. My chapter on Thoreau. (*He finds a bundle of papers (script) in right drawer and takes them to table and looks through them.*)

ABBY (*at center*). Well, when Elaine comes back I think we ought to have a little celebration. We must drink to your happiness. Martha, isn't there some of that Lady Baltimore cake left?

(*During last few speeches* MARTHA *has picked up pail from sideboard and her cape, hat and gloves from table in upstage left corner.*)

MARTHA (*crossing downstage left*). Oh, yes!

ABBY. And I'll open a bottle of wine.

MARTHA (*as she exits to kitchen*). Oh, and to think it happened in this room!

MORTIMER (*has finished looking through papers, is gazing around room*). Now where could I have put that?

ABBY. Well, with your fiancée sitting beside you tonight, I do hope the play will be something you can enjoy for once. It may be something romantic. What's the name of it?

MORTIMER. "Murder Will Out."

ABBY. Oh, dear! (*She disappears into kitchen as* MORTIMER *goes on talking.*)

MORTIMER. When the curtain goes up the first thing you'll see will be a dead body. (*He lifts window-seat and sees one. Not believing it, he drops window-seat again and starts downstage. He suddenly stops with a "take," then goes back, throws window-seat open and stares in. He goes slightly mad for a moment. He backs away, then hears* ABBY *humming on her way into the room. He drops window-seat again and holds it down, staring around the room.* ABBY *enters carrying a silencer and tablecloth which she puts on armchair, then picks up bundle of papers and returns them to drawer in sideboard.* MORTIMER *speaks in a somewhat strained voice.*) Aunt Abby!

ABBY (*at sideboard*). Yes, dear?

MORTIMER. You were going to make plans for Teddy to go to that . . . sanitarium—Happy Dale—

ABBY (*bringing legal papers from sideboard to* MORTIMER). Yes, dear, it's all arranged. Dr. Harper was here today and brought the papers for Teddy to sign. Here they are.

(*He takes them from her.*)

MORTIMER. He's got to sign them right away.

ABBY. (*Arranging silencer on table.* MARTHA *enters from kitchen door with table silver and plates on a tray. She sets tray on sideboard. Goes to table right.*) That's what Dr. Harper thinks. Then there won't be any legal difficulties after we pass on.

MORTIMER. He's got to sign them this minute. He's down in the cellar— get him up here right away.

MARTHA. (*Unfolding tablecloth. She's above table on right.*) There's no such hurry as that.

ABBY. No. When Teddy starts working on the canal you can't get his mind on anything else.

MORTIMER. Teddy's got to go to Happy Dale now—tonight.

MARTHA. Oh, no, dear, that's not until after we're gone.

MORTIMER. Right away, I tell you—right away!

ABBY (*turning to* MORTIMER). Why, Mortimer, how can you say such a thing? Why, as long as we live we'll never be separated from Teddy.

MORTIMER (*trying to be calm*). Listen, darlings, I'm frightfully sorry, but I've got some shocking news for you. (*The* AUNTS *stop work and look at him with some interest.*) Now we've all got to try and keep our heads. You know we've sort of humored Teddy because we thought he was harmless.

MARTHA. Why he *is* harmless!

MORTIMER. He *was* harmless. That's why he has to go to Happy Dale. Why he has to be confined.

ABBY (*stepping to* MORTIMER). Mortimer, why have you suddenly turned against Teddy?—your own brother?

MORTIMER. You've got to know sometime. It might as well be now, Teddy's—killed a man!

MARTHA. Nonsense, dear.

(MORTIMER *rises and points to window-seat.*)

MORTIMER. There's a body in the window-seat!

ABBY. Yes, dear, we know.

(MORTIMER *"takes" as* ABBY *and* MARTHA *busy themselves again at table.*)

MORTIMER. You *know?*

MARTHA. Of course, dear, but it has nothing to do with Teddy. (*Gets tray from sideboard—arranges silver and plates on table: three places, upstage, left, and right.*)

ABBY. Now, Mortimer, just forget about it—forget you ever saw the gentleman.

MORTIMER. *Forget?*

ABBY. We never dreamed you'd peek.

MORTIMER. But who is he?

ABBY. His name's Hoskins—Adam Hoskins. That's really all I know about him—except that he's a Methodist.

MORTIMER. That's all you know about him? Well, what's he doing here? What happened to him?

MARTHA. He died.

MORTIMER. Aunt Martha, men don't just get into window-seats and die.

ABBY (*silly boy*). No, he died first.

MORTIMER. Well, how?

ABBY. Oh, Mortimer, don't be so inquisitive. The gentleman died because he drank some wine with poison in it.

MORTIMER. How did the poison get in the wine?

MARTHA. Well, we put it in wine because it's less noticeable—when it's in tea it has a distinct odor.

MORTIMER. *You* put it in the wine?

ABBY. Yes. And I put Mr. Hoskins in the window-seat because Dr. Harper was coming.

MORTIMER. So you knew what you'd done! You didn't want Dr. Harper to see the body!

ABBY. Well, not at tea—that wouldn't have been very nice. Now, Mortimer, you know the whole thing, just forget about it. I do think Martha and I have the right to our own little secrets. (*She crosses to sideboard to get two goblets from left cupboard as* MARTHA *comes to table from sideboard with salt dish and pepper shaker.*)

MARTHA. And don't you tell Elaine! (*She gets third goblet from sideboard, then turns to* ABBY *who takes tray from sideboard.*) Oh, Abby, while I was out I dropped in on Mrs. Schultz. She's much better but she would like us to take Junior to the movies again.

ABBY. Well, we must do that tomorrow or next day.

MARTHA. Yes, but this time we'll go where we want to go. (*She starts for kitchen door.* ABBY *follows.*) Junior's not going to drag me into another one of those scary pictures. (*They exit into kitchen as* MORTIMER *wheels around and looks after them.* ABBY *shuts door.*)

MORTIMER. (*Dazed, looks around the room. His eyes come to rest on phone on desk; he crosses to it and dials a number. Into phone*) City desk! (*There is a pause.*) Hello, Al. Do you know who this is? (*Pause.*) That's right. Say, Al, when I left the office, I told you where I was going, remember?—Well, where did I say? (*Pause.*) Uh-huh. Well, it would take me about half an hour to get to Brooklyn. What time have you got? (*He looks at his watch.*) That's right. I must be there. (*He hangs up, sits for a moment, then suddenly leaps off stool toward kitchen.*) Aunt Abby! Aunt Martha! Come in here! (*He backs up to center stage as the two* AUNTS *bustle in.* MARTHA *has tray with plates, cups, saucers, and soup cups.*) What are we going to do? What are we going to do?

MARTHA (*right of table*). What are we going to do about what, dear?

MORTIMER (*pointing to window-seat*). There's a body in there.

ABBY (*upstage left of* MORTIMER). Yes—Mr. Hoskins.

MORTIMER. Well, good heavens, I can't turn you over to the police! But what am I going to do?

MARTHA. Well, for one thing, dear, stop being so excited.

ABBY. And for pity's sake stop worrying. We told you to forget the whole thing.

MORTIMER. Forget! My dear Aunt Abby, can't I make you realize that something has to be done?

ABBY (*a little sharply*). Now, Mortimer, you behave yourself. You're too old to be flying off the handle like this.

MORTIMER. But Mr. Hotchkiss—

(ABBY, *on her way to sideboard, stops and turns to* MORTIMER.)

ABBY. Hoskins, dear. (*She continues on her way to sideboard and gets napkins and rings from left drawer.* MARTHA *puts her tray, with cups, plates, etc., on table.* MORTIMER *continues speaking through this.*)

MORTIMER. Well, whatever his name is, you can't leave him there.

MARTHA. We don't intend to, dear.

ABBY (*crossing to table left with napkins and rings*). No, Teddy's down in the cellar now digging the lock.

MORTIMER. You mean you're going to bury Mr. Hotchkiss in the cellar?

MARTHA (*stepping to him*). Oh, yes, dear,—that's what we did with the others.

MORTIMER (*walking away to right*). No! You can't bury Mr.—(*Double take. Turns back to them.*)—others?

ABBY. The other gentlemen.

MORTIMER. When you say others—do you mean—others? More than one others?

MARTHA. Oh, yes, dear. Let me see, this is eleven. (*To* ABBY *upstage left of table*) Isn't it, Abby?

ABBY. No, dear, this makes twelve.

(MORTIMER *backs away from them, stunned, toward phone stool at desk.*)

MARTHA. Oh, I think you're wrong, Abby. This is only eleven.

ABBY. No, dear, because I remember when Mr. Hoskins first came in, it occurred to me that he would make just an even dozen.

MARTHA. Well, you really shouldn't count the first one.

ABBY. Oh, *I* was counting the first one. So that makes it twelve.

(*Phone rings.* MORTIMER, *in a daze, turns toward it and without picking up receiver, speaks.*)

MORTIMER. *Hello!* (*He comes to, picks up receiver.*) Hello. Oh, hello, Al. My, it's good to hear your voice.

(ABBY, *at table, is still holding out for a "twelve" count.*)

ABBY. Well, anyway, they're all down in the cellar —

MORTIMER (*to* AUNTS). Ssshhh — (*Into phone, as* AUNTS *cross to sideboard and put candelabras from top to bottom shelf*) Oh, no, Al, I'm sober as a lark. I just called you because I was feeling a little Pirandello — Piran — you wouldn't know, Al. Look, I'm glad you called. Get hold of George right away. He's got to review the play tonight. I can't make it. No, Al, you're wrong. I'll tell you all about it tomorrow. Well, George has got to cover the play tonight! This is my department and I'm running it! You get ahold of George! (*He hangs up and sits a moment trying to collect himself.*) Now let's see, where were we? (*He suddenly leaps from stool.*) TWELVE!

MARTHA. Yes, Abby thinks we ought to count the first one and that makes twelve. (*She goes back to sideboard.*)

(MORTIMER *takes chair right of table and faces it toward right stage, then takes* MARTHA *by the hands, leads her to the chair and sets her in it.*)

MORTIMER. All right — now — who was the first one?

ABBY (*crossing from above table to* MORTIMER). Mr. Midgely. He was a Baptist.

MARTHA. Of course, I still think we can't claim full credit for him because he just died.

ABBY. Martha means without any help from us. You see, Mr. Midgely came here looking for a room —

MARTHA. It was right after you moved to New York.

ABBY. —And it didn't seem right for that lovely room to be going to waste when there were so many people who needed it —

MARTHA. —He was such a lonely old man. . . .

ABBY. All his kith and kin were dead and it left him so forlorn and unhappy —

MARTHA. —We felt so sorry for him.

ABBY. And then when his heart attack came — and he sat dead in that chair (*pointing to armchair*). Looking so peaceful — remember, Martha — we made up our minds then and there that if we could help other lonely old men to that same peace — we would!

MORTIMER (all ears). He dropped dead right in that chair! How awful for you!

MARTHA. Oh, no, dear. Why, it was rather like old times. Your grandfather always used to have a cadaver or two around the house. You see, Teddy had been digging in Panama and he thought Mr. Midgely was a Yellow Fever victim.

ABBY. That meant he had to be buried immediately.

MARTHA. So we all took him down to Panama and put him in the lock. (She rises, puts her arm around ABBY.) Now that's why we told you not to worry about it because we know exactly what's to be done.

MORTIMER. And that's how all this started — that man walking in here and dropping dead.

ABBY. Of course, we realized we couldn't depend on that happening again. So —

MARTHA (crossing to MORTIMER). You remember those jars of poison that have been up on the shelves in Grandfather's laboratory all these years — ?

ABBY. You know your Aunt Martha's knack for mixing things. You've eaten enough of her piccalilli.

MARTHA. Well, dear, for a gallon of elderberry wine I take one teaspoonful of arsenic, then add a half teaspoonful of strychnine and then just a pinch of cyanide.

MORTIMER (appraisingly). Should have quite a kick.

ABBY. Yes! As a matter of fact one of our gentlemen found time to say "How delicious!"

MARTHA (stepping upstage). Well, I'll have to get things started in the kitchen.

ABBY (to MORTIMER). I wish you could stay for dinner.

MARTHA. I'm trying out a new recipe.

MORTIMER. I couldn't eat a thing.

(MARTHA goes out to kitchen.)

ABBY (calling after MARTHA). I'll come and help you, dear. (She pushes chair right into table.) Well, I feel so much better now. Oh, you have to wait for Elaine, don't you? (She smiles.) How happy you must be. (She goes to kitchen doorway.) Well, dear, I'll leave you alone with your thoughts. (She exits, shutting door.)

(The shutting of the door wakes MORTIMER from his trance. He crosses *to window-seat, kneels down, raises cover, looks in. Not believing, he lowers cover, rubs his eyes, raises cover again. This time he really sees Mr. Hoskins. Closes window-seat hastily, rises, steps back. Runs over and closes drapes over window. Backs up to above table. Sees water glass on table, picks it up, raises it to lips, suddenly remembers that poisoned wine comes in glasses, puts it down quickly. Crosses to cellar door, opens it. ELAINE enters right, he closes cellar door with a bang. As ELAINE puts her bag on top of desk he looks at her, and it dawns on him that he knows her. He speaks with faint surprise.)*

MORTIMER. Oh, it's you. (*He drops downstage.* ELAINE *crosses to him, takes his hand.*)

ELAINE. Don't be cross, darling! Father could see that I was excited — so I told him about us and that made it hard for me to get away. But listen, darling — he's not going to wait up for me tonight.

MORTIMER (*looking at window-seat*). You run along home, Elaine, and I'll call you up tomorrow.

ELAINE. Tomorrow!

MORTIMER (*irritated*). You know I always call you up every day or two.

ELAINE. But we're going to the theater tonight.

MORTIMER. No — no we're not!

ELAINE. Well, why not?

MORTIMER (*turning to her*). Elaine, something's come up.

ELAINE. What, darling? Mortimer — you've lost your job!

MORTIMER. No-no — I haven't lost my job. I'm just not covering that play tonight. (*Pushing her right*) Now you run along home, Elaine.

ELAINE. But I've got to know what's happened. Certainly you can tell me.

MORTIMER. No, dear, I can't.

ELAINE. But if we're going to be married —

MORTIMER. Married?

ELAINE. Have you forgotten that not fifteen minutes ago you proposed to me?

MORTIMER (*vaguely*). I did? Oh — yes! Well, as far as I know that's still on. (*Urging her right again*) Now you run along home, Elaine. I've got to do something.

ELAINE. Listen, you can't propose to me one minute and throw me out of the house the next.

MORTIMER (*pleading*). I'm not throwing you out of the house, darling. Will you get out of here?

ELAINE. No, I won't get out of here. (MORTIMER *crosses toward kitchen.* ELAINE *crosses below to window-seat.*) Not until I've had some kind of explanation. (ELAINE *is about to sit on window-seat.* MORTIMER *grabs her by the hand. Phone rings.*)

MORTIMER. Elaine! (*He goes to phone, dragging* ELAINE *with him.*) Hello! Oh, hello, Al. Hold on a minute, will you?—All right, it's important! But it can wait a minute, can't it? Hold on! (*He puts receiver on desk. Takes* ELAINE's *bag from top of desk and hands it to her. Then takes her by hand and leads her to door right and opens it.*) Look, Elaine, you're a sweet girl and I love you. But I have something on my mind now and I want you to go home and wait until I call you.

ELAINE (*in doorway*). Don't try to be masterful.

MORTIMER (*annoyed to the point of being literate*). When we're married and I have problems to face I hope you're less tedious and un-inspired!

ELAINE. And when we're married *if* we're married—I hope I find you adequate! (*She exits.* MORTIMER *does take, then runs out on porch after her, calling—*)

MORTIMER. Elaine! Elaine! (*He runs back in, shutting door, crosses and kneels on window-seat to open window. Suddenly remembers contents of window-seat and leaps off it. Dashes into kitchen but remembers Al is on phone, re-enters immediately and crosses to phone.*) Hello, Al? Hello . . . hello. . . . (*He pushes hook down and starts to dial when doorbell rings. He thinks it's the phone.* ABBY *enters from kitchen.*) Hello. Hello, Al?

ABBY (*crossing to right door and opening it*). That's the doorbell, dear, not the telephone. (MORTIMER *pushes hook down . . . dials.* MR. GIBBS *steps in doorway right.*) How do you do? Come in.

GIBBS. I understand you have a room to rent.

(MARTHA *enters from kitchen. Puts "Lazy Susan" on sideboard, then gets to right of table.*)

ABBY. Yes. Won't you step in?

GIBBS (*stepping into room*). Are you the lady of the house?

ABBY. Yes, I'm Miss Brewster. And this is my sister, another Miss Brewster.

GIBBS. My name is Gibbs.

ABBY (*easing him to chair right of table*). Oh, won't you sit down? I'm sorry we were just setting the table for dinner.

MORTIMER (*into phone*). Hello—let me talk to Al again. City desk.

(*Loud*) AL!! CITY DESK! WHAT? I'm sorry, wrong number. (*He hangs up and starts dialing again as* GIBBS *looks at him.* GIBBS *turns to* ABBY.)

GIBBS. May I see the room?

MARTHA (*downstage left of table*). Why don't you sit down a minute and let's get acquainted.

GIBBS. That won't do much good if I don't like the room.

ABBY. Is Brooklyn your home?

GIBBS. Haven't got a home. Live in a hotel. Don't like it.

MORTIMER (*into phone*). Hello. City desk.

MARTHA. Are your family Brooklyn people?

GIBBS. Haven't got any family.

ABBY (*another victim*). All alone in the world?

GIBBS. Yep.

ABBY. Well, Martha—(MARTHA *goes happily to sideboard, gets bottle of wine from upstage left cupboard, and a wine glass, and sets them on table, upstage end.* ABBY *eases* GIBBS *into chair right of table and continues speaking to him, then to above table.*) Well, you've come to just the right house. Do sit down.

MORTIMER (*into phone*). Hello, Al? Mort. We got cut off. Al, I can't cover the play tonight—that's all there is to it, I can't!

MARTHA (*left of table*). What church do you go to? There's an Episcopal church practically next door. (*Her gesture toward window brings her to window-seat and she sits.*)

GIBBS. I'm Presbyterian. Used to be.

MORTIMER (*into phone*). What's George doing in Bermuda? (*Rises and gets loud.*) Certainly I told him he could go to Bermuda—it's my department, isn't it? Well, you've got to get somebody. Who else is there around the office? (*He sits on second chair.*)

GIBBS. (*Annoyed. Rises and crosses table to left of it.*) Is there always this much noise?

MARTHA. Oh, he doesn't live with us.

(ABBY *sits above table.*)

MORTIMER (*into phone*). There must be somebody around the place. Look, Al, how about the office boy? You know the bright one—the one we don't like? Well, you look around the office, I'll hold on.

GIBBS. I'd really like to see the room.

ABBY. (*After seating* GIBBS *right of table she has sat in chair above table.*) It's upstairs. Won't you try a glass of our wine before we start up?

GIBBS. Never touch it.

MARTHA. We make this ourselves. It's elderberry wine.

GIBBS (*to* MARTHA). Elderberry wine. Hmmph. Haven't tasted elderberry wine since I was a boy. Thank you. (*He pulls armchair around and sits as* ABBY *uncorks bottle and starts to pour wine.*)

MORTIMER (*into phone*). Well, there must be some printers around. Look Al, the fellow who sets my copy. He ought to know about what I'd write. His name is Joe. He's the third machine from the left. But, Al, he might turn out to be another Burns Mantle!

GIBBS (*to* MARTHA). Do you have your own elderberry bushes?

MARTHA. No, but the cemetery is full of them.

MORTIMER (*rising*). No, I'm not drinking, but I'm going to start now.

GIBBS. Do you serve meals?

ABBY. We might, but first just see whether you like our wine. (MORTIMER *hangs up, puts phone on top of desk and crosses left. He sees wine on table. Goes to sideboard, gets glass, brings it to table and pours drink.* GIBBS *has his glass in hand and is getting ready to drink.*)

MARTHA. (*Sees* MORTIMER *pouring wine.*) Mortimer! Eh eh eh eh! (GIBBS *stops and looks at* MARTHA. MORTIMER *pays no attention.*) Eh eh ch eh!

(*As* MORTIMER *raises glass to lips with left hand,* ABBY *reaches up and pulls his arm down.*)

ABBY. Mortimer. Not that. (MORTIMER, *still dumb, puts his glass down on table. Then he suddenly sees* GIBBS *who has just got glass to his lips and is about to drink. He points across table at* GIBBS *and gives a wild cry.* GIBBS *looks at him, putting his glass down.* MORTIMER, *still pointing at* GIBBS, *goes around above table toward him.* GIBBS, *seeing a madman, rises slowly and backs toward center, then turns and runs for exit right,* MORTIMER *following him.* GIBBS *opens right door, and* MORTIMER *pushes him out, closing door after him. Then he turns and leans on door in exhausted relief. Meantime,* MARTHA *has risen and crossed to below armchair, while* ABBY *has risen and crossed to downstage center.*)

ABBY (*great disappointment*). Now you've spoiled everything. (*She goes to sofa and sits.*)

(MARTHA *sits in armchair.* MORTIMER *crosses to center and looks from one to the other . . . then speaks to* ABBY.)

MORTIMER. You can't do things like that. I don't know how to explain this to you, but it's not only against the law. It's wrong! (*To* MARTHA) It's not a nice thing to do.

(MARTHA *turns away from him as* ABBY *has done in his lines to her.*) People wouldn't understand. (*Points to door after* GIBBS.) *He* wouldn't understand.

MARTHA. Abby, we shouldn't have told Mortimer.

MORTIMER. What I mean is—well, this has developed into a very bad habit.

ABBY (*rises*). Mortimer, we don't try to stop you from doing things you like to do. I don't see why you should interfere with us.

(*Phone rings.* MORTIMER *answers.* MARTHA *rises to below table.*)

MORTIMER. Hello? (*It's Al again.*) All right, I'll see the first act and I'll pan the hell out of it. But look, Al, you've got to do something for me. Get hold of O'Brien—our lawyer, the head of our legal department. Have him meet me at the theater. Now, don't let me down. Okay. I'm starting now. (*He hangs up and turns to* AUNTS.) Look I've got to go to the theater, I can't get out of it. But before I go will you promise me something?

MARTHA (*crossing to* ABBY *at center*). We'd have to know what it was first.

MORTIMER. I love you very much and I know you love me. You know I'd do anything in the world for you and I want you to do just this little thing for me.

ABBY. What do you want us to do?

MORTIMER. Don't *do* anything. I mean don't do *anything.* Don't let anyone in this house—and leave Mr. Hoskins right where he is.

MARTHA. Why?

MORTIMER. I want time to think—and I've got quite a little to think about. You know I wouldn't want anything to happen to you.

ABBY. Well, what on earth could happen to us?

MORTIMER (*beside himself*). Anyway—you'll do this for me, won't you?

MARTHA. Well—we were planning on holding services before dinner.

MORTIMER. Services!

MARTHA (*a little indignant*). Certainly. You don't think we'd bury Mr. Hoskins without a full Methodist service, do you? Why he was a Methodist.

MORTIMER. But can't that wait until I get back?

ABBY. Oh, then you could join us.

MORTIMER (*going crazy himself*). Yes! Yes!

ABBY. Oh, Mortimer, you'll enjoy the services—especially the hymns.

(*To* MARTHA) Remember how beautifully Mortimer used to sing in the choir before his voice changed?

MORTIMER. And remember, you're not going to let anyone in this house while I'm gone—it's a promise!

MARTHA. Well—

ABBY. Oh, Martha, we can do that now that Mortimer's cooperating with us. (*To* MORTIMER) Well, all right, Mortimer.

(MORTIMER *heaves a sigh of relief. Crosses to sofa and gets his hat. Then on his way to opening right door, he speaks.*)

MORTIMER. Have you got some paper? I'll get back just as soon as I can. (*Taking legal papers from coat pocket as he crosses*) There's a man I've got to see.

(ABBY *has gone to desk for stationery. She hands it to* MORTIMER.)

ABBY. Here's some stationery. Will this do?

MORTIMER (*taking stationery*). That'll be fine. I can save time if I write my review on the way to the theater. (*He exits right.*)

(*The* AUNTS *stare after him.* MARTHA *crosses and closes door.* ABBY *goes to sideboard and brings two candelabras to table. Then gets matches from sideboard—lights candles during lines.*)

MARTHA. Mortimer didn't seem quite himself today.

ABBY (*lighting candles*). Well, that's only natural—I think I know why.

MARTHA (*lighting floor lamp*). Why?

ABBY. He's just become engaged to be married. I suppose that always makes a man nervous.

Who are the rebels in this play and what rules do they challenge?

How do the aunts view the deaths of the lodgers? How does the aunts' view of death compare with the poet's attitude toward Uncle Sol's death in "nobody loses all the time"?

The Catbird Seat

JAMES THURBER

Mr. Martin bought the pack of Camels on Monday night in the most crowded cigar store on Broadway. It was theater time and seven or eight men were buying cigarettes. The clerk didn't even glance at Mr. Martin, who put the pack in his overcoat pocket and went out. If any of the staff at F & S had seen him buy the cigarettes, they would have been astonished, for it was generally known that Mr. Martin did not smoke, and never had. No one saw him.

It was just a week to the day since Mr. Martin had decided to rub out Mrs. Ulgine Barrows. The term "rub out" pleased him because it suggested nothing more than the correction of an error — in this case an error of Mr. Fitweiler. Mr. Martin had spent each night of the past week working out his plan and examining it. As he walked home now he went over it again. For the the hundredth time he resented the element of imprecision, the margin of guesswork that entered into the business. The project as he had worked it out was casual and bold, the risks were considerable. Something might go wrong anywhere along the line. And therein lay the cunning of his scheme. No one would ever see in it the cautious, painstaking hand of Erwin Martin, head of the filing department at F & S, of whom Mr. Fitweiler had once said, "Man is fallible but Martin isn't." No one would see his hand, that is, unless it were caught in the act.

Sitting in his apartment, drinking a glass of milk, Mr. Martin reviewed his case against Mrs. Ulgine Barrows, as he had every night for seven nights. He began at the beginning. Her quacking voice and braying laugh had first profaned the halls of F & S on March 7, 1941 (Mr.

Martin had a head for dates). Old Roberts, the personnel chief, had introduced her as the newly appointed special adviser to the president of the firm, Mr. Fitweiler. The woman had appalled Mr. Martin instantly, but he hadn't shown it. He had given her his dry hand, a look of studious concentration, and a faint smile. "Well," she had said, looking at the papers on his desk, "are you lifting the oxcart out of the ditch?" As Mr. Martin recalled that moment, over his milk, he squirmed slightly. He must keep his mind on her crimes as a special adviser, not on her peccadillos as a personality. This he found difficult to do, in spite of entering an objection and sustaining it. The faults of the woman as a woman kept chattering on in his mind like an unruly witness. She had, for almost two years now, baited him. In the halls, in the elevator, even in his own office, into which she romped now and then like a circus horse, she was constantly shouting these silly questions at him. "Are you lifting the oxcart out of the ditch? Are you tearing up the pea patch? Are you hollering down the rain barrel? Are you scraping around the bottom of the pickle barrel? Are you sitting in the catbird seat?"

It was Joey Hart, one of Mr. Martin's two assistants, who had explained what the gibberish meant. "She must be a Dodger fan," he had said. "Red Barber announces the Dodger games over the radio and he uses those expressions—picked 'em up down South." Joey had gone on to explain one or two. "Tearing up the pea patch" meant going on a rampage; "sitting in the catbird seat" meant sitting pretty, like a batter with three balls and no strikes on him. Mr. Martin dismissed all this with an effort. It had been annoying, it had driven him near to distraction, but he was too solid a man to be moved to murder by anything so childish. It was fortunate, he reflected as he passed on to the important charges against Mrs. Barrows, that he had stood up under it so well. He had maintained always an outward appearance of polite tolerance. "Why, I even believe you like the woman," Miss Paird, his other assistant, had once said to him. He had simply smiled.

A gavel rapped in Mr. Martin's mind and the case proper was resumed. Mrs. Ulgine Barrows stood charged with willful, blatant, and persistent attempts to destroy the efficiency and system of F & S. It was competent, material, and relevant to review her advent and rise to power. Mr. Martin had got the story from Miss Paird, who seemed always able to find things out. According to her, Mrs. Barrows had met Mr. Fitweiler at a party, where she had rescued him from the embraces of a powerfully built drunken man who had mistaken the president of

F & S for a famous retired Middle Western football coach. She had led him to a sofa and somehow worked upon him a monstrous magic. The aging gentleman had jumped to the conclusion there and then that this was a woman of singular attainments, equipped to bring out the best in him and in the firm. A week later he had introduced her into F & S as his special adviser. On that day confusion got its foot in the door. After Miss Tyson, Mr. Brundage, and Mr. Bartlett had been fired and Mr. Munson had taken his hat and stalked out, mailing in his resignation later, old Roberts had been emboldened to speak to Mr. Fitweiler. He mentioned that Mr. Munson's department had been "a little disrupted" and hadn't they perhaps better resume the old system there? Mr. Fitweiler had said certainly not. He had the greatest faith in Mrs. Barrows' ideas. "They require a little seasoning, a little seasoning, is all," he had added. Mr. Roberts had given it up. Mr. Martin reviewed in detail all the changes wrought by Mrs. Barrows. She had begun chipping at the cornices of the firm's edifice and now she was swinging at the foundation stones with a pickaxe.

Mr. Martin came now, in his summing up, to the afternoon of Monday, November 2, 1942—just one week ago. On that day, at 3:00 P.M., Mrs. Barrows had bounced into his office. "Boo!" she had yelled. "Are you scraping around the bottom of the pickle barrel?" Mr. Martin had looked at her from under his green eyeshade, saying nothing. She had begun to wander about the office, taking it in with her great, popping eyes. "Do you really need *all* these filing cabinets?" she had demanded suddenly. Mr. Martin's heart had jumped. "Each of these files," he had said, keeping his voice even, "plays an indispensable part in the system of F & S." She had brayed at him, "Well, don't tear up the pea patch!" and gone to the door. From there she had bawled, "But you sure have got a lot of fine scrap in here!" Mr. Martin could no longer doubt that the finger was on his beloved department. Her pickaxe was on the upswing, poised for the first blow. It had not come yet; he had received no blue memo from the enchanted Mr. Fitweiler bearing nonsensical instructions deriving from the obscene woman. But there was no doubt in Mr. Martin's mind that one would be forthcoming. He must act quickly. Already a precious week had gone by. Mr. Martin stood up in his living room, still holding his milk glass. "Gentlemen of the jury," he said to himself, "I demand the death penalty for this horrible person."

The next day Mr. Martin followed his routine, as usual. He polished his glasses more often and once sharpened an already sharp pencil, but not even Miss Paird noticed. Only once did he catch sight of his victim; she swept past him in the hall with a patronizing "Hi!" At five-thirty he walked home, as usual, and had a glass of milk, as usual. He had never drunk anything stronger in his life—unless you could count ginger ale. The late Sam Schlosser, the S of F & S, had praised Mr. Martin at a staff meeting several years before for his temperate habits. "Our most efficient worker neither drinks nor smokes," he had said. "The results speak for themselvers." Mr. Fitweiler had sat by, nodding approval.

Mr. Martin was still thinking about that red-letter day as he walked over to the Schrafft's on Fifth Avenue near Forty-Sixth Street. He got there, as he always did, at eight o'clock. He finished his dinner and the financial page of the *Sun* at a quarter to nine, as he always did. It was his custom after dinner to take a walk. This time he walked down Fifth Avenue at a casual pace. His gloved hands felt moist and warm, his forehead cold. He transferred the Camels from his overcoat to a jacket pocket. He wondered, as he did so, if they did not represent an unnecessary note of strain. Mrs. Barrows smoked only Luckies. It was his idea to puff a few puffs on a Camel (after the rubbing-out), stub it out in the ashtray holding her lipstick-stained Luckies, and thus drag a small red herring across the trail. Perhaps it was not a good idea. It would take time. He might even choke, too loudly.

Mr. Martin had never seen the house on West Twelfth Street where Mrs. Barrows lived, but he had a clear enough picture of it. Fortunately, she had bragged to everybody about her ducky first-floor apartment in the perfectly darling three-story red-brick. There would be no doorman or other attendants; just the tenants of the second and third floors. As he walked along, Mr. Martin realized that he would get there before nine-thirty. He had considered walking north on Fifth Avenue from Schrafft's to a point from which it would take him until ten o'clock to reach the house. At that hour people were less likely to be coming in or going out. But the procedure would have made an awkward loop in the straight thread of his casualness, and he had abandoned it. It was impossible to figure when people would be entering or leaving the house, anyway. There was great risk at any hour. If he ran into anybody, he would simply have to place the rubbing-out of Ulgine Barrows in the inactive file forever. The same thing would hold true if there were someone in her apartment. In that case he would just say that he had been passing by, recognized her charming house, and thought to drop in.

It was eighteen minutes after nine when Mr. Martin turned into Twelfth Street. A man passed him, and a man and a woman, talking. There was no one within fifty paces when he came to the house, halfway down the block. He was up the steps and in the small vestibule in no time, pressing the bell under the card that said "Mrs. Ulgine Barrows." When the clicking in the lock started, he jumped forward against the door. He got inside fast, closing the door behind him. A bulb in a lantern hung from the hall ceiling on a chain seemed to give a monstrously bright light. There was nobody on the stair, which went up ahead of him along the left wall. A door opened down the hall in the wall on the right. He went toward it swiftly, on tiptoe.

"Well, for God's sake, look who's here!" bawled Mrs. Barrows, and her braying laugh rang out like the report of a shotgun. He rushed past her like a football tackle, bumping her. "Hey, quit shoving!" she said, closing the door behind them. They were in her living room, which seemed to Mr. Martin to be lighted by a hundred lamps. "What's after you?" she said. "You're as jumpy as a goat." He found he was unable to speak. His heart was wheezing in his throat. "I—yes," he finally brought out. She was jabbering and laughing as she started to help him off with his coat. "No, no," he said. "I'll put it here." He took it off and put it on a chair near the door. "Your hat and gloves, too," she said. "You're in a lady's house." He put his hat on top of the coat. Mrs. Barrows seemed larger than he had thought. He kept his gloves on. "I was passing by," he said. "I recognized—is there anyone here?" She laughed louder than ever. "No," she said. "We're all alone. You're as white as a sheet, you funny man. Whatever *has* come over you? I'll mix you a toddy." She started toward a door across the room. "Scotch-and-soda be all right? But say, you don't drink, do you?" She turned and gave him her amused look. Mr. Martin pulled himself together. "Scotch-and-soda will be all right," he heard himself say. He could hear her laughing in the kitchen.

Mr. Martin looked quickly around the living room for the weapon. He had counted on finding one there. There were andirons and a poker and something in a corner that looked like an Indian club. None of them would do. It couldn't be that way. He began to pace around. He came to a desk. On it lay a metal paper knife with an ornate handle. Would it be sharp enough? He reached for it and knocked over a small brass jar. Stamps spilled out of it and it fell to the floor with a clatter. "Hey," Mrs. Barrows yelled from the kitchen, "are you tearing up the pea patch?" Mr. Martin gave a strange laugh. Picking up the knife, he tried its point against his left wrist. It was blunt. It wouldn't do.

When Mrs. Barrows reappeared, carrying two highballs, Mr. Martin, standing there with his gloves on, became acutely conscious of the fantasy he had wrought. Cigarettes in his pocket, a drink prepared for him—it was all too grossly improbable. It was more than that; it was impossible. Somewhere in the back of his mind a vague idea stirred, sprouted. "For heaven's sake, take off those gloves," said Mrs. Barrows. "I always wear them in the house," said Mr. Martin. The idea began to bloom, strange and wonderful. She put the glasses on a coffee table in front of a sofa and sat on the sofa. "Come over here, you odd little man," she said. Mr. Martin went over and sat beside her. It was difficult getting a cigarette out of the pack of Camels, but he managed it. She held a match for him, laughing. "Well," she said, handing him his drink, "this is perfectly marvelous. You with a drink and a cigarette."

Mr. Martin puffed, not too awkwardly, and took a gulp of the highball. "I drink and smoke all the time," he said. He clinked his glass against hers. "Here's nuts to that old windbag, Fitweiler," he said, and gulped again. The stuff tasted awful, but he made no grimace. "Really, Mr. Martin," she said, her voice and posture changing, "you are insulting our employer." Mrs. Barrows was now all special adviser to the president. "I am preparing a bomb," said Mr. Martin, "which will blow the old goat higher than hell." He had only had a little of the drink, which was not strong. It couldn't be that. "Do you take dope or something?" Mrs. Barrows asked coldly. "Heroin," said Mr. Martin. "I'll be coked to the gills when I bump that old buzzard off." "Mr. Martin!" she shouted, getting to her feet. "That will be all of that. You must go at once." Mr. Martin took another swallow of his drink. He tapped his cigarette out in the ashtray and put the pack of Camels on the coffee table. Then he got up. She stood glaring at him. He walked over and put on his hat and coat. "Not a word about this," he said, and laid an index finger against his lips. All Mrs. Barrows could bring out was "Really!" Mr. Martin put his hand on the doorknob. "I'm sitting in the catbird seat," he said. He stuck his tongue out at her and left. Nobody saw him go.

Mr. Martin got to his apartment, walking, well before eleven. No one saw him go in. He had two glasses of milk after brushing his teeth, and he felt elated. It wasn't tipsiness, because he hadn't been tipsy. Anyway, the walk had worn off all effects of the whiskey. He got in bed and read a magazine for a while. He was asleep before midnight.

Mr. Martin got to the office at eight-thirty the next morning, as usual. At a quarter to nine, Ulgine Barrows, who had never before arrived at work before ten, swept into his office. "I'm reporting to Mr. Fitweiler now!" she shouted. "If he turns you over to the police, it's no more than you deserve!" Mr. Martin gave her a look of shocked surprise. "I beg your pardon?" he said. Mrs. Barrows snorted and bounced out of the room, leaving Miss Paird and Joey Hart staring after her. "What's the matter with that old devil now?" asked Miss Paird. "I have no idea," said Mr. Martin, resuming his work. The other two looked at him and then at each other. Miss Paird got up and went out. She walked slowly past the closed door of Mr. Fitweiler's office. Mrs. Barrows was yelling inside, but she was not braying. Miss Paird could not hear what the woman was saying. She went back to her desk.

Forty-five minutes later, Mrs. Barrows left the president's office and went into her own, shutting the door. It wasn't until half an hour later that Mr. Fitweiler sent for Mr. Martin. The head of the filing department, neat, quiet, attentive, stood in front of the old man's desk. Mr. Fitweiler was pale and nervous. He took his glasses off and twiddled them. He made a small, brushing sound in his throat. "Martin," he said, "you have been with us more than twenty years." "Twenty-two, sir," said Mr. Martin. "In that time," pursued the president, "your work and your—uh—manner have been exemplary." "I trust so, sir," said Mr. Martin. "I have understood, Martin," said Mr. Fitweiler, "that you have never taken a drink or smoked." "That is correct, sir," said Mr. Martin. "Ah, yes." Mr. Fitweiler polished his glasses. "You may describe what you did after leaving the office yesterday, Martin," he said. Mr. Martin allowed less than a second for his bewildered pause. "Certainly, sir," he said. "I walked home. Then I went to Schrafft's for dinner. Afterward I walked home again. I went to bed early, sir, and read a magazine for a while. I was asleep before eleven." "Ah, yes," said Mr. Fitweiler again. He was silent for a moment, searching for the proper words to say to the head of the filing department. "Mrs. Barrows," he said finally, "Mrs. Barrows has worked hard, Martin, very hard. It grieves me to report that she has suffered a severe breakdown. It has taken the form of a persecution complex accompanied by distressing hallucinations." "I am very sorry, sir," said Mr. Martin. "Mrs. Barrows is under the delusion," continued Mr. Fitweiler, "that you visited her last evening and behaved yourself in an—uh—unseemly manner." He raised his hand to silence Mr. Martin's little pained outcry. "It is the nature of these psychological diseases," Mr.

Fitweiler said, "to fix upon the least likely and most innocent party as the—uh—source of persecution. These matters are not for the lay mind to grasp, Martin. I've just had my psychiatrist, Doctor Fitch, on the phone. He would not, of course, commit himself, but he made enough generalizations to substantiate my suspicions. I suggested to Mrs. Barrows, when she had completed her—uh—story to me this morning, that she visit Doctor Fitch, for I suspected a condition at once. She flew, I regret to say, into a rage, and demanded—uh—requested that I call you on the carpet. You may not know, Martin, but Mrs. Barrows had planned a reorganization of your department—subject to my approval, of course, subject to my approval. This brought you, rather than anyone else, to her mind—but again that is a phenomenon for Doctor Fitch and not for us. So, Martin, I am afraid Mrs. Barrows' usefulness here is at an end." "I am dreadfully sorry, sir," said Mr. Martin.

It was at this point that the door to the office blew open with the suddenness of a gas-main explosion and Mrs. Barrows catapulted through it. "Is the little rat denying it?" she screamed. "He can't get away with that!" Mr. Martin got up and moved discreetly to a point beside Mr. Fitweiler's chair. "You drank and smoked at my apartment," she bawled at Mr. Martin, "and you know it! You called Mr. Fitweiler an old windbag and said you were going to blow him up when you got coked to the gills on your heroin!" She stopped yelling to catch her breath and a new glint came into her popping eyes. "If you weren't such a drab, ordinary little man," she said, "I'd think you'd planned it all. Sticking your tongue out, saying you were sitting in the catbird seat, because you thought no one would believe me when I told it! My God, it's really too perfect!" She brayed loudly and hysterically, and the fury was on her again. She glared at Mr. Fitweiler. "Can't you see how he has tricked us, you old fool? Can't you see his little game?" But Mr. Fitweiler had been surreptitiously pressing all the buttons under the top of his desk and employees of F & S began pouring into the room. "Stockton," said Mr. Fitweiler, "you and Fishbein will take Mrs. Barrows to her home. Mrs. Powell, you will go with them." Stockton, who had played a little football in high school, blocked Mrs. Barrows as she made for Mr. Martin. It took him and Fishbein together to force her out of the door into the hall, crowded with stenographers and office boys. She was still screaming imprecations at Mr. Martin, tangled and contradictory imprecations. The hubbub finally died down in the corridor.

"I regret that this has happened," said Mr. Fitweiler. "I shall ask you to dismiss it from your mind, Martin." "Yes, sir," said Mr. Martin, anticipating his chief's "That will be all" by moving to the door. "I will dismiss it." He went out and shut the door, and his step was light and quick in the hall. When he entered his department he had slowed down to his customary gait, and he walked quietly across the room to the W20 file, wearing a look of studious concentration.

Is Mrs. Ulgine Barrows an impostor? Does she represent a genuine force for change within the company? Why or why not?

Is Mr. Martin a traditional or a rebellious character? Why?

Many heroes in romance defeat their enemies because of their superhuman strength. How do Mutsmag and Mr. Martin defeat their opponents?

BUSU

A Japanese Nō Play
Translated by DONALD KEENE

Characters

MASTER

TARŌ KAJA

JIRŌ KAJA

The MASTER, TARŌ KAJA, *and* JIRŌ KAJA *enter the stage along the Bridge.* TARŌ KAJA *and* JIRŌ KAJA *seat themselves by the Name-Saying Seat. The* MASTER *as he introduces himself goes to the Waki's Pillar.*

MASTER. I am a gentleman of this vicinity. I plan to go away to the mountains for a few days, and now I shall summon my servants to give them instructions about what to do during my absence. Taro kaja, where are you?

TARŌ. Here, Master. (*He gets up and goes toward the* MASTER, *then bows.*)

MASTER. Call Jiro kaja too.

TARŌ. Yes, Master. Jiro kaja, the master wants you.

JIRŌ. I obey. (*He also comes forward and bows.*)

TOGETHER. We are before you, Master.

MASTER. I have called you because I am going to the mountains for a few days, and I want you both to take good care of the house while I am away.

TARŌ. Your orders will be obeyed, Master, but you have always taken one of us with you on your journeys, and today too . . .

TOGETHER. One of us would like to accompany you.

MASTER. No, that is out of the question. Today I have something important to leave in your care, and both of you must guard it. Wait here.

TOGETHER. Very good, Master.

(The MASTER goes to the Flute Pillar where he picks up a round lacquered cask about two feet high. He deposits it in the center of the stage, and returns to his former position.)

MASTER. This is what is known as *busu,* a deadly poison. If even a wind blowing from its direction should strike you, it will mean instant death. Be on your guard.

TARŌ. Yes, Master.

JIRŌ. Excuse me, Master, but I would like to ask you something.

MASTER. What is it?

JIRŌ. Why do you keep such a dreadful poison in the house?

MASTER. The *busu* loves its master, and as long as it is the master who handles it, there is not the slightest danger. But if either of you so much as approach it, you will suffer instant death. Beware even of being touched by the wind from its direction.

JIRŌ. Yes, Master.

MASTER. Now I shall be leaving.

TARŌ. May you have a pleasant journey.

TOGETHER. And come back soon.

MASTER. Thank you.

(The MASTER goes to the Bridge, where he seats himself at the First Pine, indicating that he has disappeared. TARŌ and JIRŌ see him off, then seat themselves at the back of the stage.)

TARŌ. He always takes one of us with him. I wonder why today he left both of us to look after the house.

JIRŌ. I wonder why.

TARŌ. At any rate, it's always lonesome being left here by oneself, but since we are both here today, we can have a pleasant talk. —Oh!

JIRŌ. What is the matter?

TARŌ. There was a gust of wind from the *busu!*

JIRŌ. How frightening!

TARŌ. Let's move a little farther away.

JIRŌ. A good idea.

(They hastily move toward Bridge, then sit.)

TARŌ. Just as you said before, why should the master keep in the house a thing so deadly that even a breath of wind from it will cause instant death?

JIRŌ. However much it may love its master, I still don't understand why he keeps it.

TARŌ. You know, I'd like to have a look at the *busu.* What do you think it can be?

JIRŌ. Have you gone mad? Don't you know that even the wind from its way means certain death?

TARŌ. Let's go up to it fanning from this side. In that way we won't get any wind from it.

JIRŌ. That's a good idea.

(The two men stand, and fanning vigorously approach the cask.)

TARŌ. Fan, fan hard.

JIRŌ. I am fanning.

TARŌ. I'm going to untie the cord around it now, so fan hard.

JIRŌ. Right!

TARŌ. I've unfastened it. Now, I'll take off the cover.

JIRŌ. Do it quickly!

TARŌ. Keep fanning!

TARŌ. It's off! *(They flee to the Bridge.)* Oh, that's a relief!

JIRŌ. What's a relief?

TARŌ. That thing—it's not an animal or it would jump out.

JIRŌ. Perhaps it is only playing dead.

TARŌ. I'll have a look.

JIRŌ. That's a good idea.

(They approach the cask as before.)

TARŌ. Fan, fan hard!

JIRŌ. I am fanning!

TARŌ. Now I'm going to have a look, so fan hard!

JIRŌ. Right!

TARŌ. I've seen it! I've seen it! *(They flee as before to the Bridge.)*

JIRŌ. What did you see?

TARŌ. Something dark gray that looked good to eat. You know, I think I'd like a taste of that *busu.*

JIRŌ. How can you think of eating something which will kill you even if you only catch a whiff of it?

TARŌ. I must be bewitched by the *busu.* I can't think of anything but eating it. I will have a taste.

JIRŌ. You mustn't.

(He takes TARŌ's *sleeve, and they struggle.)*

TARŌ. Let me go!

JIRŌ. I won't let you go!

TARŌ. I tell you, let me go!

JIRŌ. I tell you, I won't let you go!

*(*TARŌ *frees himself and approaches the cask. He uses his fan to scoop out the contents.)*

TARŌ *(singing).* Shaking off with sorrow the sleeves of parting,
  I come up to the side of the *busu.*

JIRŌ. Alas! Now he will meet his death.

TARŌ. Oh, I am dying. I am dying. *(He falls over.)*

JIRŌ. I knew it would happen. Tarō kaja! What is it? *(He rushes to him.)*

TARŌ. It's so delicious, I'm dying. *(He gets up.)*

JIRŌ. What can it be?

TARŌ. It's sugar!

JIRŌ. Let me have a taste.

TARŌ. Go ahead.

JIRŌ. Thank you. It really is sugar!

(The two of them eat, using their fans to scoop out the busu. TARŌ, *seeing that* JIRŌ *is too busy eating to notice, carries off the cask to the Waki's Pillar. While he is eating,* JIRŌ *comes up and takes the cask to the Facing Pillar.)*

TARŌ. You mustn't eat it all by yourself. Let me have it!

JIRŌ. No, you were eating before I did. Give me some more.

TARŌ. Let's both eat it.

JIRŌ. A good idea.

(They put the cask between them.)

TARŌ. Delicious, isn't it?

JIRŌ. Really delicious.

TARŌ. The master told us that it was *busu*, thinking we wouldn't eat it then. That was really most disagreeable of him. Eat up! Eat up!

JIRŌ. It was disagreeable of him to have told us that we would die instantly if we got so much as a whiff of it. Eat up! Eat up!

TARŌ. I can't stop eating.

JIRŌ. It feels as if our chins are sagging, doesn't it?

TARŌ. Eat up! Oh, it's all gone!

JIRŌ. Yes, all gone.

TARŌ. Well, you can be proud of yourself.

JIRŌ. *I* can be proud of myself? It was *you* who first looked at the *busu* and first ate it. I'll tell the master as soon as he gets back.

TARŌ. I was only joking. Now, tear up this *kakemono*.[1]

JIRŌ. Very well. (*He goes to the Waki's Pillar and makes motions of tearing a* kakemono.) *Sarari. Sarari. Pattari.*

TARŌ. Bravo! First you looked at the *busu*, then you ate it, and now you've torn up the master's *kakemono*. I'll inform him of that as soon as he returns.

JIRŌ. I only did it because you told me. And I shall inform the master of that.

TARŌ. I was joking again. Now smash this bowl.

JIRŌ. No, I've had enough.

TARŌ. Then let's smash it together.

JIRŌ. All right.

(*They go to the Facing Pillar and make motions of picking up a large bowl and dashing it to the ground.*)

TOGETHER. *Garari chin.*

TARŌ. Ah—it's in bits.

JIRŌ. Now what excuse will we make?

TARŌ. When the master returns, the first thing to do is to burst into tears.

JIRŌ. Will tears do any good?

TARŌ. They will indeed. He'll be coming back soon. Come over here.

JIRŌ. Very well.

(*They go to the stage and sit there. The* MASTER *stands up and speaks at the First Pine.*)

1. **kakemono:** picture or writing on silk or paper.

MASTER. I have completed my business now. I imagine that my servants must be waiting for my return. I shall hasten home. Ah, here I am already. Tarō kaja, Jirō kaja, I've returned! (*He goes to the Waki's Pillar.*)

TARŌ. He's back! Now start weeping! (*They weep.*)

MASTER. Tarō kaja, Jirō kaja! Where are you? What is the matter here? Instead of being glad that I have returned they are both weeping. If something has happened, let me know at once.

TARŌ. Jirō kaja, you tell the master.

JIRŌ. Tarō kaja, you tell the master.

MASTER. Whichever of you it is, tell me quickly.

TARŌ. Well, then, this is what happened. I thought that it wouldn't do for me to sleep while on such important duty, but I got sleepier and sleepier. To keep me awake I had a wrestling match with Jirō kaja. He is so strong that he knocked me over, and to keep from falling, I clutched at that *kakemono,* and ripped it as you can see.

MASTER. What a dreadful thing to happen! (*He looks at the Waki's Pillar in amazement.*) How could you tear up a precious *kakemono* that way?

TARŌ. Then he threw me back and spun me over the stand with the bowl on it and the bowl was smashed to bits.

MASTER. What a dreadful thing! (*He looks at the Facing Pillar in amazement.*) You even smashed my precious bowl. What am I going to do?

TARŌ. Knowing that you would soon return, we thought that we could not go on living, so we ate up the *busu,* hoping thus to die. Isn't that so, Jirō kaja?

JIRŌ. Exactly.

TARŌ (*singing*). One mouthful and still death did not come.

JIRŌ (*singing*). Two mouthfuls and still death did not come.

TARŌ (*singing*). Five mouthfuls.

TARŌ (*singing*). More than ten mouthfuls.

(*They get up and begin to dance.*)

TOGETHER (*singing*). We ate until there wasn't any left,
    But still death came not, strange to tell,
    Ah, what a clever head!

(*They approach the* MASTER *while fanning, then suddenly strike him on the head with their fans. They run off laughing.*)

MASTER. What do you mean "clever head"? You brazen things! Where are you going? Catch them! You won't get away with it! (*He runs after them to Bridge.*)

TOGETHER. Forgive us! Forgive us!

Why do the servants escape punishment for disobeying the rules of their master?

The clever servant who outwits his master is a character-type that has appeared in literature for centuries. Can you think of other examples of this character-type in literature, movies, or on television?

"All for a lady fair"

HE: "My death I love, my life I hate, all for a lady fair;
That she is bright as morning light, too well I am aware:
Like summer leaf whose greenness goes, I wither in despair.
To whom then, thought availing not, shall I make known my care?

"Sighing, grief and deadly sorrow hold my heart so fast,
I fear I shall become distracted if it longer last.
With just a word from you, my love, my care and grief were past.
What gain to you to blight my life and make it stand aghast?"

SHE: "Scholar, be quiet! You are a fool. No more I wish to chide you.
You'll never see that day alive when I shall lie beside you.
If you are taken in my bower, scandal shall deride you.
Better to plod on foot than on an evil horse to ride you."

HE: "Alas, why say you so? I am your man, so pity me,
For you are always in my thoughts, wherever I may be.
The scandal would be yours if love for you were death of me;
So let me live and be your love, and you my lover be."

SHE: "Be quiet, fool, I named you rightly; can't you stop that din?
By day and night in wait for you lie Father and all his kin.
If in my bower you're caught they will not stop, from fear of sin,
Imprisoning me and killing you, and then your death you'll win!"

HE: "Sweetest lady, change your mind; you fill me with distresses,
And now I am as full of woes as once I was of blisses:
Yet at your window fifty times we clung exchanging kisses,
Whose pledge has power to make a lover hide his spirit's stresses."

SHE: "Alas, why say you so? You thus my pain of love renew.
A scholar was my lover once; his love to me was true;
The day he had no sight of me, he never gladness knew.
I loved him better than my life; what good does lying do?"

HE: "While I was a scholar at school, I learned all kinds of lore;
And now with pangs of love for you I suffer anguish sore,
An outlaw in the forest far from home and human door.
Sweet lady, show me pity now, for I can say no more."

SHE: "You seem indeed to be a scholar, you speak so soft and still:
For love of me you never shall endure such pain and ill.
Father, mother and all my kin shall never thwart my will;
So you be mine, and I'll be yours, and all your joy fulfill."

A medieval lyric
Translated by BRIAN STONE

How does the fate of this suitor differ from that of Freddie Widgeon in "Goodbye to All Cats"? Who or what do you think is responsible for the difference?

"All the Sweet Buttermilk . . ."

DONAGH MAC DONAGH

The most lonesome place I was ever posted to was a little town twenty miles from the nearest railway, in the County Mayo, where there was neither cinema, theater, nor anything else; the only entertainment was a chat and a smoke, a drink and an occasional dance. I was always a great one to fish and take life easy, so it suited me fine, but the Sergeant didn't fancy it at all.

Sergeant Finnegan was a dour looking man and very close. I never rightly discovered what it was had him shifted to that place, but it can't have been want of zeal. He was the most energetic man and the most enthusiastic man in his search for crime that ever I met. Of course he was wasting his time looking for crime in Coolnamara, but what he couldn't find he invented.

Hanlon and Flaherty and myself used to have a grand easy life of it in old Sergeant Moloney's time; there wasn't a bicycle lamp in the district, the pubs closed when the last customer went home, and that was earlier than you'd think, and if there was any poteen made nobody came worrying us about it. But Sergeant Finnegan soon changed all that. He wasn't a month in the place till every lad in the county had a lamp on his bike, I even bought one myself; and there was such a row kicked up about the pubs staying open that nobody went home till midnight. They suddenly realized that there must be a great charm in after-hours drinking.

The Sergeant used to have me cross-eyed chasing round the country in search of illicit stills, and as soon as ever I'd get settled down for the evening with my pipe going nicely and the wireless behind my head, he'd be in with some new list of outrages, cattle straying on the road, a camp of tinkers that whipped a couple of chickens, or some nonsense like that.

"Take your feet down off that mantelpiece," he'd say, "and get out on patrol. Who knows what malicious damage or burglary or larceny is going on under the cover of night!" And up I'd have to get, put on my coat and go in next door to listen to the news.

He was a great man for objecting to dance-hall licences, and if he'd had his way there wouldn't have been a foot put on a floor within the four walls of Ireland. On the night of a dance he'd be snooping around to see was there any infringement of the regulations, and his finger itching on the pencil to make notes for a prosecution.

One night there was an all-night dance over in Ballyduv and he sent me over to keep an eye on it.

"I think I better go in mufti, Sergeant," says I. "There's no use in drawing their attention to the Civic Guards being present."

"True. True. Quite true!" says he. So up I went and changed, chuckling to myself. I could have worn a beard and a major-general's outfit and every hog, dog and devil in the place would have known me. But I always enjoyed a dance and I didn't want to be encumbered with a uniform for the stretch of the evening.

When I got to the dance hall it was about half-ten but hardly anyone had arrived yet. At an all-night dance they're never in much of a hurry to get started, and besides the lads have to get washed and changed after the day's work. I stood chatting to Callaghan, that owned the hall, for a bit, and then we went over to Hennessy's for a couple of pints. Of course it was well after hours by this time, but with the Sergeant safe in Coolnamara nobody was worrying too much about that. Around about half-eleven we heard the band getting into its stride, so we came back to see how the fun was going.

As soon as I stepped in through the door I saw the grandest looking girl you'd want to see, bronze colored hair, green eyes, and an American dress that was made for her figure.

"Who's that?" says I to Callaghan. "She must be down from Dublin."

"Dublin nothing!" says he, "She's from the mountain beyond. There's a whole family of them, and they're as wild as a lot of mountain goats. Lynch's they are."

"Give us a knock-down," says I, "I'll surely die if I don't meet that one!"

"I will," says he, "but I better say nothing about you being in the Guards."

"And why not?"

"Now never mind. It's what I'm telling you." So he brought me over and introduced me to her.

Well, we got on grand. There was a waltz just starting and I asked her out, and we danced from that out without a break, and when we were tired dancing we went out for a bit of a walk, and I can tell you I wasn't wasting my time.

She told me all about the sister in America, and how anxious she was to get to Dublin, and I could see she was dying down dead to find out what I was, but after Jack Callaghan's warning I made her no wiser.

On about one o'clock we were whirling around when what should I see sloping in through the door but the Sergeant, and he in mufti, too. He gave me a very cold nod and I didn't pretend to take the least bit of notice of him.

"Who's your friend?" says she. "I never saw him before."

"Any more than you saw me!" says I, giving her a squeeze and avoiding the question.

"Who is he, though?" she said again, so I saw there was no way out of it.

"That's Sergeant Finnegan from Coolnamara," says I, "and a greater trouble maker there isn't in the country."

"And what else would he be only a trouble maker, if he's a Guard. If there's one thing I hate in this world it's a Guard, and if there's a thing I hate more it's a Sergeant." I could see I was on very delicate ground and took all the trouble I could not to be any way awkward with my big feet.

"And why is that?" says I, but she only tossed her head and shot the Sergeant dead with both her green eyes.

After a bit some great gawk of a countryman managed to prise her away from me, and off she went, though I felt she'd rather stay. No sooner had she gone than I could feel the Sergeant breathing down the back of my neck.

"Come outside here till I talk to you," says he, and I could see she had her eyes buried in us as we went out the door.

"Do you know who that is?" says he.

"That's a girl called Maeve Lynch," says I. "Isn't she a grand looking thing."

"Her father's the greatest poteen maker in the County of Mayo, and I thought you were long enough in the county to know that."

"Well, that's news to me. He was never prosecuted in my time. How do you know?"

"From information received. Now you keep away from that girl, or it might be worse for you. And keep your mind on your business. Don't you know you have no right to be dancing?"

"I was just seeing could I pick up any information. But things are very quiet."

"Things are never as quiet as they appear. I hope you investigated Hennessy's after closing time."

"You can be bound I did!" says I without a smile.

We went back into the hall, and as soon as I got the Sergeant's back turned I gave Maeve the beck to come on out. As she passed the Sergeant she gave him a glare that must have rocked him back on his heels.

"Are you not going to dance?" says she to me, but instead of answering I drew her out into the dark and slipped an arm around her. We walked along for a while without saying a word. Then she gave my hand a squeeze.

"What did the Sergeant want with you?"

"Ah, he was just chatting."

"You seem to be terrible great with him."

"I wouldn't say that. I just know him."

"Did he say anything about me?"

"What would he say? He doesn't know you, does he?"

"Oh, the dear knows. They're a very nosey crowd, the Guards. Come on back and dance."

"No," I said, "I'm tired. Let's sit down." So we sat down.

When we got back to the dance it was near breaking up and the Sergeant was gone. I was all for taking her home, but there were some cousins of hers there who said they'd take her in a trap, so I arranged to meet her the next Sunday at a dance a few miles away, and away I went singing "The Red Haired Girl" and whistling back at the birds.

I had an early breakfast and was off to the lake with my rod and line long before the Sergeant or Hanlon or Flaherty were stirring. I spent half the day fishing and half the day dreaming, and when I got back in the afternoon the Sergeant was fit to be tied.

"Where were you all day?" says he, "I'll report you to the Superintendent for being absent without leave."

"Oh, indeed I wasn't, Sergeant," says I, "I was on duty all day. I was down at the lake keeping an eye open for poachers." It was fortunate that I had left the half-dozen trout down the town on my way home.

"Poachers!" says he. "And who ever heard of poachers on Cool Lake?"

"You'd never know when they might start. I took the precaution of bringing along a rod as a camouflage!" I could see he was only half convinced, but he let it go.

"Get up on your bike there," says he. "We have work to do." But I told him I'd have to get something to eat first. I had such an appetite that minute that I'd have nearly eaten the sour face off himself. I downed a good meal in record time and the two of us started off.

For a couple of miles the Sergeant never said a word, and I said no more. After a bit I realized we were heading toward the mountains, a part of the world I wasn't very well acquainted with.

"Where are we off to, Sergeant?" says I.

"We're off on a job that may get you your Sergeant's stripes if you play your cards right. It's that old Maurice Lynch. I have information that he's after running enough poteen to set the whole countryside drunk. He thinks he's as safe as Gibraltar, stuck up here on his mountainside, but it isn't old Sergeant Moloney he has to deal with now. Callaghan told me last night the daughter didn't know about you being in the Guards."

"That's true enough."

"Well, maybe it's just as well you were so busy chasing after her. You'll be able to keep them in chat while I have a look around. You can pretend you came on a social call."

I cursed my day's fishing when I realized that it was too late now to get any word to Maeve. If I'd been in the station when the Sergeant first decided on this expedition I could have sent a message through Callaghan, but here I was now on an empty bog road with the Sergeant glued to my side and every stroke on the pedals bringing us nearer. There was a big push being made against poteen all through the country, and I knew it would go hard with old Lynch if he was caught.

At last we got into the mountains, and after a while we had to get down and walk, and heavy climbing it was.

"There it is now," says the Sergeant. "We'll have to dump the bikes and take to the fields. But you go ahead and I'll follow after at a safe distance."

Here's my chance, said I to myself, and I started hot-foot for the farmhouse. Just as I got up to the gate, a fine handsome girl with red hair came out the door and leaned against the jamb, showing off her figure. I was just going to wave to her when I realized that it wasn't Maeve.

"What can we do for you?" says she, looking very bold at me.

"Listen!" says I, "this is urgent. If you have any poteen about the place, for God's sake tell me where it is till I get rid of it. There's a Sergeant of the Guards on his way across the fields now."

"Poteen?" says she. "Poteen? I seem to have heard of the stuff."

"Look!" I said, "this is no time for fooling. Show me where it is quick till I destroy it. God knows I'm taking enough risk." She stretched her arms over her head and yawned.

"Is your father here?" I said.

"He is not."

"Is Maeve?"

"She is not."

"Well then, show me where it is quick. The Sergeant will be in on top of us in a minute."

"He'll find nothing here."

"Very well then, I give up. But you'll be a sorry girl if your father gets six months or a year in jail."

"Be off with you now, you have the look of a spy about you. By the big boots I'd take you for a peeler. Go on now before I let out Shep."

I gave a sigh and turned out the gate again. The Sergeant was just coming up the field, his uniform standing out against the country like a scarecrow in the corn.

"Why aren't you inside keeping them out of the way?" says he.

"There's no one there."

"Better and better. Come on and help me now." And he was off like a retriever for the barn. I pretended to help him in his search, but he found no more than I did.

"I'll tell you a little trick I know," says he, and he caught up a dung-fork that was lying against the wall. "Come out here now and I'll show you." So I followed him out again. He went across to the heap of manure that was lying in the backyard and started to probe around in it with the fork. I was just standing, admiring the fine sight of a Sergeant at work when there was the noise of the fork striking something, and the next moment the Sergeant was standing up holding a two-gallon jar. He pulled out the cork and gave the first real smile I ever saw on his face.

"Poteen!" says he, and the way he said it you'd think it was a poem.

Then he whipped it behind his back quick and I looked round and saw Maeve's sister just coming round the corner of the house. When she saw the Sergeant's uniform she shook her fist at the two of us.

"I knew what you were," she said, "I knew! Let you get out of this now before my father gets back or it'll be the worse for the pair of you."

"Be careful, young woman!" says the Sergeant. "It is a very dangerous thing to obstruct a Guard officer in the discharge of his duty. We are here in search of illicit spirits, and if there is any on the premises it is wiser to tell us now."

I was leaning against the door of the barn, looking out over the Mayo mountains, and wondering how long would poor old Lynch get at the District Court, when what should I see peeping up over the hedge but another red head. And this time it was Maeve sure enough. She had been there all the time watching every move. She gave me a wicked glare. I winked back. The Sergeant was standing with his back turned to her, rocking from his heels to his toes playing cat-and-mouse with the sister, and waggling the jar gently behind his back. There wasn't a prouder Sergeant on the soil of Ireland that minute.

I could see that Maeve wasn't quite sure whether I was just a pal of the Sergeant's that came out to keep him company, or a Guard on duty, and she kept glancing from me to the jar that the Sergeant was so busy hiding. She seemed to be asking me a question with her eyes. As there wasn't anything I could do to help her I gave her another wink and a big grin. She looked hard at me, then ducked out of sight behind the hedge. I was just beginning to wonder what had happened to her when she stood up straight, and my heart nearly stopped when I saw the big lump of a rock she had in her fist. I'm not a very narrow-minded man, and I had no particular regard for the Sergeant, but I wasn't going to have him murdered in cold blood before my eyes. If a thing like that came out at the inquest it would look very bad on my record. I was in two minds whether to shout out or not, weighing the trouble Maeve and her family would get into if I did against the trouble I'd get into if I didn't, when she drew back her arm, took wicked and deliberate aim, and let fly. I closed my eyes tight and turned away. When I heard a scream of agony from the Sergeant I closed them even tighter, but I opened them again when I heard what he was shouting.

"Blast it! Blast it! Blast it to hell!" he was roaring, and then I saw the heap of broken crockery at his feet. The sister was in kinks of laughter and there wasn't a sign of Maeve. There was a most delightful smell of the very best poteen on the air, and when the Sergeant threw the handle of the jar on the ground in a rage I realized that it was the jar and not the Sergeant's head that had received the blow. I burst out laughing.

"Who did that?" he shouted at me. "Who did that, you grinning imbecile?" But I shook my head.

"I was just day-dreaming," I said, "I didn't see a thing."

"You'll pay for this!" he said. "You'll pay dearly for this, you inefficient lout! Dereliction of duty! Gross imbecility! Crass stupidity! I'll have the coat off your back for this day's work!" Of course the poor man didn't know what he was saying, but in a way I was nearly sorry for him. He was so sure that he had the case all sewn up. But now, without the contents of the jar any chance of a prosecution was ballooned from the beginning. The Law requires very strict proof in these matters.

The Sergeant and myself searched all through the farm that day. And every day for a week afterward Flaherty and Hanlon and myself searched it again. But it was labor in vain. It was great weather, though, and I used to spend most of the day lying out in the hay, and after the first day I managed to get Maeve to join me. I had a terrible job persuading her that all Guards aren't as bad as she thought, and that the Sergeant was quite exceptional. Fortunately, Flaherty and Hanlon were in no great hurry to get the searching finished, so I had plenty of time to devote to persuading her. For some reason old Lynch didn't seem to care if we searched till doomsday, and himself and myself struck up a great friendship when I told him about my conversation with Maeve's sister, Mary. So that when Maeve agreed to marry me he put up no objection.

The Sergeant did his level best to have me drummed out of the Guards for marrying a poteen-maker's daughter, but, as I pointed out to the Superintendent, there was no proof that Maurice Lynch ever ran a drop of poteen, and even if he did, wouldn't a Guard in the family be the greatest deterrent against illicit distilling. The Superintendent saw my point, but I'm not so sure that I was right. I've often said that my father-in-law makes the smoothest run of mountain dew it has ever been my good luck to taste.

It was just as well the Sergeant was moved soon after. He was very bitter about the broken jar and would have stopped at nothing to get a conviction. Things have been very quiet and peaceful since he left and crime has practically disappeared from the district.

An obsessed character who dwells on one idea continually or repeats the same behavior over and over is a frequent source of amusement and ridicule in comic writing. What is the Sergeant obsessed with? What other characters in this book are ruled by obsessions?

The young comic hero in this story wins two victories. What are they? What personal characteristics contribute to his success?

Why do you think people enjoy stories in which policemen, or other authority figures, are outwitted?

Using some of the stock character-types you have met in these first two units, write a short skit or story, poem, or song, or draw a cartoon or comic strip. Follow the familiar plot of the comic hero whose desires are blocked by an inflexible authority figure, whom the hero eventually outwits and exposes. Go back over the names used for the heroes or heroines in this book so far, and choose an appropriate name for your "hero."

The central conflict in comedy is between a youthful hero, or one who has the resourcefulness of youth, and some blocking character or group of characters who consider his claims on life subversive and try to thwart him. In the first phase of comedy the blocking characters succeed, and the hero's desires are not realized. In the second phase of comedy, the hero has more success. He may not manage to change the society around him to suit his wishes, but he does manage to defeat the blocking characters and to get what he wants for himself.

Since the hero is trying to take or maintain his rightful place in society, his opponents seem to be impostors who lay claim to more than is rightfully theirs. In simpler comic folk tales, there is an easy way for the hero to get rid of the impostor who tries to block him from making his way in the world—just kill him off. This is, in fact, Mutsmag's final solution. But death is a hard thing to treat lightly, and so in most comedy the hero does not have to go to such an extreme. It is enough to dislodge the impostor or blocking character from his position of influence.

What really stands in the hero's way is that the impostor is a person with authority in the established order, whereas the hero is not. It is with an almost audible sigh of relief that Mr. Martin in "The Catbird Seat" realizes that it is not necessary to murder Mrs. Barrows after all. He has merely to make her seem demented and Mr. Fitweiler will no longer be influenced by her. In "The Umbrella Oracle," the umbrella is a kind of impostor god, and it takes the irreverent impatience of the young widow to deflate its authority over the superstitious villagers. In none of these cases does the impostor change at the end into a better, more balanced, more generous person, but the laughter to which he is exposed frees those around him from his moral influence.

Set against the cunning and special influence by which the blocking characters try to enforce their authority, the hero may appear somewhat naive and innocent. But innocence has two sides to it. On the one hand, it suggests a kind of beautiful simplicity of spirit, like that which persuades the two aunts in "The Body in the Window-seat" that a peaceful death is kinder than the lonely, deprived existence of the men who come looking for lodgings in their home. But innocence can also mean ignorance, and this is no advantage to the comic hero. In order to triumph, he must not be ignorant of the dog-eat-dog principle that dominates in the world around him. He must quickly learn to be more clever and resourceful than his enemies. These are the qualities that enable Mr. Martin to outsmart Mrs. Barrows, Mutsmag to fool the giant and the witch, and the servants in "Busu" to lie their way out of trouble with their Master. Failure to size up the nature of the opposition could mean defeat, as it did for Pal Smurch in "The Greatest Man in the World."

Yet the hero must never become as corrupt, greedy, or petty as his opponents. Otherwise, he would lose his moral advantage, and there would be little sense of comic triumph at the end. If he is clever, he tends to employ the impostor's own corruptness or folly against him. But in some cases, like that of the kindly aunts in "The Body in the Window-seat," the hero's very simplicity of soul cannot comprehend the wickedness or stupidity of the world at all. People like this must then be rescued from danger by other kindly, but more worldly, friends like Nephew Mortimer who understands, as the law would not, that his aunts meant no harm. The young guard in "All the Sweet Buttermilk . . ." is a perfect comic hero because he possesses just the right combination of good-naturedness, intelligence, and humor to baffle the cranky Sergeant and to restore his society to its natural, peaceful ways.

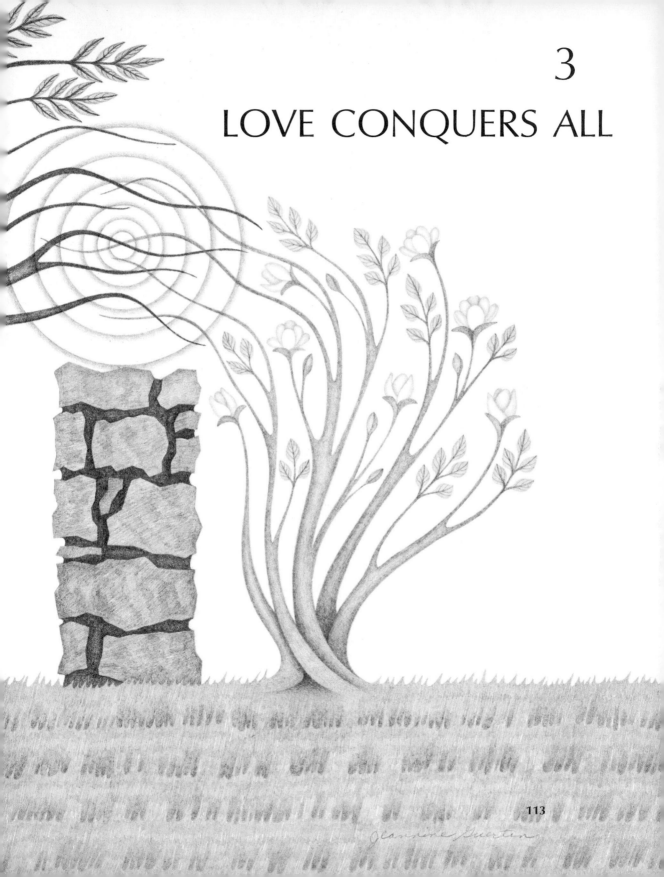

3

LOVE CONQUERS ALL

Jeannine Guertin

Song

Love and harmony combine
And around our souls intwine
While thy branches mix with mine,
And our roots together join.

Joys upon our branches sit,
Chirping loud and swinging sweet;
Like gentle streams beneath our feet
Innocence and virtue meet.

Thou the golden fruit dost bear,
I am clad in flowers fair;
Thy sweet boughs perfume the air,
And the turtle buildeth there.

There she sits and feeds her young.
Sweet I hear her mournful song;
And thy lovely leaves among,
There is love: I hear his tongue.

There his charming nest doth lay,
There he sleeps the night away.
There he sports along the day,
And doth among our branches play.

WILLIAM BLAKE

With what are the two lovers in this poem identified? What images are used
to suggest that the lovers are joined together as one person?

Cupid and Psyche

A Greek myth
Retold by JAY MACPHERSON

There was once a king living in the west country who had three daughters, Psyche, the youngest, being so beautiful that citizens and strangers joined in paying her divine honors, half believing her to be a new birth of the love goddess Venus who once rose from the foaming sea. The people pressed about Psyche as she walked through the town, calling her by the goddess's name and titles and offering her flowery garlands. As her fame spread, travelers came from farther and farther away to see her, until the shrines of Venus, even that at Cythera itself, lay neglected and her altars stood untended and covered with old ashes.

Venus became angry at this, and swore to be avenged. "What, shall I who am the kindling spirit of all the world share my worship with a mortal girl who must one day die?" She called to her aid her winged son Cupid, who does all kinds of mischief without caring for anyone, and pointed out Psyche to him where she sat in her father's house. "My dear son, I adjure you by a mother's love, punish this disobedient beauty that offends me. Make the girl fall into a desperate passion for the most wretched creature living, something so foul and sick and deformed that nothing can compare with it." So saying, she embraced her son and set off toward the sea, attended by nymphs singing and playing about her.

Psyche meantime, loved by all, nevertheless pined in her unfortunate beauty; for Venus's displeasure kept suitors away from her. She was praised and admired like some painted image, rather than sought as a young woman of flesh and blood. Her two elder sisters were splendidly married to kings, while she sat lonely at home and hated the sad chance that set her apart from the ordinary fate of women.

Her father, fearing that some god was the cause of her misfortune, made a journey to an oracle of Apollo, which gave this alarming reply:

King, lead your daughter to the mountain-side
Appareled for her harsh fate like a bride.
He who shall claim her is no mortal brood,
But horrid dragon furious and rude
Who beats the upper air with iron wings,
Who wearies and breaks down the strongest things.
He frights great Jove and gods on high that dwell,
Rivers, and rugged rocks, and shades of Hell.

When they heard the god's answer, the unhappy family spent several days in mourning as the time of the funereal marriage approached. The torches burned with feebly flickering light, the wedding-music was broken by lamentations, the bride wiped away the tears with her veil; the whole city mourned with her parents. Psyche reproached them: "When all the people paid me divine honors, calling me the new Venus, then you should have wept and grieved for me; now dry your useless tears and lead me to the place." The people accompanied her to the top of the mountain where she was to meet her strange fate, and there they left her. Then when she was left alone, weeping and trembling on the rock, gentle Zephyr caught her up with her robes and carried her through the air, setting her down after some time in a deep valley on a bed of softest flowers.

Looking about her, Psyche found herself beside a crystal stream and a green wood, and in the heart of the wood rose a stately palace, more finely wrought and decorated than the work of man, shining with precious stones like the light of the sun. At the pleasant sight Psyche took heart and entered; and as she walked through the courts and rooms, which all lay open without lock or bar, she saw many delightful things but no person at all. When she had seen everything, she heard a voice that said, "Lady, why do you marvel at these treasures? All that you see is at your command, and we who speak are here to serve you; take therefore some rest, and bathe and refresh yourself, and whatever dishes you care for shall be set before you when you please." Then Psyche thanked the gods who watched over her, and refreshed herself as the voice had said. At table she was served by invisible hands and entertained by invisible musicians, and all was done for her that she could desire.

At night Psyche went to the chamber prepared for her and lay down

to sleep; and there after a while someone came to her, known only by his voice and touch in the darkness. This was the master of the palace and its treasures, and he greeted her with great kindness. Night after night he came to her room, always leaving her again before the morning light.

In this way and with this strange companionship, which became very dear to her, Psyche lived in happiness for many weeks. One night her lover told her that her sisters were searching for her, but that if she heard their lamentations she must pay no attention unless she wished to bring great sorrow on herself and him. Then Psyche remembered her home and family, and suddenly her fine palace seemed to her a prison if she could not speak to her sisters; so she begged and implored him to have them carried to the valley to visit her. At last he gave in to her pleading, but warned her again about taking them into her confidence.

When gentle Zephyr set her dear sisters down in the valley, Psyche made them welcome with great joy, entertaining them with the best the palace could afford. When they saw her happiness and how splendidly she was served, envy took hold in their hearts, and they pressed her for an account of her husband; but she put them off with a tale of his being a fair young man who passed the days hunting on the hills. Then filling their laps with jewels and golden ornaments, she commanded Zephyr to carry them home again.

Away from her their envy at her good fortune increased beyond all measure, and they complained to each other that she was giving herself airs like the consort of a god. Once more Psyche's husband warned her against them, and told her, moreover, that as a testimony of their love she was now carrying his child, who was destined to become one of the immortal gods if only she concealed his secret. Then Psyche was more joyful than before, and loved her husband more dearly than ever.

But those wicked sisters commanded Zephyr to bring them back to the valley, and after congratulating Psyche on the child she would soon bear, they pretended to be concerned for her safety: "for we have learned that he who comes to you every night is a monstrous serpent, who watches over you and caresses you only until your child is born, when he means to devour you both together." Forgetting all the tenderness of her husband, his admonitions, and her promises, poor Psyche was very much frightened, and she begged her sisters to advise her in her extremity. Their counsel was to hide a sharp knife and a burning lamp in her room, and at night, after her unknown lover had fallen asleep, to bring out the lamp and strike him by its light. Then having done their work they went away.

At night Psyche made her preparations, trembling still with fear for herself and her unborn child. When her lover slept, she brought out the lamp and carried it toward the bed: and there she saw lying the fair body of her husband, Cupid, the god of love himself, still ignorant of her treachery. Now it was with shame and fondness that she trembled, and in her haste to hide the lamp she let a drop of burning oil fall on his shoulder, waking him with the pain. Without a word he caught up his bow and quiver and rose into the air on his white-plumaged wings, flying in a moment far out of sight.

Cupid made his way straight to his mother's chamber, where he lay uneasily waiting for his burned shoulder to heal, enduring Venus's reproaches for flouting her commands. Meanwhile faithful Psyche wandered about searching for him, often weary with her burden but taking no rest. From altar to altar of the lady goddesses she traveled, performing humble services in their temples and imploring their help. Juno, Ceres, all, pitied her repentance and her condition, but none would advise her for fear of the anger of Venus, who of all the divine powers is best able to avenge a slight.

In her distress, Psyche resolved to approach the offended goddess herself, whom she might yet placate by her humility and tears. As she came within sight of the house of Venus, one of the servants ran out and seized her, dragging her by the hair into the presence of the goddess, who beat and struck her and reviled her as a shameless wench. Then she spilled out on the floor a great quantity of wheat, barley, lentils, and other grains and ordered her to sort them before night. Psyche did not even begin, but as soon as she was left alone sat down and wept. Immediately an ant, pitying the sorrows of the woman married to a god, called to all her sisters, daughters of the ground that is mother of all, to sort the seeds into separate piles. When the task was done they slipped out of the house and disappeared. But Venus when she came in was furious: "No mortal could have accomplished the task: that scapegrace son of mine must have helped you." She threw her a crust of bread and let her sleep in a corner, while she devised another trial.

In the morning Venus sent Psyche into a thick forest to bring back some golden wool from the fierce sheep that fed there. When Psyche reached the forest, her first thought was to throw herself into the river that ran by and end her griefs, but a green reed on the river bank,

stirred into murmuring music by the wind, whispered to her that this task was an easy one, if only she waited till the heat of the day was past and the sheep came down to the water to drink, leaving tufts of their fleece caught on the bushes. This she could gather and carry back to Venus's house.

Still, when she had done so, Venus accused her of using trickery, and now she set her a harder task yet. From a black rock on top of a high mountain there flowed down a freezing stream whose flow became the dreary Stygian shallows and Cocytus's angry river: with that water she was to fill a crystal vial. The rock proved impossible to climb, and was moreover guarded by crawling dragons that rolled their sleepless bloodshot eyes. As Psyche stood there, cold and rigid like any stone, Jupiter's royal bird, the eagle, who had an old obligation to Cupid, swept down on his broad wings and offered to fill her flask as required with the dreadful water of Styx of which the gods themselves are afraid. When Psyche carried it back to Venus, she was received with worse insults than ever. "You must be a black sorceress, to carry out these tasks and return safely: let us see you perform one more. Take this box and descend to Hell and the house of shadows, and ask Proserpina to send me a little of her beauty: and come back with it as quickly as you can."

At this command Psyche was in the deepest despair. Without pausing even to think of how to carry it out, she hastened up to the top of a high tower intending to throw herself down. Then the tower gave forth a voice and spoke to her: "Wretched woman, do not take the shortest way to Pluto's house and give up your hope of return; but inquire along the roads the path to Taenarus in the waste, where you will find a pit, the breathing-place of Hell. There you can enter, taking in your hands two honey cakes and in your mouth two pieces of money. On the downward path you will meet people who ask you for help: those you must ignore. At the deadly river, let Charon the ferryman take a coin from your mouth, and he will then carry you over in his rickety boat. As you cross, an old man swimming in the river will hold out to you his rotting hands and cry to you to take him into the boat, but do not heed his crying. When you meet the dog Cerberus that guards the desolate house of death, cast him a honey cake, and the other one on your return. Proserpina when you enter will make you welcome and offer you a soft seat and delicate foods: be sure that you sit down on the hard ground and accept nothing but a crust of bread. When you have obtained what you came for, go back to the upper

world by the way you came. But above all, be careful not to look into the box that Proserpina has filled, nor be too curious about the treasure of the divine beauty."

Psyche immediately made ready for the descent, following the tower's instructions. She passed by in silence all those who would detain her, paid Charon's fee, refused the dead old man in the river, stopped Cerberus's mouth with a honey cake, and so came into the presence of Proserpina, where she sat down on the hard ground and contented herself with a crust of bread. On her way back, when she had almost reached the house of Venus, she was overcome with a great desire, saying to herself, "Am I not a fool, knowing that I carry the divine beauty, not to take a little of it so that I may please my lover?" And thereupon she opened the box, which seemed to be empty: but a deadly sleep came stealing out of it and covered her face, so that she fell down in the pathway like one dead.

Meanwhile Cupid had recovered from his burn and flown out by the window from the room where Venus thought to keep him shut up, and was now searching to find what had become of his Psyche. When he saw her lying in the path, he wiped the dreadful sleep from her face and put it back in the box, waking her with gentle words. Then he sprang into the air, while Psyche carried to Venus the present of Proserpina.

Won over at last by the long patience of his wife, Cupid flew straight to his father Jupiter to declare his cause. When he had heard all, Jupiter replied with some severity, "My son, you have never treated me so dutifully as you ought, seeing that I am both your father and the law-giver of the universe: it is your fault that my reputation has been stained by wicked intrigues, to say nothing of transformations at various times into the lowly forms of beasts and birds. However, I will do for you what I can." So saying, he called a council of all the dwellers on high Olympus. He reminded the gods of the wrongs they had suffered at Cupid's hands and from the painful prick of his arrows: now, he said, it was time that the mischievous boy should settle down to a man's responsibilities, and to that end they were gathered together to celebrate his marriage with a virtuous young woman of tried fidelity. Even Venus could not cross the will of great Jove, who pacified her with gracious speeches. Then calling Psyche before him, he gave her to drink the divine nectar, so that she might remain forever with her husband Cupid, ageless and deathless like the immortal gods and honored like them in the temples and hearts of men.

Now the great marriage feast was prepared, and Cupid sat at the head of the table with his dear bride in his arms. The Hours had decked all the house with garlands of roses, the Graces perfumed it, the Muses sang sweetly in time to the harping of Apollo their leader, and Venus danced in the midst of them. And when in due time her child was born into happiness and the bright looks of his parents, Psyche named him Pleasure.

Why do Venus and Psyche's sisters oppose her union with Cupid? How are these sisters like those in the folk tale "Mutsmag" and the fairy tale "Cinderella"?

What obstacles does Psyche conquer in this myth? Who helps make the marriage between Cupid and Psyche possible, and why?

How does the natural world respond to Cupid and Psyche, Mutsmag, and to the lovers in "Song"?

In what ways does this myth resemble "Making the Right Connections" and "Goodbye to All Cats"? How does it differ from them?

The Boor

ANTON CHEKHOV
Translated by AVRAHM YARMOLINSKY

Characters

YELENA IVANOVNA POPOVA,
a little widow with dimpled cheeks, a landowner

GRIGORY STEPANOVICH SMIRNOV,
a middle-aged gentleman farmer

LUKA,
MADAME POPOVA'S *footman, an old man*

The drawing room in MME. POPOVA'S *manor house.* MME. POPOVA, *in deep mourning, her eyes fixed on a photograph.* LUKA *is on stage.*

LUKA. It isn't right, madam. You're just killing yourself. The maid and the cook have gone berrying, every living thing rejoices, even the cat knows how to enjoy life and wanders through the courtyard catching birds, but you stay in the house as if it were a convent and take no pleasure at all. Yes, really! It's a whole year now, I figure, that you haven't left the house!

MME. POPOVA. And I never will leave it . . . What for? My life is over. He lies in his grave, and I have buried myself within these four walls. We are both dead.

LUKA. There you go again! I oughtn't to listen to you, really. Nikolay Mihailovich is dead; well, there is nothing to do about it, it's the will of God; may the kingdom of Heaven be his. You have grieved over it, and that's enough; there's a limit to everything. One can't cry and wear mourning forever. The time came when my old woman, too, died. Well? I grieved over it, I cried for a month, and that was enough for her, but to go on wailing all my life, why, the old woman isn't worth it. (*Sighs.*) You've forgotten all your neighbors. You don't go out and you won't receive anyone. We live, excuse me, like spiders—we never see the light of day. The mice have eaten the livery. And it isn't as if there were no nice people around—the county is full of gentlemen. A regiment is quartered at Ryblov and every officer is a good-looker; you can't take your eyes off them. And every Friday there's a ball at the camp, and 'most every day the military band is playing. Eh, my dear lady, you're young and pretty, just peaches and cream, and you could lead a life of pleasure. Beauty doesn't last forever, you know. In ten years' time you'll find yourself wanting to strut like a peahen and dazzle the officers, but it will be too late.

MME. POPOVA (*resolutely*). I beg you never to mention this to me again! You know that since Nikolay Mihailovich died, life has been worth nothing to me. You think that I am alive, but it only seems so to you! I vowed to myself that never to the day of my death would I take off my mourning or see the light. Do you hear me? Let his shade see how I love him! Yes, I know, it is no secret to you that he was often unjust to me, cruel, and . . . even unfaithful, but I shall be true to the end and prove to him how I can love. There, in the other world, he will find me just the same as I was before he died. . . .

LUKA. Instead of talking like that, you ought to go and take a walk in the garden or have Toby or Giant put in the shafts and drive out to pay calls on the neighbors.

MME. POPOVA. Oh! (*Weeps.*)

LUKA. Madam! Dear madam! What's wrong? Bless you!

MME. POPOVA. He was so fond of Toby! When he drove out to the Korchagins and the Vlasovs it was always with Toby. What a wonderful driver he was! How graceful he was when he pulled at the reins with all his might! Do you remember? Toby, Toby! Tell them to give him an extra measure of oats today.

LUKA. Very well, madam. (*The doorbell rings sharply.*)

MME. POPOVA (*startled*). Who is it? Say that I am at home to no one.

LUKA. Very good, madam. (*Exits.*)

MME. POPOVA (*looking at the photograph*). You shall see, Nicolas, how I can love and forgive. My love will die only with me, when my poor heart stops beating. (*Laughs through her tears.*) And aren't you ashamed? I am a good, faithful little wife; I've locked myself in and shall remain true to you to the grave, and you . . . aren't you ashamed, you naughty boy? You were unfaithful to me, you made scenes, you left me alone for weeks. . . . (LUKA *enters.*)

LUKA (disturbed). Madam, someone is asking for you, wants to see you. . . .

MME. POPOVA. But you told him, didn't you, that since my husband's death I receive no one?

LUKA. Yes, I did, but he wouldn't listen to me; he says it's a very urgent matter.

MME. POPOVA. I do not receive anyone!

LUKA. I told him, but . . . he's a perfect devil . . . he curses and barges right in . . . he's in the dining room now.

MME. POPOVA (annoyed). Very well, ask him in. . . . What rude people! (Exit LUKA.) How irritating! What do they want of me? Why do they have to intrude on my solitude? (Sighs.) No, I see I shall really have to enter a convent. (Pensively) Yes, a convent . . . (Enter SMIRNOV and LUKA.)

SMIRNOV (to LUKA). Blockhead, you talk too much. You jackass! (Seeing MME. POPOVA, with dignity) Madam, I have the honor to introduce myself: Landowner Grigory Stepanovich Smirnov, lieutenant of the artillery, retired. I am compelled to disturb you in connection with a very weighty matter.

MME. POPOVA (without offering her hand). What do you wish?

SMIRNOV. At his death your late husband, with whom I had the honor of being acquainted, was in my debt to the amount of twelve hundred rubles, for which I hold two notes. As I have to pay interest on a loan to the Land Bank tomorrow, I must request you, madam, to pay me the money today.

MME. POPOVA. Twelve hundred. . . . And for what did my husband owe you the money?

SMIRNOV. He used to buy oats from me.

MME. POPOVA (sighing, to LUKA). So don't forget, Luka, to tell them to give Toby an extra measure of oats. (Exit LUKA.) (To SMIRNOV) If Nikolay Mihailovich owed you money, I shall pay you, of course, but you must excuse me, I haven't any ready cash today. The day after tomorrow my steward will be back from town and I will see that he pays you what is owing to you, but just now I cannot comply with your request. Besides, today is exactly seven months since my husband's death and I am in no mood to occupy myself with money matters.

SMIRNOV. And I am in the mood to be carried out feet foremost if I don't pay the interest tomorrow. They'll seize my estate!

MME. POPOVA. The day after tomorrow you will receive your money.

SMIRNOV. I need the money today, not the day after tomorrow.

MME. POPOVA. I am sorry, but I cannot pay you today.

SMIRNOV. And I can't wait till the day after tomorrow.

MME. POPOVA. But what can I do if I don't have the money now!

SMIRNOV. So you can't pay me?

MME. POPOVA. No, I can't.

SMIRNOV. H'm . . . So that's your last word?

MME. POPOVA. My last word.

SMIRNOV. Your last word? Positively?

MME. POPOVA. Positively.

SMIRNOV. Many thanks. I'll make a note of it. *(Shrugs his shoulders.)* And they want me to keep cool! I meet the tax commissioner on the road, and he asks me: "Why are you always in a bad humor, Grigory Stepanovich?" But in heaven's name, how can I help being in a bad humor? I'm in desperate need of money. I left home yesterday morning at dawn and called on all my debtors and not one of them paid up! I wore myself out, slept the devil knows where, in some inn next to a barrel of vodka. . . . Finally I come here, fifty miles from home, hoping to get something, and I'm confronted with a "mood." How can I help getting in a temper?

MME. POPOVA. I thought I made it clear to you that you will get your money as soon as my steward returns from town.

SMIRNOV. I didn't come to your steward, but to you! What the devil — pardon the expression — do I care for your steward!

MME. POPOVA. Excuse me, sir, I am not accustomed to such language or to such a tone. I won't listen to you any more. *(Exits rapidly.)*

SMIRNOV. That's a nice thing! Not in the mood . . . husband died seven months ago! What about me? Do I have to pay the interest or don't I? I'm asking you: do I have to pay the interest or don't I? Well, your husband died, you're not in the mood, and all that . . . and your steward, devil take him, has gone off somewhere, but what do you want me to do? Am I to escape my creditors in a balloon, eh? Or take a running start and dash my head against a wall? I call on Gruzdev, he's not at home; Yaroshevich is hiding; I had an awful row with Kuritzyn and nearly threw him out of the window; Mazutov has an upset stomach, and this one isn't in the mood! Not one scoundrel will pay up! And it's all because I've spoiled them, because I'm a milksop, a softy, a weak sister. I'm too gentle with them altogether! But wait! You'll find out what I'm like! I won't let you make a fool of me, devil take it! I'll stay right here till she pays up!

Ugh! I'm in a perfect rage today, in a rage! Every one of my nerves is trembling with fury, I can hardly breathe. Ouf! Good Lord, I even feel sick! *(Shouts.)* You there! *(Enter* LUKA.*)*

LUKA. What do you wish?

SMIRNOV. Give me some kvass or a drink of water! *(Exit* LUKA.*)* No, but the logic of it! A fellow is in desperate need of cash, is on the point of hanging himself, but she won't pay up, because, you see, she isn't in the mood to occupy herself with money matters! Real petticoat logic! That's why I've never liked to talk to women, and I don't now. I'd rather sit on a powder keg than talk to a woman. Brr! I'm getting gooseflesh — that skirt made me so furious! I just have to see one of these poetic creatures from a distance and my very calves begin to twitch with rage. It's enough to make me yell for help. *(Enter* LUKA.*)*

LUKA *(handing* SMIRNOV *a glass of water).* Madam is ill and will see no one.

SMIRNOV. Get out! *(Exit* LUKA.*)* Ill and will see no one! All right, don't see me. I'll sit here until you pay up. If you're sick for a week, I'll stay a week; if you're sick a year, I'll stay a year. I'll get my own back, my good woman. You won't get round me with your widow's weeds and your dimples. . . . We know those dimples! *(Shouts through the window)* Semyon, take out the horses! We're not leaving so soon! I'm staying on! Tell them at the stables to give the horses oats. You blockhead, you've let the left outrider's leg get caught in the reins again! *(Mimicking the coachman)* "It don't matter." . . . I'll show you "don't matter." *(Walks away from the window.)* It's horrible . . . the heat is terrific, nobody has paid up, I slept badly, and here's this skirt in mourning, with her moods! I have a headache. Shall I have some vodka? Yes, I think I will. *(Shouts.)* You there! *(Enter* LUKA.*)*

LUKA. What do you wish?

SMIRNOV. Give me a glass of vodka. *(Exit* LUKA.*)* Ouf! *(Sits down and looks himself over.)* I cut a fine figure, I must say! All dusty, boots dirty, unwashed, uncombed, straw on my vest. The little lady must have taken me for a highwayman. *(Yawns.)* It's a bit uncivil to barge into a drawing room in such shape, but never mind. . . . I'm no caller, just a creditor, and there are no rules as to what the creditor should wear. *(Enter* LUKA.*)*

LUKA *(handing* SMIRNOV *the vodka).* You allow yourself too many liberties, sir. . . .

"*Your bell sounds lovely this evening.*"

SMIRNOV (crossly). What?

LUKA. I . . . nothing . . . I just meant . . .

SMIRNOV. To whom do you think you're talking? Shut up!

LUKA (aside). There's a demon in the house. . . . The Evil Spirit must have brought him. . . . (Exit LUKA.)

SMIRNOV. Oh, what a rage I'm in! I'm mad enough to grind the whole world to powder. I feel sick. (Shouts.) You there! (Enter MME. POPOVA.)

MME. POPOVA (with downcast eyes). Sir, in my solitude I've long since grown unaccustomed to the human voice, and I cannot bear shouting. I beg you not to disturb my peace!

SMIRNOV. Pay me my money and I'll drive off.

MME. POPOVA. I told you in plain language, I have no ready cash now. Wait till the day after tomorrow.

SMIRNOV. And I had the honor of telling you in plain language that I need the money today, not the day after tomorrow. If you don't pay me today, I'll have to hang myself tomorrow.

MME. POPOVA. But what shall I do if I have no money? How odd!

SMIRNOV. So you won't pay me now, eh?

MME. POPOVA. I can't.

SMIRNOV. In that case I stay and I'll sit here till I get the money. (Sits down.) You'll pay me the day after tomorrow? Excellent. I'll sit here till the day after tomorrow. (Jumps up.) I ask you. Do I have to pay the interest tomorrow or don't I? Or do you think I'm joking?

MME POPOVA. Sir, I beg you not to shout. This is no stable.

SMIRNOV. Never mind the stable, I'm asking you: Do I have to pay the interest tomorrow or not?

MME. POPOVA. You don't know how to behave in the presence of ladies!

SMIRNOV. No, madam, I do know how to behave in the presence of ladies!

MME. POPOVA. No, you do not! You are a rude, ill-bred man! Decent people don't talk to women that way!

SMIRNOV. Admirable! How would you like me to talk to you? In French, eh? (Rages, and lisps) Madame, je vous prie, I am delighted that you do not pay me my money. . . . Ah, pardonnez-moi if I have discommoded you! It's such delightful weather today! And how your mourning becomes you! (Scrapes his foot.)

MME. POPOVA. That's rude and silly.

SMIRNOV (mimicking her). Rude and silly! I don't know how to behave in the presence of ladies! Madam, I've seen more ladies than you've seen sparrows! I've fought three duels on account of women; I've jilted twelve women and been jilted by nine! Yes, madam! Time was when I played the fool, sentimentalized, used honeyed words, went out of my way to please, bowed and scraped. . . . I used to love, pine, sigh at the moon, feel blue, melt, freeze. . . . I loved passionately, madly, all sorts of ways, devil take me; I chattered like a magpie about the emancipation of women; I wasted half my fortune on affairs of the heart, but now, please excuse me! Now you won't bamboozle me! Enough! Dark eyes, burning eyes, ruby lips, dimpled cheeks, the moon, whispers, timid breathing. . . . I wouldn't give a brass farthing for all this now, madam. Present company excepted, all women, young or old, put on airs, pose, gossip, are liars to the marrow of their bones, are malicious, vain, petty, cruel, revoltingly unreasonable, and as for this *(taps his forehead),* pardon my frankness, a sparrow can give ten points to any philosopher in skirts! You look at one of these poetic creatures: She's all muslin and fluff, an airy demigoddess, a million transports, but look into her soul and what do you see but a common crocodile! *(Grips the back of his chair so that it cracks and breaks.)* But what is most revolting, this crocodile for some reason imagines that the tender feelings are her special province, her privilege, her monopoly! Why, devil take it, hang me by my feet on that nail, but can a woman love anything except a lap dog? When she's in love all she can do is whimper and turn on the waterworks! While a man suffers and makes sacrifices, her love finds expression only in swishing her train and trying to get a firmer grip on your nose. You, madam, have the misfortune of being a woman, so you know the nature of women down to the ground. Tell me honestly, then, did you ever see a woman who was sincere, faithful and constant. You'll sooner come across a horned cat or a white woodcock than a constant woman!

MME. POPOVA. Allow me to ask, then, who, in your opinion, is faithful and constant in love? Not man?

SMIRNOV. Yes, madam, man!

MME. POPOVA. Man! *(With bitter laughter)* Man is faithful and constant in love! That's news! *(Hotly)* What earthly right do you have to say that? Men faithful and constant! If such is the case, let me tell you that of all the men I have ever known my late husband was the best. I loved him passionately, with my whole soul, as only a young, deep-natured woman can love. I gave him my youth, my happiness, my life, my fortune; I loved and breathed by him; I worshiped him like a heathen, and . . . and what happened? This best of men deceived me shamelessly at every step! After his death I found a whole drawerful of love letters in his desk, and while he was alive—I can't bear to recall it!—he would leave me alone for weeks on end; he made love to other women before my very eyes, and he was unfaithful to me; he squandered my money and mocked my feelings. And in spite of it all, I loved him and was faithful to him. More than that, he died, and I am still faithful to him, still constant. I have buried myself forever within these four walls, and I will not take off my mourning till I go to my grave.

SMIRNOV (laughing scornfully). Mourning! I wonder who you take me for! As if I didn't know why you are masquerading in black like this and why you've buried yourself within four walls! Of course I do! It's so mysterious, so poetic! Some cadet or some puny versifier will ride past the house, glance at the windows, and say to himself: "Here lives the mysterious Tamara who, for love of her husband, has buried herself within four walls." We know those tricks!

MME. POPOVA (flaring up). What! How dare you say this to me!

SMIRNOV. You've buried yourself alive, but you haven't forgotten to powder your nose.

MME. POPOVA. How dare you talk to me like that!

SMIRNOV. Please don't scream, I'm not your steward! Allow me to call a spade a spade. I'm no woman and I'm used to talking straight from the shoulder! So please don't shout!

MME. POPOVA. I'm not shouting, you are shouting! Please leave me alone!

SMIRNOV. Pay me my money, and I'll go.

MME. POPOVA. I won't give you any money.

SMIRNOV. No, madam, you will!

MME. POPOVA. Just to spite you, I won't give you a penny. Only leave me alone!

SMIRNOV. I haven't the pleasure of being either your husband or your fiancé, so kindly, no scenes. (Sits down.) I don't like them.

MME. POPOVA (choking with rage). You've sat down?

SMIRNOV. I've sat down.

MME. POPOVA. I ask you to leave.

SMIRNOV. Give me my money. . . . (Aside) Oh, what a rage I'm in, what a rage!

MME. POPOVA. Such impudence! I don't want to talk to you. Please get out. (Pause.) Are you going? No?

SMIRNOV. No.

MME. POPOVA. No?

SMIRNOV. No!

MME. POPOVA. Very well, then. (*Enter* LUKA.)

MME. POPOVA. Luka, show this gentleman out!

LUKA (*approaching* SMIRNOV). Sir, be good enough to leave when you are asked to. Don't be —

SMIRNOV (*jumping to his feet*). Shut up! Who do you think you're talking to! I'll make hash of you!

LUKA (*clutching at his heart*). Mercy on us! Holy saints! (*Drops into an armchair.*) Oh, I'm sick, I'm sick! I can't get my breath!

MME. POPOVA. But where is Dasha? Dasha? (*Shouts.*) Dasha! Pelageya! Dasha! (*Rings.*)

LUKA. Oh, they've all gone berrying. . . . There's no one here. . . . I'm sick, water!

MME. POPOVA (*to* SMIRNOV). Please, get out!

SMIRNOV. Can't you be a little more civil?

MME. POPOVA (*clenching her fists and stamping her feet*). You're a boor! A brute, a bully, a monster!

SMIRNOV. What! What did you say?

MME. POPOVA. I said that you were a brute, a monster.

SMIRNOV (*advancing upon her*). Excuse me, but what right have you to insult me?

MME. POPOVA. Yes, I insulted you. What of it? Do you think I'm afraid of you?

SMIRNOV. And you think, just because you're a poetic creature, you can insult people with impunity, eh? I challenge you!

LUKA. Mercy on us! Holy saints! Water!

SMIRNOV. We'll shoot it out!

MME. POPOVA. Just because you have big fists and bellow like a bull, you think I'm afraid of you, eh? Bully!

SMIRNOV. I challenge you! I won't allow anybody to insult me, and it makes no difference to me that you're a woman, a member of the weaker sex.

MME. POPOVA (*trying to outshout him*). Brute, brute, brute!

SMIRNOV. It's high time to abandon the prejudice that men alone must pay for insults. Equal rights are equal rights, devil take it! I challenge you!

MME. POPOVA. You want to shoot it out? Well and good.

SMIRNOV. This very minute.

MME. POPOVA. This very minute. I have my husband's pistols. I'll bring them directly. *(Walks rapidly away and turns back.)* What pleasure it will give me to put a bullet into your brazen head! Devil take you! *(Exits.)*

SMIRNOV. I'll bring her down like a duck. I'm no boy, no sentimental puppy. There's no weaker sex as far as I'm concerned.

LUKA *(to SMIRNOV).* Master, kind sir! *(Going down on his knees)* Have pity on an old man, do me a favor—go away from here! You've frightened me to death, and now you want to fight a duel!

SMIRNOV *(not listening to him).* A duel! That's equal rights, that's emancipation! That's equality of the sexes for you! I'll bring her down as a matter of principle. But what a woman! *(Mimics her)* "Devil take you . . . I'll put a bullet into your brazen head." What a woman! She flushed and her eyes shone! She accepted the challenge! Word of honor, it's the first time in my life that I've seen one of that stripe.

LUKA. Kind master, please go away, and I will pray for you always.

SMIRNOV. That's a woman! That's the kind I understand! A real woman! Not a sour-faced, spineless crybaby, but a creature all fire and gunpowder, a cannon ball! It's a pity I have to kill her!

LUKA *(crying).* Sir, kind sir, please go away!

SMIRNOV. I positively like her! Positively! Even though she has dimples in her cheeks, I like her! I am even ready to forgive her the debt. . . . And I'm not angry any more. A remarkable woman! *(Enter MME. POPOVA with the pistols.)*

MME. POPOVA. Here are the pistols. But before we fight, please show me how to shoot. I never held a pistol in my hands before.

LUKA. Lord, have mercy on us! I'll go and look for the gardener and the coachman. Why has this calamity befallen us? *(Exits.)*

SMIRNOV *(examining the pistols).* You see, there are several makes of pistols. There are Mortimers, specially made for dueling, they are fired with the percussion cap. What you have here are Smith and Wesson triple-action, central-fire revolvers with extractors. Excellent pistols! Worth ninety rubles a pair at least. You hold the revolver like this. . . . *(Aside)* The eyes, the eyes! A woman to set you on fire!

MME. POPOVA. Like this?

SMIRNOV. Yes, like this. Then you cock the trigger . . . and you take aim like this . . . throw your head back a little! Stretch your arm out properly. . . . Like this. . . . Then you press this gadget with this finger, and that's all there is to it. . . . The main thing is: Keep cool and take aim slowly. . . . And try not to jerk your arm.

MME. POPOVA. Very well. It's inconvenient to shoot indoors; let's go into the garden.

SMIRNOV. All right. Only I warn you, I'll fire into the air.

MME. POPOVA. That's all that was wanting. Why?

SMIRNOV. Because . . . because. . . . It's my business why.

MME. POPOVA. You're scared, eh? Ah, ah, ah! No, sir, don't try to get out of it! Be so good as to follow me. I shan't rest until I've drilled a hole in your forehead . . . this forehead that I hate so! Scared?

SMIRNOV. Yes, I am scared.

MME. POPOVA. You're lying! Why do you refuse to fight?

SMIRNOV. Because . . . because I . . . like you.

MME. POPOVA (laughing bitterly). He likes me! He dares to say that he likes me! (Shows him the door.) You may go.

SMIRNOV (silently puts down the revolver, takes his cap and walks to the door; there he stops and for half a minute the pair look at each other without a word; then he says, hesitantly approaching MME. POPOVA). Listen . . . are you still angry? I'm in a devil of a temper myself, but you see . . . it's this way . . . in fact. . . . (Shouts.) Well, am I to blame if I like you? (Clutches the back of his chair; it cracks and breaks.) The devil! What fragile furniture you have! I like you. You understand. I've almost fallen in love.

MME. POPOVA. Go away from me. I hate you.

SMIRNOV. God, what a woman! Never in my life have I seen anything like her! I'm lost. I'm done for. I'm trapped like a mouse.

MME. POPOVA. Go away or I'll shoot.

SMIRNOV. Shoot! You can't understand what happiness it would be to die before those enchanting eyes . . . to die of a revolver shot fired by this little velvet hand! I've lost my mind. Think a moment and decide right now, because if I leave this house, we'll never see each other again. Decide. I'm a landed gentleman, a decent fellow, with an income of ten thousand a year; I can put a bullet through a penny thrown into the air; I have a good stable. Will you be my wife?

MME. POPOVA (indignant, brandishing the revolver). We'll shoot it out! Come along! Get your pistol.

SMIRNOV. I've lost my mind. I don't understand anything. (Shouts.) You there! Some water!

MME. POPOVA (shouts). Come! Let's shoot it out!

SMIRNOV. I've lost my mind. I've fallen in love like a boy, like a fool. (Seizes her by the hand; she cries out with pain.) I love you. (Goes down on his knees.) I love you as I've never loved before. I jilted twelve women and was jilted by nine. But I didn't love one of them as I do you. I've gotten sentimental. I'm melting. I'm weak as water. Here I am on my knees like a fool, and I offer you my hand. It's a shame, a disgrace! For five years I've not been in love. I took a vow. And suddenly I'm bowled over, swept off my feet. I offer you my hand— yes or no? You won't? Then don't! (*Rises and walks rapidly to the door.*)

MME. POPOVA. Wait a minute.

SMIRNOV (*stops*). Well?

MME. POPOVA. Never mind. Go . . . but no, wait a minute. . . . No, go, go! I detest you! Or no . . . don't go! Oh, if you knew how furious I am, how furious! (*Throws the revolver on the table.*) My fingers are cramped from holding this vile thing. (*Tears her handkerchief in a fit of temper.*) What are you standing there for? Get out!

SMIRNOV. Good-by.

MME. POPOVA. Yes, yes, go! (*Shouts.*) Where are you going? Wait a minute. . . . But no, go away. . . . Oh, how furious I am! Don't come near me, don't come near me!

SMIRNOV (*approaching her*). I'm disgusted with myself! Falling in love like a mooncalf, going down on my knees. It gives me gooseflesh. (*Rudely*) I love you. What on earth made me fall in love with you? Tomorrow I have to pay the interest. And we've started mowing. And here are you! . . . (*Puts his arm around her waist.*) I shall never forgive myself for this.

MME. POPOVA. Get away from me! Hands off! I hate you! Let's shoot it out!

(*A prolonged kiss. Enter* LUKA *with an axe, the gardener with a rake, the coachman with a pitchfork, and hired men with sticks.*)

LUKA (*catching sight of the pair kissing*). Mercy on us! Holy saints! (*Pauses.*)

MME. POPOVA (*dropping her eyes*). Luka, tell them at the stables that Toby isn't to have any oats at all today.

Who presented obstacles to a union between Popova and Smirnov?

Were you surprised when the couple fell in love at the end of the play? Why or why not? Was this outcome believable or not?

The couple in this play are examples of character-types which could be called "fighting lovers." Can you think of other couples of this type you have encountered in literature, movies, or on television?

How is the woman portrayed in the typical love story like "Cupid and Psyche"? Is Popova a different type of woman? Why or why not?

Aucassin
and Nicolette

A French legend
Retold by BARBARA LEONIE PICARD

Long ago there ruled in Beaucaire an old count who had but one child, his son Aucassin, a comely youth with gray eyes and curling golden hair. Gracious he was, and generous, and of great courtesy, as a youth of noble birth should be, but for those other qualities which become the son of a count he cared nothing. He never rode a-hunting, he never donned helmet and hauberk to joust, on the tourney field and in the tilting yard he was never seen, and for the honors of knighthood he had no wish. But ever would he spend his days in the company of the maiden whom he loved, or when that might not be, he would sit alone and dream of her.

In the city of Beaucaire the Count had a vassal who, fifteen years before, knowing nothing of her birth or parentage, had out of pity bought from Saracen pirates a little girl. He had baptized this child and called her Nicolette, and brought her up with kindness in his own house, intending, when she came of an age to be married, to give her as a wife to some honest man-at-arms or merchant. But Aucassin had once seen Nicolette and loved her straightway, so that he cared for nothing else, and at all hours of every day he would be at the vassal's house, seeking speech with Nicolette, and for her part, she was very glad of this.

The Count of Beaucaire was ill-pleased by his son's love for a maiden who had once been sold as a slave and about whom nothing else was known, and he spoke to him of marriage with one of his own rank, the daughter of a count or a duke, or even of a king. But Aucassin answered him, "I will have Nicolette for my wife, or no one else."

Angered, the Count bade his vassal send Nicolette far off where his son might no more see her. "If you do not obey me in this," he said, "it will go ill with you. And as for this wretched girl, she shall be burnt."

So the vassal, afraid, locked Nicolette away, with only an old woman for company, in a room at the very top of his house, with no more than one little window, looking down upon the garden.

When Aucassin found that Nicolette was gone, and no man could tell him where, he sought out his father's vassal and asked what had become of her. "Lord," said the vassal, "it is your father's wish that you should see and speak with her no more." And though Aucassin argued and pleaded with him, it was in vain. "I fear the Count too much, lord. For if I disobey him in this matter, Nicolette will be burnt, and perhaps I also."

So with a heavy heart Aucassin returned to his father's castle, cast himself down on his bed, and wept. And there he remained, sighing for Nicolette and paying no heed to any who sought to reason with him.

For some time the Count of Valence had waged war upon the Count of Beaucaire, and hardly a day had passed when he had not made an attack upon his lands. Since Aucassin's father was too old for fighting, often had he tried to persuade his son to lead the men of Beaucaire to battle. But caring for nothing save his love for Nicolette, Aucassin had taken no part in the war. But now there came a day when the Count of Valence said, "This war has lasted long enough. We must make an end of it." And with all his forces he attacked the city of Beaucaire, meaning not to cease until it was in his hands.

The Count of Beaucaire went to Aucassin, where he grieved, lying upon his bed. "Are you a coward?" he asked. "Or would you be shamed for ever, that you lie here, when, at any hour, our city may be taken? Rise up and put on your armor and lead our men to battle. It will give them fresh courage against the enemy, if they see you at their head."

But Aucassin only answered, "I care nothing for the city if I may not have my Nicolette."

"And I would rather lose my city and all my lands, than see my son wedded with a maiden who comes from no one knows where." The Count turned away in anger and would have left the room, but suddenly Aucassin sat up upon his bed. "Father," he said, "let us make a bargain. If I do this thing for you, and put on my armor and lead out your men, when I return, will you let me see my Nicolette, and speak a word or two to her and give her one kiss?"

"I will do that," said the Count.

Joyfully Aucassin put on armor and girded on a sword, taking up lance and shield with a merry heart. The gates of the city were opened, and on a huge war horse, Aucassin rode out at the head of his father's men. But he gave not one thought to the battle or the enemy, remembering only his father's promise: how in a little while he would see Nicolette again. In his eagerness he spurred on his horse and it galloped forward, all alone, right to where the men of Valence stood thickest, and Aucassin, his eyes blind to all about him saw only his Nicolette, and deaf to all else, heard only her sweet voice in his ears.

And then he came back to reality, to find himself surrounded by the enemy, his lance and his shield being dragged from his grasp, without his having struck one blow. Bewildered, he looked about him, while the men of Valence rejoiced and jeered. "It is the son of the Count of Beaucaire. Let us take and hang him." And they sent to their lord of Valence that he might see it done.

Then the thought suddenly came to Aucassin, "If they hang me, I shall never see my Nicolette again." He saw that they had not yet taken his sword from him, and before they knew what he was about, he had drawn it, and hacking and striking all around him, he won his way back toward the city. The Count of Valence, seeing his prize escaping, rode after him and sought to recapture him, but Aucassin fought mightily, thinking of his Nicolette, and he flung the Count from his horse and took him captive, dragging him into the city, to his father's feet.

"Here is your enemy, my father. See how I have ended the war for you. Now quickly fulfill your promise and let me speak with Nicolette."

"Might I be cursed if I kept to such a bargain," said the Count of Beaucaire. "If I had Nicolette before me now, I would order her burnt, that there might be an end to this foolish love of yours."

When Aucassin saw how he had been cheated by his father, he released the Count of Valence from his bonds, gave him a horse, and saw him safely from the city. "Let this be your ransom," he said, "that you never call my father friend."

Then, in his wrath, the Count of Beaucaire had Aucassin cast into a dungeon, deep below a tower, where only one small barred window let in the light of day, and there he remained, weeping for his Nicolette.

One summer night soon after, as Nicolette lay unsleeping on her bed in the room where she was imprisoned, she thought of how the Count had sworn to burn her if he ever found her, and fearing lest he should discover where she had been hidden, she determined to escape and leave the city. So, hearing from her snores that the old woman who guarded her was sleeping, she rose quietly and dressed herself; then knotting together the sheets and the coverlet from her bed, she fastened one end of the rope she had made to the window frame and climbed down into the garden. Lightly she ran across the garden, and out through the garden gate.

In the streets, wrapped in her dark cloak, she kept close to the houses, in the shadows, making for the city walls. In this fashion, by chance she came by the tower below which Aucassin lay bound. Through the small window of his dungeon she heard his voice, sighing for her. She knelt down and spoke to him through the bars. "Aucassin, dear love, it is I, your Nicolette. Since your father will never permit us to marry, and since he has sworn to kill me, should he ever find me, I am leaving the city to seek safety in another place." And she cut off a tress of her hair and dropped it down to him.

"You will go to another land, and there another man will make you his wife, and I shall die for love of you," said Aucassin.

"Alas," said Nicolette, "what else can I do?" With tears they bade each other farewell, and Nicolette went on her way. She found a spot where the city walls had been damaged in the siege, and with great pain she climbed them, and then with much labor and in fear she crossed the moat and somehow reached the other side, and made for the nearby forest. On the edge of the forest she hid among the bushes and slept, for she was very weary.

At dawn she awoke to the sound of voices, and coming out from her hiding place, she saw three or four shepherd lads eating their breakfast. She went to them. "Good shepherds, if Aucassin, the Count's son, should ever chance this way, tell him, I beg of you, that in this forest there is a fair quarry for his hunting, such that he would not part with for five hundred golden marks."

They stared at her, and one of them answered, "There is no beast in all this forest worth one golden mark. You must be out of your mind, or a fairy woman, to speak such words. But should the Lord Aucassin ride this way, I will tell him what you said."

Nicolette thanked him and went on into the forest, and there, among the trees, she built herself a bower of leaves and branches.

When he found that Nicolette was gone from his house, the Count's vassal went to his lord and said,"I have done as you bade me, and Nicolette is no longer in my keeping." And thinking her to have been sent far away, the Count was glad, and in his gladness forgave his son and released him from the dungeon. Aucassin mounted a horse and rode out of the city and away to the forest, to be alone with his grief. On the edge of the forest he came upon the shepherd lads, and they spoke to him. "Are you not Lord Aucassin, the son of our Count?"

"I am," he said.

"There has passed this way," said one of the shepherds, "a maiden, be she mortal or fairy I know not, who left a strange message for you. She said that in this forest there is a quarry for your hunting, such as you would not part with for five hundred golden marks. Yet I cannot tell what she meant by her words."

But Aucassin knew at once that it was Nicolette they spoke of, and hopefully he rode on into the forest. All day he searched, and that night he came upon the bower she had built, and found Nicolette herself within. Their joy in being together once again knew no bounds, but Nicolette said, "We cannot stay here, for if your father sends his men to search for you, and they find me with you, I shall be taken and burnt."

"In the morning," said Aucassin, "we shall go far from my father's lands."

At dawn he mounted his horse, set Nicolette before him, and together they rode from Beaucaire, and away to the coast. There they found a ship setting sail for a foreign land. They went aboard her and soon reached the island of Torelore, where they were welcomed by the King. And there they dwelt happily for a time.

But there came a day when the fleet of the King of Carthage raided the island, taking much booty and many prisoners to sell as slaves. And among those they took were Aucassin and Nicolette. Nicolette was led to the ship of the King of Carthage himself, while Aucassin was taken on board another vessel. When the spoils and prisoners were all bestowed, the fleet set sail for Carthage, but once out at sea, a storm arose. Blown from her course, and parted from the other vessels, the ship which carried Aucassin was wrecked upon the coast of France, close by the county of Beaucaire. Aucassin was saved by some fisher folk, and from them he learned that his father was dead, so that he was now the count and ruler of Beaucaire. He went at once to his own lands and was received with great joy, for all had thought him dead. His vassals came to do him homage, and in all his realm was peace and happiness, but his own heart was heavy, for he did not know what had become of Nicolette.

Yet indeed, no ill had come to her, for when the King of Carthage and his twelve sons saw her, for some reason they could not guess, she seemed familiar to them, and they held her in all honor and questioned her as to who she was and whence she came. But all she could tell them was that she had been stolen from her home by pirates when she was a very little child and had since lived in Beaucaire. After several days at sea, the coast of Carthage came in sight, and as soon as she saw the harbor and the buildings and the country that lay round about, Nicolette cried out that she had seen it all before. And the King of Carthage embraced her, saying, "You will be my lost daughter, who was stolen from me, fifteen years ago."

He took her to his palace, giving her rich clothes to wear and costly gifts, and he looked about him at all his noblest lords, seeking a husband worthy of her. But Nicolette thought only of how she might return to Aucassin. And when a means had come into her mind, she asked that she might learn to play the lute, and it was granted her. When she had mastered the art, she cut off her hair and stained her skin with walnut juice, and in the garb of a boy she slipped from the palace and down to the harbor. There she sought out the captain of a ship that was to go to France, and asked to sail with him. And because she sang sweetly and played so well upon the lute, he gave her passage willingly, and set her ashore on the coast of Provence.

From there she traveled as a minstrel to Beaucaire, to see if she might hear news of Aucassin, and in the city of Beaucaire she found that he ruled as count, his father being dead. But she had no way of telling whether he still loved her, so, going to the castle, she asked if she might sing before the Count.

She played upon her lute and sang a song that she had made, of the love of Aucassin and Nicolette: how they had fled away together, and how they had been parted, and how Nicolette was the daughter of the King of Carthage. When the song was done, Aucassin called her to him and spoke to her apart. "Sir minstrel," he said, "tell me what more you know of this lady, Nicolette."

"Lord," she said, "I know that her father would give her as a wife to the highest in his land. But she would rather die than be the wife of any but the one she loves."

"And I," said Aucassin, "will have no wife at all, unless I can have my Nicolette." And he wept, remembering her.

And Nicolette, knowing that he still loved her, told him who she was, and in great joy he took her in his arms. And so at last they were married and lived long and happily in Beaucaire.

How does the plot of this story resemble the plot of "Cupid and Psyche"?

In many love stories the young couple go to the forest or other rural setting. Why is the forest an appropriate retreat for young lovers? Can you think of other examples of lovers who court in a forest or other rural setting?

Why do you think writers so often have parents serve as blocking figures who object to the mates their children choose?

In many comedies the evading or breaking of a cruel law or restriction is often a very narrow squeeze. How could the doom that hung over Psyche, Aucassin, or Nicolette have resulted in tragedy? Try rewriting the end of one of the stories so that it ends in tragedy.

Gertrude the Governess; or, Simple Seventeen

STEPHEN LEACOCK

Synopsis of Previous Chapters:
There are no Previous Chapters.

It was a wild and stormy night on the West Coast of Scotland. This, however, is immaterial to the present story, as the scene is not laid in the West of Scotland. For the matter of that the weather was just as bad on the East Coast of Ireland.

But the scene of this narrative is laid in the South of England and takes place in and around Knotacentinum Towers (pronounced as if written Nosham Taws), the seat of Lord Knotacent (pronounced as if written Nosh).

But it is not necessary to pronounce either of these names in reading them.

Nosham Taws was a typical English home. The main part of the house was an Elizabethan structure of warm red brick, while the elder portion, of which the Earl was inordinately proud, still showed the outlines of a Norman Keep, to which had been added a Lancastrian Jail and a Plantagenet Orphan Asylum. From the house in all directions stretched magnificent woodland and park with oaks and elms of immemorial antiquity, while nearer the house stood raspberry bushes and geranium plants which had been set out by the Crusaders.

About the grand old mansion the air was loud with the chirping of the thrushes, the cawing of patridges and the clear sweet note of the rook, while deer, antelope, and other quadrupeds strutted about the lawn so tame as to eat off the sun-dial. In fact, the place was a regular menagerie.

From the house downwards through the park stretched a beautifully broad avenue laid out by Henry VII.

Lord Nosh stood upon the hearthrug of the library. Trained diplomat and statesman as he was, his stern aristocratic face was upside down with fury.

"Boy," he said, "you shall marry this girl or I disinherit you. You are no son of mine."

Young Lord Ronald, erect before him, flung back a glance as defiant as his own.

"I defy you," he said. "Henceforth you are no father of mine. I will get another. I will marry none but a woman I can love. This girl that we have never seen—"

"Fool," said the Earl, "would you throw aside our estate and name of a thousand years? The girl, I am told, is beautiful; her aunt is willing; they are French; pah! they understand such things in France."

"But your reason—"

"I give no reason," said the Earl. "Listen, Ronald, I give one month. For that time you remain here. If at the end of it you refuse me, I cut you off with a shilling."

Lord Ronald said nothing; he flung himself from the room, flung himself upon his horse, and rode madly off in all directions.

As the door of the library closed upon Ronald, the Earl sank into a chair. His face changed. It was no longer that of the haughty nobleman, but of the hunted criminal. "He must marry the girl," he muttered. "Soon she will know all. Tutchemoff has escaped from Siberia. He knows and will tell. The whole of the mines pass to her, this property with it, and I—but enough." He rose, walked to the sideboard, drained a dipper full of gin and bitters, and became a highbred English gentleman.

It was at this moment that a high dogcart, driven by a groom in the livery of Earl Nosh, might have been seen entering the avenue of Nosham Taws. Beside him sat a young girl, scarce more than a child, in fact, not nearly so big as the groom.

The apple-pie hat which she wore, surmounted with black willow plumes, concealed from view a face so facelike in its appearance as to be positively facial.

It was—need we say it—Gertrude the Governess, who was this day to enter upon her duties at Nosham Taws.

At the same time that the dogcart entered the avenue at one end there might have been seen riding down it from the other a tall young man, whose long, aristocratic face proclaimed his birth and who was mounted upon a horse with a face even longer than his own.

And who is this tall young man who draws nearer to Gertrude with every revolution of the horse? Ah, who, indeed? Ah, who, who? I wonder if any of my readers could guess that this was none other than Lord Ronald.

The two were destined to meet. Nearer and nearer they came. And then still nearer. Then for one brief moment they met. As they passed Gertrude raised her head and directed toward the young nobleman two eyes so eyelike in their expression as to be absolutely circular, while Lord Ronald directed toward the occupant of the dogcart a gaze so gazelike that nothing but a gazelle, or a gas pipe, could have emulated its intensity.

Was this the dawn of love? Wait and see. Do not spoil the story.

Let us speak of Gertrude. Gertrude De Mongmorenci McFiggin had known neither father nor mother. They had both died years before she was born. Of her mother she knew nothing, save that she was French, was extremely beautiful, and that all her ancestors and even her business acquaintances had perished in the Revolution.

Yet Gertrude cherished the memory of her parents. On her breast the girl wore a locket in which was enshrined a miniature of her mother, while down her neck inside at the back hung a daguerreotype of her father. She carried a portrait of her grandmother up her sleeve and had pictures of her cousins tucked inside her boot, while beneath her—but enough, quite enough.

Of her father Gertrude knew even less. That he was a high-born English gentleman who had lived as a wanderer in many lands, this was all she knew. His only legacy to Gertrude had been a Russian grammar, a Rumanian phrase-book, a theodolite, and a work on mining engineering.

From her earliest infancy Gertrude had been brought up by her aunt. Her aunt had carefully instructed her in Christian principles. She had also taught her Mohammedanism to make sure.

When Gertrude was seventeen her aunt had died of hydrophobia.

The circumstances were mysterious. There had called upon her that day a strange bearded man in the costume of the Russians. After he had left, Gertrude had found her aunt in a syncope from which she passed into an apostrophe and never recovered.

To avoid scandal it was called hydrophobia. Gertrude was thus thrown upon the world. What to do? That was the problem that confronted her.

It was while musing one day upon her fate that Gertrude's eye was struck with an advertisement.

"Wanted a governess; must possess a knowledge of French, Italian, Russian, Rumanian, Music, and Mining Engineering. Salary 1 pound, 4 shillings and 4 pence half-penny per annum. Apply between half-past eleven and twenty-five minutes to twelve at No. 41 A Decimal Six, Belgravia Terrace. The Countess of Nosh."

Gertrude was a girl of great natural quickness of apprehension, and she had not pondered over this announcement more that half an hour before she was struck with the extraordinary coincidence between the list of items desired and the things that she herself knew.

She duly presented herself at Belgravia Terrace before the Countess, who advanced to meet her with a charm which at once placed the girl at her ease.

"You are proficient in French?" she asked.

"*Oh, oui,*" said Gertrude modestly.

"And Italian?" continued the Countess.

"*Oh, si,*" said Gertrude.

"And German?" said the Countess in delight.

"*Ah, ja,*" said Gertrude.

"And Russian?"

"*Yaw.*"

"And Rumanian?"

"*Jep.*"

Amazed at the girl's extraordinary proficiency in modern languages, the Countess looked at her narrowly. Where had she seen those lineaments before? She passed her hand over her brow in thought, and spit upon the floor, but no, the face baffled her.

"Enough," she said, "I engage you on the spot; tomorrow you go down to Nosham Taws and begin teaching the children. I must add that in addition you will be expected to aid the Earl with his Russian correspondence. He has large mining interests at Tschminsk."

Tschminsk! Why did the simple word reverberate upon Gertrude's ears? Why? Because it was the name written in her father's hand on the title page of his book on mining. What mystery was here?

It was on the following day that Gertrude had driven up the avenue.

She descended from the dogcart, passed through a phalanx of liveried servants drawn up seven-deep, to each of whom she gave a sovereign as she passed and entered Nosham Taws.

"Welcome," said the Countess, as she aided Gertrude to carry her trunk upstairs.

The girl presently descended and was ushered into the library, where she was presented to the Earl. As soon as the Earl's eye fell upon the face of the new governess he started visibly. Where had he seen those lineaments? Where was it? At the races, or the theater—on a bus —no. Some subtler thread of memory was stirring in his mind. He strode hastily to the sideboard, drained a dipper and a half of brandy, and became again the perfect English gentleman.

While Gertrude has gone to the nursery to make the acquaintance of the two tiny golden-haired children who are to be her charges, let us say something here of the Earl and his son.

Lord Nosh was the perfect type of the English nobleman and statesman. The years that he had spent in the diplomatic service at Constantinople, St. Petersburg, and Salt Lake City had given to him a peculiar finesse and noblesse, while his long residence at St. Helena, Pitcairn Island, and Hamilton, Ontario, had rendered him impervious to external impressions. As deputy-paymaster of the militia of the county he had seen something of the sterner side of military life, while his hereditary office of Groom of the Sunday Breeches had brought him into direct contact with Royalty itself.

His passion for outdoor sports endeared him to his tenants. A keen sportsman, he excelled in fox-hunting, dog-hunting, pig-killing, bat-catching, and the pastimes of his class.

In this latter respect Lord Ronald took after his father. From the start the lad had shown the greatest promise. At Eton he had made a splendid showing at battledore and shuttlecock, and at Cambridge had been first in his class at needlework. Already his name was whispered in connection with the All England ping-pong championship, a triumph which would undoubtedly carry with it a seat in Parliament.

Thus was Gertrude the Governess installed at Nosham Taws.

The days and the weeks sped past.

The simple charm of the beautiful orphan girl attracted all hearts. Her two little pupils became her slaves. "Me loves oo," the little Rasehellfrida would say, leaning her golden head in Gertrude's lap. Even the servants loved her. The head gardener would bring a bouquet of beautiful roses to her room before she was up, the second gardener a bunch of early cauliflowers, the third a spray of late asparagus, and even the tenth and eleventh a sprig of mangelwurzel or an armful of hay. Her room was full of gardeners all the time, while at evening the aged butler, touched at the friendless girl's loneliness, would tap softly at her door to bring her a rye whiskey and seltzer or a box of Pittsburg Stogies. Even the dumb creatures seemed to admire her in their own dumb way. The dumb rooks settled on her shoulder and every dumb dog around the place followed her.

And Ronald! Ah, Ronald! Yes, indeed! They had met. They had spoken.

"What a dull morning," Gertrude had said. *"Quel triste matin! Was fur ein allerverdamnter Tag!"*

"Beastly," Ronald had answered.

"Beastly! !" The word rang in Gertrude's ears all day.

After that they were constantly together. They played tennis and ping-pong in the day, and in the evening, in accordance with the stiff routine of the place, they sat down with the Earl and Countess to twenty-five cent poker, and later still, they sat together on the veranda, and watched the moon sweeping in great circles around the horizon.

It was not long before Gertrude realized that Lord Ronald felt toward her a warmer feeling than that of mere ping-pong. At times in her presence he would fall, especially after dinner, into a fit of profound substraction.

Once at night, when Gertrude withdrew to her chamber and before seeking her pillow, prepared to retire as a preliminary to disrobing — in other words, before going to bed, she flung wide the casement (opened the window) and perceived (saw) the face of Lord Ronald. He was sitting on a thorn bush beneath her, and his upturned face wore an expression of agonized pallor.

Meanwhile the days passed. Life at the Taws moved in the ordinary routine of a large English household. At seven a gong sounded for rising, at eight a horn blew for breakfast, at eight-thirty a whistle sounded for prayers, at one a flag was run up at half-mast for lunch, at four a gun was fired for afternoon tea, at nine a first bell sounded for dressing, at nine-fifteen a second bell for going on dressing, while at nine-thirty a rocket was sent up to indicate that dinner was ready. At midnight dinner was over, and at one A.M. the tolling of a bell summoned the domestics to evening prayers.

Meanwhile the month allotted by the Earl to Lord Ronald was passing away. It was already July 15, then within a day or two it was July 17, and, almost immediately afterward, July 18.

At times the Earl, in passing Ronald in the hall, would say sternly, "Remember, boy, your consent, or I disinherit you."

And what were the Earl's thoughts of Gertrude? Here was the one drop of bitterness in the girl's cup of happiness. For some reason that she could not divine the Earl showed signs of marked antipathy.

Once as she passed the door of the library he threw a bootjack at her. On another occasion at lunch alone with her he struck her savagely across the face with a sausage.

It was her duty to translate to the Earl his Russian correspondence. She sought in it in vain for the mystery. One day a Russian telegram was handed to the Earl. Gertrude translated it to him aloud.

"Tutchemoff went to the woman. She is dead."

On hearing this the Earl became livid with fury; in fact this was the day that he struck her with the sausage.

Then one day while the Earl was absent on a bat-hunt, Gertrude, who was turning over his correspondence, with that sweet feminine instinct of interest that rose superior to ill-treatment, suddenly found the key to the mystery.

Lord Nosh was not the rightful owner of the Taws. His distant cousin of the older line, the true heir, had died in a Russian prison to which the machinations of the Earl, while Ambassador at Tschminsk, had consigned him. The daughter of this cousin was the true owner of Nosham Taws.

The family story, save only that the documents before her withheld the name of the rightful heir, lay bare to Gertrude's eye.

Strange is the heart of woman. Did Gertrude turn from the Earl with spurning? No. Her own sad fate had taught her sympathy.

Yet still the mystery remained! Why did the Earl start perceptibly each time that he looked into her face? Sometimes he started as much as four centimetres, so that one could distinctly see him do it. On such occasions he would hastily drain a dipper of rum and vichy water and become again the correct English gentleman.

The denouement came swiftly. Gertrude never forgot it.

It was the night of the great ball at Nosham Taws. The whole neighborhood was invited. How Gertrude's heart had beat with anticipation, and with what trepidation she had overhauled her scant wardrobe in order to appear not unworthy in Lord Ronald's eyes. Her resources were poor indeed, yet the inborn genius for dress that she inherited from her French mother stood her in good stead. She twined a single rose in her hair and contrived herself a dress out of a few old papers and the inside of an umbrella that would have graced a court. Round her waist she bound a single braid of bag-string, while a piece of old lace that had been her mother's was suspended to her ear by a thread.

Gertrude was the cynosure of all eyes. Floating to the strains of the music she presented a picture of bright girlish innocence that no one could see undisenraptured.

The ball was at its height. It was away up!

Ronald stood with Gertrude in the shrubbery. They looked into one another's eyes.

"Gertrude," he said, "I love you."

Simple words, and yet they thrilled every fiber in the girl's costume.

"Ronald!" she said, and cast herself about his neck.

At this moment the Earl appeared standing beside them in the moonlight. His stern face was distorted with indignation.

"So!" he said, turning to Ronald, "it appears that you have chosen!"

"I have," said Ronald with hauteur.

"You prefer to marry this penniless girl rather than the heiress I have selected for you?"

Gertrude looked from father to son in amazement.

"Yes," said Ronald.

"Be it so," said the Earl, draining a dipper of gin which he carried, and resuming his calm. "Then I disinherit you. Leave this place, and never return to it."

"Come, Gertrude," said Ronald tenderly, "let us flee together."

Gertrude stood before them. The rose had fallen from her head. The lace had fallen from her ear and the bagstring had come undone from her waist. Her papers were crumpled beyond recognition. But disheveled and illegible as she was, she was still mistress of herself.

"Never," she said firmly. "Ronald, you shall never make this sacrifice for me." Then to the Earl, in tones of ice, "There is a pride, sir, as great even as yours. The daughter of Metschnikoff McFiggin need crave a boon from no one."

With that she hauled from her bosom the daguerreotype of her father and pressed it to her lips.

The Earl started as if shot. "That name!" he cried, "That face! That photograph! Stop!"

There! There is no need to finish; my readers have long since divined it. Gertrude was the heiress.

The lovers fell into one another's arms. The Earl's proud face relaxed. "God bless you," he said. The Countess and the guests came pouring out upon the lawn. The breaking day illuminated a scene of gay congratulations.

Gertrude and Ronald were wed. Their happiness was complete. Need we say more? Yes, only this. The Earl was killed in the hunting-field a few days later. The Countess was struck by lightning. The two children fell down a well. Thus the happiness of Gertrude and Ronald was complete.

In what other stories or plays you have read has the revelation of a secret or mysterious identity of a character been a crucial element in the plot?

Make a list of other recurring patterns (like the mysterious identity) of the comic love story that you find in "Gertrude the Governess" and in other selections in this unit. Try writing a love story of your own using some of these familiar patterns.

How would you describe the tone of "Gertrude the Governess"? How does it differ from "Cupid and Psyche" or "Aucassin and Nicolette"?

You might try dramatizing this tale of Gertrude and Lord Ronald. Pay particular attention to costuming and the way the characters act. Exaggeration is essential. The play could all be done in mime, using a narrator.

Benjamin Braddock, a recent college graduate, is determined to marry Elaine Robinson, a student at Berkeley, despite her parents' strong opposition. The Robinsons have pushed Elaine into a marriage with Carl Smith, a medical student, although Elaine really loves Benjamin.

There Goes the Bride

From The Graduate
CHARLES WEBB

Just before dawn Benjamin landed at the San Francisco airport and hurried off the plane and into a phone booth. There was only one Carl Smith in the directory. He called but there was no answer. Then he tore the page out of the phone book and had a taxi take him to the address. The front door of the apartment building was unlocked. Benjamin pushed it open and hurried up the three flights of stairs and down a darkened hall to the door of Carl Smith's apartment. Just as he was about to knock he noticed a white envelope thumbtacked to the wood of the door next to the doorknob. He tore it off and ran back down the hall with it to a window. On the front of the envelope the name *Bob* was written. Benjamin ripped it open, pulled out a sheet of paper from inside and read it quickly by the gray light coming in through the dirty glass of the window.

Bob,

Prepare yourself for a real jolt, old boy. Believe it or not I am getting hitched. Elaine Robinson, the girl I brought up to your party last month, has accepted my proposal and in fact insists that we tie the knot this very weekend. I cannot believe my luck and am, needless to say, in quite a daze at the moment so I know you will forgive me for canceling out on our plans.

It was all arranged in a midnight visit from her and her father. There are many strange and bizarre circumstances surrounding the whole thing which I don't have time to go into now. Elaine is down in Santa Barbara staying with my folks and I am on my way down. We will be married in the First Presbyterian Church on Allen Street in S.B. at eleven o'clock Saturday morning. If perchance you find this note soon enough, be sure and hop it down there as I think I can promise you a pretty good show. Janie is frantically trying to dig up bridesmaids and Mother is telegramming invitations to everyone in sight. Dad is too stunned to do anything.

I will be back early in the week, bride in tow, and will see you then if not before, Hallelulia!

Carl

His airplane touched down in a small airport in the outskirts of Santa Barbara just at eleven o'clock. Benjamin was the first out of its door and down the ramp. Several minutes later his taxi pulled to a stop in front of the First Presbyterian Church on Allen Street. He jumped out and handed the driver a bill through the window.

The church was in a residential section of large houses and neat green lawns and was itself an extremely large building with a broad expanse of stained-glass windows across the front and wide concrete stairs leading up to a series of doors, all of which were closed. Benjamin squeezed between the bumpers of two limousines parked in front of the church and hurried up the stairs. He grabbed the handles of two doors and pulled. They were locked. He rushed to the next pair of handles and pulled again. They were also locked. He began banging with his fist on one of the doors, then turned around and ran down the steps. He ran to the side of the church. A stairway led up the wall of the church to a door. Benjamin hurried back along the wall, then ran two steps at a time up to the top of the stairs. He tried the door. It opened. Thick organ music poured out from inside the building. He ran down a hall to a door and pushed it open, then hurried through it and stopped.

Beneath him were the guests. They were standing. Nearly all of them were turned part way around and looking back toward the rear of the church under the balcony where he was standing. Most of the women were wearing white gloves. One was holding a handkerchief up to her eye. A man with a red face near the front of the church was turned around and was smiling broadly toward the back. Carl Smith and another boy were standing at the front of the church. Both were wearing black tuxedos with white carnations in their lapels. Benjamin saw Mrs. Robinson. She was standing in the first pew in the church and wearing a small hat on her head. He stared at her a moment, then a girl wearing a bright green dress came walking slowly under him and down the aisle of the church toward the altar. Another girl appeared, also wearing a bright green dress, then another and another. Then suddenly Elaine appeared. Benjamin rushed closer to the railing and leaned over to stare down at a piece of white lace on the top of her head. He began clenching and unclenching his hands in front of him. She was walking with her arm in her father's arm and wearing a white wedding dress whose long train followed her slowly over the thick red carpet and toward the front of the church. Benjamin began shaking his head, still staring at her and clenching and unclenching his hands. The guests turned slowly as she passed them. The girls in green dresses formed two rows at either side of the altar. Then Benjamin slammed his hands down on the railing of the balcony and yelled.

"Elaine!!!"

The organ music stopped.

He slammed his hands down again. "Elaine!!! Elaine!!! Elaine!!!"

From the altar the minister looked up quickly. The girls in green all looked up toward the back of the church. Mrs. Robinson stepped part way into the aisle, stared up at him, then took another step toward him and began shaking her head. The man with the red face near the front of the church looked up and stopped smiling.

Benjamin slammed his hands down on the wooden railing. "Elaine!!!"

Elaine had turned around and was staring up at him. Behind her Carl Smith was looking up at him with his head tilted slightly to the side. Mr. Robinson made a move toward the back of the church. Then he turned around quickly and took Elaine's hand. He pulled her up toward the front of the church and to the minister. He said something to the minister, the minister bent slightly forward, he said it again, gesturing at Carl Smith, then the minister nodded. Mr. Robinson took Carl Smith's arm and brought him over beside Elaine in front of the minister. The minister opened a small book he was holding.

"No!!!"

Benjamin turned in a circle. Then he lifted one of his legs up and put it over the railing. A woman screamed. Several guests immediately beneath him began pushing and shoving each other to get out of the way. Elaine turned around and took several steps down the aisle toward the back of the church and stared up at him, holding her hands up over part of her face. Then her father grabbed her arm and pulled her back up to the minister again.

Benjamin removed his leg from over the railing. He ran across the balcony to the door and through the door and down through a wooden hallway leading to the front part of the church. At the end of the hallway were two doors. He threw one of them open and a man wearing black clergyman's clothes looked up at him over a desk and began rising from his chair. Benjamin turned around and pushed open the other door. It opened onto a flight of wooden stairs. He ran down. There were two more doors. He grabbed the doorknob of one and pushed it open.

Mr. Robinson was waiting for him. He was standing crouched in front of Benjamin with his arms spread out beside him. Behind Mr. Robinson Elaine was standing staring at him with her hands still up beside her face. Benjamin jumped one way to get around him but Mr. Robinson moved in front of him. He jumped the other. Mr. Robinson dove in toward him and grabbed him around the waist. Benjamin twisted away but before he could reach Elaine he felt Mr. Robinson grabbing at his neck and then grabbing at the collar of his shirt and pulling him backward and ripping the shirt down his back. He spun around and slammed his fist into Mr. Robinson's face. Mr. Robinson reeled backward and crumpled into a corner.

Benjamin hurried forward. Elaine stepped toward him and he grabbed her hand. "Come on," he said. "Don't faint."

He pulled her part way back toward the door but then suddenly the man in black clergyman's clothes from upstairs stepped in through it and closed it behind him.

"Get out of my way," Benjamin said.

The man didn't move. Benjamin bent his knees slightly and was about to move toward the door when he felt an arm closing around his neck. He thrashed away. Carl Smith was standing behind him breathing heavily. His carnation had fallen off. Benjamin looked quickly back and forth from Carl Smith to the man still standing in front of the door then he grabbed a large bronze cross from off an altar beside him and raised it up beside his ear. He rushed at Carl Smith.

Carl Smith stumbled backward, then turned and fled back down to the other guests. Benjamin gripped Elaine's hand as tightly as he could and pulled her toward the door.

"Move!!!" he said. He drew the cross farther back behind his head. The man in clergyman's clothes hurried away from the door. Benjamin dropped the cross and pulled Elaine through the door and across the hallway and out another door onto a sidewalk in back of the church.

"Run!" he said. He pulled her after him. "Run, Elaine! Run!"

She tripped and fell. "Benjamin, this dress!" she said.

"Come on!" he said. He pulled her up.

They ran for several blocks. Crossing one street a car had to slam on its brakes and turn up onto the curb to avoid hitting them. Finally Benjamin saw a bus stopped half a block ahead of them loading passengers.

"There!" he said, pointing at it as he ran.

The doors of the bus closed just as they reached it. Benjamin banged against them with his free hand and they were opened. He pushed Elaine up ahead of him and carried the train of her dress in after her.

"Where does this bus go," he said to the driver, trying to catch his breath.

The driver was staring at Elaine and didn't answer.

"Where does this bus go!"

"Morgan Street," he said.

"All right then," Benjamin said. He pulled a handful of change out of one of his pockets and dropped it in the coin box. Then he let go of Elaine's dress and took her hand again to lead her toward the back of the bus. The driver got up out of his seat to watch them. Most of the passengers stood part way up in their seats and stared at Benjamin's torn shirt hanging down around his knees and then turned their heads to stare down at the train of Elaine's dress as it dragged slowly past over the ends of cigarettes and gum wrappers in the aisle. There was a little girl sitting by herself on the seat at the rear.

"Excuse me," Benjamin said. He helped Elaine in next to the window and sat down beside her.

Most of the passengers were standing, turned around in their seats. One old man was bending his head around someone and out into the aisle to look back at them. The driver was still standing in the front next to the coin box staring at them.

"Get this bus moving!" Benjamin said.

The driver stood where he was.

"Get it moving!" Benjamin said, beginning to rise up again from the seat. "Get this bus moving!"

The driver waited a moment, then turned around and climbed back up into his seat. He pulled a handle and the doors of the bus closed. Benjamin sat back down.

Elaine was still trying to catch her breath. She turned her face to look at him. For several moments she sat looking at him, then she reached over and took his hand.

"Benjamin?" she said.

"What."

The bus began to move.

In old romances, the knight often undergoes a crucial struggle in order to rescue his imprisoned bride. How is this plot updated and used in the story of Benjamin and Elaine?

Why do you think our sympathies are on the side of Benjamin, Aucassin, and Psyche and against their opposers?

This is the end of the novel *The Graduate*. What do you imagine might happen next? What do you think Elaine has to say to Benjamin?

Why do you think the story of lovers overcoming all obstacles recurs so often in different times and cultures?

Comedy celebrates the power of nature to renew itself and the power of the spirit of life to overthrow the threat of death. As far as individuals are concerned, these powers are embodied in the ability to create children. And for society, this implies the institutions of marriage and the family. It is not surprising, then, to discover that the central phases of comedy concern an event as old as the human race itself—boy falls in love with girl.

Most stories in this phase center on courtship. Since a young man's object in courtship is to win the girl he loves, the blocking figure he encounters is often a parent, or some other relative, who, for a variety of reasons, considers the match unsuitable. In the tale of "Aucassin and Nicolette," Aucassin's father thinks that Nicolette comes from the wrong social class. In "Gertrude the Governess," financial problems impel Lord Ronald's father to arrange a match against his son's wishes. However, the blocking character is not always a member of the hero's family. He may, for instance, be a rival suitor. In "There Goes the Bride," Benjamin's rival actually gets his girl to the altar, and Benjamin has to break into the church to reclaim her.

Whatever blocks the union of the two young people must be removed, so the comic action is largely concerned with the maneuvers and manipulations that the hero or heroine must engineer in order to win his or her beloved. Psyche goes on a series of dangerous and difficult adventures, even braving the terrors of the underworld, before she moves Jupiter to overrule Venus and restore Cupid to her. Aucassin must fight his father's enemy, and even brave his father's wrath, to join his love. Nicolette too has to suffer shipwreck and travel great distances before she is united with Aucassin.

The triumph of love over all obstacles reminds us that the power that propels a lover to gain his mate is related to the urge of the human race to continue.

In myth this power is symbolized by the goddess Venus and her son Cupid, who at her command shoots burning arrows into the hearts of young men and women, and even of gods and goddesses. Blake's "Song" locates this power in all of nature, and its overwhelming effect can be seen in "The Boor," where two seemingly sensible, middle-aged people, who think they have become completely disillusioned with the opposite sex, find themselves falling in love almost against their will. So powerful is this force of attraction, in fact, that even Cupid himself succumbs when he sees Psyche.

It is also this powerful urge to survive that gives the plot of a comic courtship a strong drive toward a happy ending. The human race must go on reproducing itself, and in order to do so, young men and women must marry and have families. And in cases where the hero does not have enough power or influence to triumph on his own accord, he must get help, as Psyche does from the ants, the river reed, and the eagle. When no helpers appear on the scene, sometimes the author himself rather obviously steps in to arrange events to the hero's advantage. Aucassin's father very conveniently dies before his return. Gertrude the Governess luckily turns out to be of the same social class as Lord Ronald, and a wealthy heiress as well.

In fact, so predictable is the happy ending of a comic romance that in "Gertrude the Governess" the narrator can rely on the standard expectations of his readers for much of the humor of the story. Happy coincidences and contrivance on the part of the author are perfectly welcome in comedy, and in the long run, they do not seem so implausible or unnatural. Nature itself decrees what the grieving widow learns in "The Boor"—"life must go on," despite our sometimes irrational attempts to put obstacles in its way.

4
THE BEAUTIFUL CHANGES

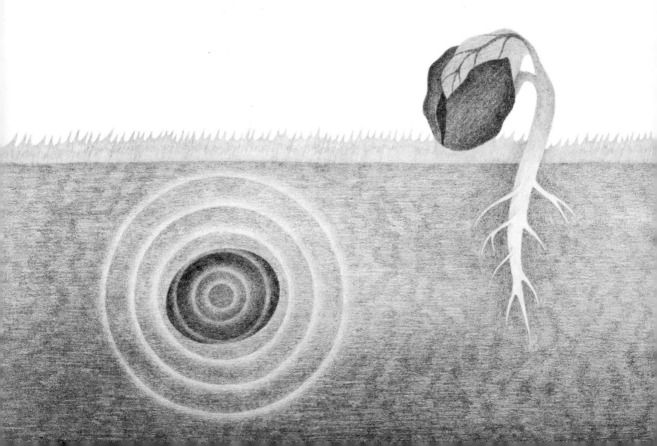

165

Putting Winter to Bed

Old Winter with an angry frown
Restationed on his head his crown,
And grew more obdurate,
As rumors every day had flown
From some officials near the throne
That he might abdicate.

Fixing his rivals with his eyes,
He thumped his chest and clapped his thighs,
And ground his Arctic heel,
Splintering the dais, just to show
That he was lord of ice and snow,
With sinews of wrought steel.

His patience had been sorely tried
By a recent blow dealt to his pride,
When March, the stripling, dared
To jeer at him with callow yells,
And shake the hoary icicles
From off the royal beard.

Then at a most indecent time,
The lusty youngster nearing prime,
Gaining in reach and height,
Had called out Winter to his face
To meet him in a neutral place,
And join in single fight.

The gage accepted, Winter drew
First blood, then beat him black and blue

With Nordic thrust and swing,
Till March at last, the wily fox,
Clipped him on the equinox,
And bashed him round the ring;

And would have clearly had him down,
Captured his domain and crown,
When three parts through the bout,
Had not the king with a trick malign,
Cracked him on the nether sign,
And March was counted out.

So now, with an Alaskan ire,
He donned in full his white attire,
Lord of the Polar waste,
And claimed before those flabby-thewed
Contenders of a Southern brood,
He would not be displaced.

And yet before the week was passed,
Neuralgic headaches thick and fast
Were blinding him with tears;
Despite the boast, he needed rest
To stop that panting in his breast,
That buzzing in his ears.

He wandered to a frozen brook
Beneath dank willows where he took
His usual noon-day nap;
He heard dull subterranean calls.
Narcotic sounds from crystal falls,
The climbing of the sap.

He laid his head against a stump,
One arm reclined upon a clump
Of glaciated boulders;
The other held his side—he had
Pleuritic pains and very bad
Rheumatic hips and shoulders.

A sorry sight indeed he lay,
A god-like being in decay—
Dead leaves were all around him:
His favorite cave of ice was streaming,
And many a fallen trunk was steaming,
The day that April found him.

With one glance at his swollen feet,
Her diagnosis was complete,
That dropsy had set in:
She felt his pulse—"Lord, what a rate!
His heart is in a parlous state,
And colic roars within.

"O shame, that March should thus surprise him,
Without a thought to acclimatize him
Towards a mellow age;
I know another way benign
To lead him through an anodyne
Into his hermitage."

She spent the morning in the search
For twigs of alder and of birch
And shoots of pussy willow;
She wove these through a maze of fern,
Added some moss on her return,
And made the downiest pillow.

Then with a bath of rain and sleet,
She took the chilblains from his feet
With tender lubrication:
She poulticed out the angry spots,
The kinks and cramps and spinal knots,
And all discoloration.

So with her first aid rendered, she
Began her ancient sorcery,
Quietly to restore
His over-burdened mind to sleep,
Dreamless and passionless and deep,
Out of her wild-wood lore.

It took three days to get his throat
Clear of that wheezy guttural note,
His brain to vaporize;
She conjured him at last to rest,
Folded his hands across his breast
And sealed up both his eyes.

Then over his lank form she threw
The lightest coverlet she knew,
Brought from her deepest glades —
The whites and greys of quiet mood,
Pale pinks and yellows all subdued
With brown and purple shades;

The choicest of her tapestries,
Spring beauties and anemones
Plucked from the winter grass,
Wake-robins too: with these she took
Trout-lilies from a woodland brook
And cool hepaticas.

With one thing more, her task was done —
Something she found hid from the sun
Within a valley low;
"Just what he needs, dawn fresh and white —
The north wind brought it overnight —
A counterpane of snow.

"So now this makes his bed complete."
She doubled it across his feet,
And tucked it neatly in;
Then taking on a mood austere,
Kneeling, she whispered in his ear,
A word of discipline.

"Take heed! Before you enter sleep,
Swear by your honor you will keep
A vow which I propose:
Listen — an oath, which if you break,
'Twill carry for you in its wake
A multitude of woes.

"For eight months now, without demur,
You give your promise not to stir,
And not to roar or wail,
Or send your north wind with its snow,
Or yet the east whose vapors blow
Their shuddering sleet and hail.

"So help you then for evermore —
If you so much as cough or snore,
My seven younger sisters,
Who follow after me in turn,
Are under strict command to burn
Your body up with blisters.

"Of autumn, too, you must beware,
For if you rise to scent the air,
Our Indian-summer maid
Will plague you past what you endure,
Until you think your temperature
One hundred Centigrade.

"But if you keep this honest vow,
I pledge their virtue, here and now,
To rouse you in December;
Then you may come on Christmas Day
With furs and bells, reindeer and sleigh —
But, hand on heart — remember!"

And now, to make the pledge come true,
She walked around the king and drew
Three circles on his breast;
Murmured a charm, then bending down,
She graciously removed the crown,
And left him to his rest.

E. J. PRATT

In what ways is Old Winter in this poem a blocking character? Who succeeds in displacing him? How is the victory attained? How is the cycle of the seasons a perfect metaphor for the comic story?

Madame La Gimp

DAMON RUNYON

One night I am passing the corner of Fiftieth Street and Broadway, and what do I see but Dave the Dude standing in a doorway talking to a busted-down old Spanish doll by the name of Madame La Gimp. Or rather Madame La Gimp is talking to Dave the Dude, and what is more he is listening to her, because I can hear him say yes, yes, as he always does when he is really listening to anybody, which is very seldom.

Now this is a most surprising sight to me, because Madame La Gimp is not such an old doll as anybody will wish to listen to, especially Dave the Dude. In fact, she is nothing but an old haybag, and generally somewhat ginned up. For fifteen years, or maybe sixteen, I see Madame La Gimp up and down Broadway, or sliding along through the Forties, sometimes selling newspapers, and sometimes selling flowers, and in all these years I seldom see her but what she seems to have about half a heat on from drinking gin.

Of course nobody ever takes the newspapers she sells, even after they buy them off of her, because they are generally yesterday's papers, and sometimes last week's, and nobody ever wants her flowers, even after they pay her for them, because they are flowers such as she gets off an undertaker over in Tenth Avenue, and they are very tired flowers, indeed.

Personally, I consider Madame La Gimp nothing but an old pest, but kind-hearted guys like Dave the Dude always stake her to a few pieces of silver when she comes shuffling along putting on the moan about her tough luck. She walks with a gimp in one leg, which is why she is called Madame La Gimp, and years ago I hear somebody say Madame La Gimp is once a Spanish dancer, and a big shot on Broadway, but that she meets up with an accident which puts her out of the dancing dodge, and that a busted romance makes her become a gin-head.

I remember somebody telling me once that Madame La Gimp is quite a beauty in her day, and has her own servants, and all this and that, but I always hear the same thing about every bum on Broadway, male and female, including some I know are bums, in spades, right from taw, so I do not pay attention to these stories.

Still, I am willing to allow that maybe Madame La Gimp is once a fair looker, at that, and the chances are has a fair shape, because once or twice I see her when she is not ginned up, and has her hair combed, and she is not so bad-looking, although even then if you put her in a claiming race I do not think there is any danger of anybody claiming her out of it.

Mostly she is wearing raggedy clothes, and busted shoes, and her gray hair is generally hanging down her face, and when I say she is maybe fifty years old I am giving her plenty the best of it. Although she is Spanish, Madame La Gimp talks good English, and in fact she can cuss in English as good as anybody I ever hear, barring Dave the Dude.

Well, anyway, when Dave the Dude sees me as he is listening to Madame La Gimp, he motions me to wait, so I wait until she finally gets through gabbing to him and goes gimping away. Then Dave the Dude comes over to me looking much worried.

"This is quite a situation," Dave says. "The old doll is in a tough spot. It seems that she once has a baby which she calls by the name of Eulalie, being it is a girl baby, and she ships this baby off to her sister in a little town in Spain to raise up, because Madame La Gimp figures a baby is not apt to get much raising-up off of her as long as she is on Broadway. Well, this baby is on her way here. In fact," Dave says, "she will land next Saturday and here it is Wednesday already."

"Where is the baby's papa?" I ask Dave the Dude.

"Well," Dave says, "I do not ask Madame La Gimp this, because I do not consider it a fair question. A guy who goes around this town asking where babies' papas are, or even who they are, is apt to get the name of being nosey. Anyway, this has nothing whatever to do with the proposition, which is that Madame La Gimp's baby, Eulalie, is arriving here.

"Now," Dave says, "it seems that Madame La Gimp's baby, being now eighteen years old, is engaged to marry the son of a very proud old Spanish nobleman who lives in this little town in Spain, and it also seems that the very proud old Spanish nobleman, and his ever-loving wife, and the son, and Madame La Gimp's sister, are all with the baby.

They are making a tour of the whole world, and will stop over here a couple of days just to see Madame La Gimp."

"It is commencing to sound to me like a movie such as a guy is apt see at a midnight show," I say.

"Wait a minute," Dave says, getting impatient. "You are too gabby to suit me. Now it seems that the proud old Spanish nobleman does not wish his son to marry any lob, and one reason he is coming here is to look over Madame La Gimp, and see that she is okay. He thinks that Madame La Gimp's baby's own papa is dead, and that Madame La Gimp is now married to one of the richest and most aristocratic guys in America."

"How does the proud old Spanish nobleman get such an idea as this?" I ask. "It is a sure thing he never sees Madame La Gimp, or even a photograph of her as she is at present."

"I will tell you how," Dave the Dude says. "It seems Madame La Gimp gives her baby the idea that such is the case in her letters to her. It seems Madame La Gimp does a little scrubbing business around a swell apartment hotel in Park Avenue that is called the Marberry, and she cops stationery there and writes her baby in Spain on this stationery saying this is where she lives, and how rich and aristocratic her husband is. And what is more, Madame La Gimp has letters from her baby sent to her in care of the hotel and gets them out of the employees' mail."

"Why," I say, "Madame La Gimp is nothing but an old fraud to deceive people in this manner, especially a proud old Spanish nobleman. And," I say, "this proud old Spanish nobleman must be something of a chump to believe a mother will keep away from her baby all these years, especially if the mother has plenty of dough, although of course I do not know just how smart a proud old Spanish nobleman can be."

"Well," Dave says, "Madame La Gimp tells me the thing that makes the biggest hit of all with the proud old Spanish nobleman is that she keeps her baby in Spain all these years because she wishes her raised up a true Spanish baby in every respect until she is old enough to know what time it is. But I judge the proud old Spanish nobleman is none too bright, at that," Dave says, "because Madame La Gimp tells me he always lives in this little town which does not even have running water in the bathrooms.

"But what I am getting at is this," Dave says. "We must have

Madame La Gimp in a swell apartment in the Marberry with a rich and aristocratic guy for a husband by the time her baby gets here, because if the proud old Spanish nobleman finds out Madame La Gimp is nothing but a bum, it is a hundred to one he will cancel his son's engagement to Madame La Gimp's baby and break a lot of people's hearts, including his son's.

"Madame La Gimp tells me her baby is daffy about the young guy, and he is daffy about her, and there are enough broken hearts in this town as it is. I know how I will get the apartment, so you go and bring me Judge Henry G. Blake for a rich and aristocratic husband, or anyway for a husband."

Well, I know Dave the Dude to do many a daffy thing but never a thing as daffy as this. But I know there is no use arguing with him when he gets an idea, because if you argue with Dave the Dude too much he is apt to reach over and lay his Sunday punch on your snoot, and no argument is worth a punch on the snoot, especially from Dave the Dude.

So I go out looking for Judge Henry G. Blake to be Madame La Gimp's husband, although I am not so sure Judge Henry G. Blake will care to be anybody's husband, and especially Madame La Gimp's after he gets a load of her, for Judge Henry G. Blake is kind of a classy old guy.

To look at Judge Henry G. Blake, with his gray hair, and his nose glasses, and his stomach, you will think he is very important people, indeed. Of course Judge Henry G. Blake is not a judge, and never is a judge, but they call him Judge because he looks like a judge, and talks slow, and puts in many long words, which very few people understand.

They tell me Judge Blake once has plenty of dough, and is quite a guy in Wall Street, and a high shot along Broadway, but he misses a few guesses at the market, and winds up without much dough, as guys generally do who miss guesses at the market. What Judge Henry G. Blake does for a living at this time nobody knows, because he does nothing much whatever, and yet he seems to be a producer in a small way at all times.

Now and then he makes a trip across the ocean with such as Little Manuel, and other guys who ride the tubs, and sits in with them on games of bridge, and one thing and another, when they need him. Very often when he is riding the tubs, Little Manuel runs into some guy he cannot cheat, so he has to call in Judge Henry G. Blake to outplay the guy on the level, although of course Little Manuel will much rather get a guy's dough by cheating him than by outplaying him on the level. Why this is, I do not know, but this is the way Little Manuel is.

Anyway, you cannot say Judge Henry G. Blake is a bum, especially as he wears good clothes, with a wing collar, and a derby hat, and most people consider him a very nice old man. Personally I never catch the judge out of line on any proposition whatever, and he always says hello to me, very pleasant.

It takes me several hours to find Judge Henry G. Blake, but finally I locate him in Derle's billiard room playing a game of pool with a guy from Providence, Rhode Island. It seems the judge is playing the guy from Providence for five cents a ball, and the judge is about thirteen balls behind when I step into the joint, because naturally at five cents a ball the judge wishes the guy from Providence to win, so as to encourage him to play for maybe twenty-five cents a ball, the judge being very cute this way.

Well, when I step in I see the judge miss a shot anybody can make blindfolded, but as soon as I give him the office I wish to speak to him, the judge hauls off and belts in every ball on the table, bingity-bing, the last shot being a bank that will make Al de Oro stop and think, because when it comes to pool, the old judge is just naturally a curly wolf.

Afterwards he tells me he is very sorry I make him hurry up this way, because of course after the last shot he is never going to get the guy from Providence to play him pool even for fun, and the judge tells me the guy sizes up as a right good thing, at that.

Now Judge Henry G. Blake is not so excited when I tell him what Dave the Dude wishes to see him about, but naturally he is willing to do anything for Dave, because he knows that guys who are not willing to do things for Dave the Dude often have bad luck. The judge tells me that he is afraid he will not make much of a husband because he tries it before several times on his own hook and is always a bust, but as long as this time it is not to be anything serious, he will tackle it. Anyway, Judge Henry G. Blake says, being aristocratic will come natural to him.

Well, when Dave the Dude starts out on any proposition, he is a wonder for fast working. The first thing he does is to turn Madame La Gimp over to Miss Billy Perry, who is now Dave's ever-loving wife which he takes out of tap-dancing in Miss Missouri Martin's Sixteen Hundred Club, and Miss Billy Perry calls in Miss Missouri Martin to help.

This is water on Miss Missouri Martin's wheel, because if there is anything she loves it is to stick her nose in other people's business, no matter what it is, but she is quite a help at that, although at first they have a tough time keeping her from telling Waldo Winchester, the scribe, about the whole cat-hop, so he will put a story in the *Morning Item* about it, with Miss Missouri Martin's name in it. Miss Missouri Martin does not believe in ever overlooking any publicity bets on the layout.

Anyway, it seems that between them Miss Billy Perry and Miss Missouri Martin get Madame La Gimp dolled up in a lot of new clothes, and run her through one of these beauty joints until she comes out very much changed, indeed. Afterward I hear Miss Billy Perry and Miss Missouri Martin have quite a few words, because Miss Missouri Martin wishes to paint Madame La Gimp's hair the same color as her own, which is a high yellow, and buy her the same kind of dresses which Miss Missouri Martin wears herself, and Miss Missouri Martin gets much insulted when Miss Billy Perry says no, they are trying to dress Madame La Gimp to look like a lady.

They tell me Miss Missouri Martin thinks some of putting the slug on Miss Billy Perry for this crack, but happens to remember just in time that Miss Billy Perry is now Dave the Dude's ever-loving wife, and that nobody in this town can put the slug on Dave's ever-loving wife, except maybe Dave himself.

Now the next thing anybody knows, Madame La Gimp is in a swell eight- or nine-room apartment in the Marberry, and the way this comes about is as follows: It seems that one of Dave the Dude's most important champagne customers is a guy by the name of Rodney B. Emerson, who owns the apartment, but who is at his summer home in Newport, with his family, or anyway with his ever-loving wife.

This Rodney B. Emerson is quite a guy along Broadway, and a great hand for spending dough and looking for laughs, and he is very popular with the mob. Furthermore, he is obligated to Dave the Dude, because Dave sells him good champagne when most guys are trying to hand him the old phonus bolonus, and naturally Rodney B. Emerson appreciates this kind treatment.

He is a short, fat guy, with a round, red face, and a big laugh, and the kind of a guy Dave the Dude can call up at his home in Newport and explain the situation and ask for the loan of the apartment, which Dave does.

Well, it seems Rodney B. Emerson gets a big bang out of the idea, and he says to Dave the Dude like this:

"You not only can have the apartment, Dave, but I will come over and help you out. It will save a lot of explaining around the Marberry if I am there."

So he hops right over from Newport, and joins in with Dave the Dude, and I wish to say Rodney B. Emerson will always be kindly remembered by one and all for his cooperation, and nobody will ever again try to hand him the phonus bolonus when he is buying champagne, even if he is not buying it off of Dave the Dude.

Well, it is coming on Saturday and the boat from Spain is due, so Dave the Dude hires a big town car, and puts his own driver, Wop Sam, on it, as he does not wish any strange driver tipping off anybody that it is a hired car. Miss Missouri Martin is anxious to go to the boat with Madame La Gimp, and take her jazz band, the Hi Hi Boys, from her Sixteen Hundred Club with her to make it a real welcome, but nobody thinks much of this idea. Only Madame La Gimp and her husband, Judge Henry G. Blake, and Miss Billy Perry go, though the judge holds out for some time for Little Manuel, because Judge Blake says he wishes somebody around to tip him off in case there are any bad cracks made about him as a husband in Spanish, and Little Manuel is very Spanish.

The morning they go to meet the boat is the first time Judge Henry G. Blake gets a load of his ever-loving wife, Madame La Gimp, and by this time Miss Billy Perry and Miss Missouri Martin give Madame La Gimp such a going-over that she is by no means the worst looker in the world. In fact, she looks first-rate, especially as she is off gin and says she is off it for good.

Judge Henry G. Blake is really quite surprised by her looks as he figures all along she will turn out to be a crow. In fact, Judge Blake hurls a couple of shots into himself to nerve himself for the ordeal, as he explains it, before he appears to go to the boat. Between these shots, and the nice clothes, and the good cleaning-up Miss Billy Perry and Miss Missouri Martin give Madame La Gimp, she is really a pleasant sight to the judge.

They tell me the meeting at the dock between Madame La Gimp and her baby is very affecting indeed, and when the proud old Spanish nobleman and his wife, and their son, and Madame La Gimp's sister, all go into action, too, there are enough tears around there to float all the battleships we once sink for Spain. Even Miss Billy Perry and Judge Henry G. Blake do some first-class crying, although the chances are the judge is worked up to the crying more by the shots he takes for his courage than by the meeting.

Still, I hear the old judge does himself proud, what with kissing Madame La Gimp's baby plenty, and duking the proud old Spanish nobleman, and his wife, and son, and giving Madame La Gimp's sister a good strong hug that squeezes her tongue out.

It turns out that the proud old Spanish nobleman has white sideburns, and is entitled Conde de Something, so his ever-loving wife is the Condesa, and the son is a very nice-looking quiet young guy any way you take him, who blushes every time anybody looks at him. As for Madame La Gimp's baby, she is as pretty as they come, and many guys are sorry they do not get Judge Henry G. Blake's job as stepfather, because he is able to take a kiss at Madame La Gimp's baby on what seems to be very small excuse. I never see a nicer-looking young couple, and anybody can see they are very fond of each other, indeed.

Madame La Gimp's sister is not such a doll as I will wish to have sawed off on me, and is up in the paints as regards to age, but she is also very quiet. None of the bunch talk any English, so Miss Billy Perry and Judge Henry G. Blake are pretty much outsiders on the way uptown. Anyway, the judge takes the wind as soon as they reach the Marberry, because the judge is now getting a little tired of being a husband. He says he has to take a trip out to Pittsburgh to buy four or five coal mines, but will be back the next day.

Well, it seems to me that everything is going perfect so far, and that it is good judgment to let it lay as it is, but nothing will do Dave the Dude but to have a reception the following night. I advise Dave the Dude against this idea, because I am afraid something will happen to spoil the whole cat-hop, but he will not listen to me, especially as Rodney B. Emerson is now in town and is a strong booster for the party, as he wishes to drink some of the good champagne he has planted in his apartment.

Furthermore, Miss Billy Perry and Miss Missouri Martin are very indignant at me when they hear about my advice, as it seems they both buy new dresses out of Dave the Dude's bank roll when they are dressing up Madame La Gimp, and they wish to spring these dresses somewhere where they can be seen. So the party is on.

I get to the Marberry around nine o'clock and who opens the door of Madame La Gimp's apartment for me but Moosh, the doorman from Miss Missouri Martin's Sixteen Hundred Club. Furthermore, he is in his Sixteen Hundred Club uniform, except he has a clean shave. I wish Moosh a hello, and he never raps to me but only bows, and takes my hat.

The next guy I see is Rodney B. Emerson in evening clothes, and the minute he sees me he yells out, "Mister O. O. McIntyre." Well, of course I am not Mister O. O. McIntyre, and never put myself away as Mister O. O. McIntyre, and furthermore there is no resemblance whatever between Mister O. O. McIntyre and me, because I am a fairly good-looking guy, and I start to give Rodney B. Emerson an argument, when he whispers to me like this:

"Listen," he whispers, "we must have big names at this affair, so as to impress these people. The chances are they read the newspapers back there in Spain, and we must let them meet the folks they read about, so they will see Madame La Gimp is a real big shot to get such names to a party."

Then he takes me by the arm and leads me to a group of people in a corner of the room, which is about the size of the Grand Central waiting room.

"Mister O. O. McIntyre, the big writer!" Rodney B. Emerson says, and the next thing I know I am shaking hands with Mr. and Mrs. Conde, and their son, and with Madame La Gimp and her baby, and Madame La Gimp's sister, and finally with Judge Henry G. Blake, who has on a swallowtail coat, and does not give me much of a tumble. I figure the chances are Judge Henry G. Blake is getting a swelled head already, not to tumble up a guy who helps him get his job, but even at that I wish to say the old judge looks immense in his swallowtail coat, bowing and giving one and all the old castor oil smile.

Madame La Gimp is in a low-neck black dress and is wearing a lot of Miss Missouri Martin's diamonds, such as rings and bracelets, which Miss Missouri Martin insists on hanging on her, although I hear afterwards that Miss Missouri Martin has Johnny Brannigan, the plain clothes copper, watching these diamonds. I wonder at the time why Johnny is there but figure it is because he is a friend of Dave the Dude. Miss Missouri Martin is no sucker, even if she is kind-hearted.

Anybody looking at Madame La Gimp will bet you all the coffee in Java that she never lives in a cellar over in Tenth Avenue, and drinks plenty of gin in her day. She has her gray hair piled up high on her head, with a big Spanish comb in it, and she reminds me of a picture I see somewhere, but I do not remember just where. And her baby,

Eulalie, in a white dress is about as pretty a little doll as you will wish to see, and nobody can blame Judge Henry G. Blake for copping a kiss off of her now and then.

Well, pretty soon I hear Rodney B. Emerson bawling, "Mister Willie K. Vanderbilt," and in comes nobody but Big Nig, and Rodney B. Emerson leads him over to the group and introduces him.

Little Manuel is standing alongside Judge Henry G. Blake, and he explains in Spanish to Mr. and Mrs. Conde and the others that "Willie K. Vanderbilt" is a very large millionaire, and Mr. and Mrs. Conde seem much interested, anyway, though naturally Madame La Gimp and Judge Henry G. Blake are jerry to Big Nig, while Madame La Gimp's baby and the young guy are interested in nobody but each other.

Then I hear, "Mister Al Jolson," and in comes nobody but Tony Bertazzola, from the Chicken Club, who looks about as much like Al as I do like O. O. McIntyre, which is not at all. Next comes "the Very Reverend John Roach Straton," who seems to be Sleets Bolivar to me, then "the Honorable Mayor James J. Walker," and who is it but Good-Time Charley Bernstein.

"Mister Otto H. Kahn" turns out to be Rochester Red, and "Mister Heywood Broun" is Nick the Greek, who asks me privately who Heywood Broun is, and gets very sore at Rodney B. Emerson when I describe Heywood Broun to him.

Finally there is quite a commotion at the door and Rodney B. Emerson announces, "Mister Herbert Bayard Swope" in an extra loud voice which makes everybody look around, but it is nobody but the Pale Face Kid. He gets me to one side, too, and wishes to know who Herbert Bayard Swope is, and when I explain to him, the Pale Face Kid gets so swelled up he will not speak to Death House Donegan, who is only "Mister William Muldoon."

Well, it seems to me they are getting too strong when they announce, "Vice-President of the United States, the Honorable Charles Curtis," and in pops Guinea Mike, and I say as much to Dave the Dude, who is running around every which way looking after things, but he only says, "Well, if you do not know it is Guinea Mike, will you know it is not Vice-President Curtis?"

But it seems to me all this is most disrespectful to our leading citizens, especially when Rodney B. Emerson calls, "The Honorable Police Commissioner, Mister Grover A. Whalen," and in pops Wild William Wilkins, who is a very hot man at this time, being wanted in several spots for different raps. Dave the Dude takes personal charge of Wild William and removes a rod from his pants pocket, because none of the guests are supposed to come rodded up, this being strictly a social matter.

I watch Mr. and Mrs. Conde, and I do not see that these names are making any impression on them, and I afterwards find out that they never get any newspapers in their town in Spain except a little local bladder which only prints the home news. In fact, Mr. and Mrs. Conde seem somewhat bored, although Mr. Conde cheers up no little and looks interested when a lot of dolls drift in. They are mainly dolls from Miss Missouri Martin's Sixteen Hundred Club, and the Hot Box, but Rodney B. Emerson introduces them as "Sophie Tucker," and "Theda Bara," and "Jeanne Eagels," and "Helen Morgan" and "Aunt Jemima," and one thing and another.

Well, pretty soon in comes Miss Missouri Martin's jazz band, the Hi Hi Boys, and the party commences getting up steam, especially when Dave the Dude gets Rodney B. Emerson to breaking out the old grape. By and by there is dancing going on, and a good time is being had by one and all, including Mr. and Mrs. Conde. In fact, after Mr. Conde gets a couple of jolts of the old grape, he turns out to be a pretty nice old skate, even if nobody can understand what he is talking about.

As for Judge Henry G. Blake, he is full of speed, indeed. By this time anybody can see that the judge is commencing to believe that all this is on the level and that he is really entertaining celebrities in his own home. You put a quart of good grape inside the old judge and he will believe anything. He soon dances himself plumb out of wind, and then I notice he is hanging around Madame La Gimp a lot.

Along about midnight, Dave the Dude has to go out into the kitchen and settle a battle there over a crap game, but otherwise everything is very peaceful. It seems that "Herbert Bayard Swope," "Vice-President Curtis" and "Grover Whalen" get a little game going, when "the Reverend John Roach Straton" steps up and cleans them in four passes, but it seems they soon discover that "the Reverend John Roach Straton" is using tops on them, which are very dishonest dice, and so they put the slug on "the Reverend John Roach Straton" and Dave the Dude has to split them out.

By and by I figure on taking the wind, and I look for Mr. and Mrs. Conde to tell them good night, but Mr. Conde and Miss Missouri Martin are still dancing, and Miss Missouri Martin is pouring conversation into Mr. Conde's ear by the bucketful, and while Mr. Conde does not savvy a word she says, this makes no difference to Miss Missouri Martin. Let Miss Missouri Martin do all the talking, and she does not care a whoop if anybody understands her.

Mrs. Conde is over in a corner with "Herbert Bayard Swope," or the Pale Face Kid, who is trying to find out from her by using hog Latin and signs on her if there is any chance for a good twenty-one dealer in Spain, and of course Mrs. Conde is not able to make heads or tails of what he means, so I hunt up Madame La Gimp.

She is sitting in a darkish corner off by herself and I really do not see Judge Henry G. Blake leaning over her until I am almost on top of them, so I cannot help hearing what the judge is saying.

"I am wondering for two days," he says, "if by any chance you remember me. Do you know who I am?"

"I remember you," Madame La Gimp says. "I remember you—oh, so very well, Henry. How can I forget you? But I have no idea you recognize me after all these years."

"Twenty of them now," Judge Henry G. Blake says. "You are beautiful then. You are still beautiful."

Well, I can see the old grape is working first-class on Judge Henry G. Blake to make such remarks as this, although at that, in the half light, with the smile on her face, Madame La Gimp is not so bad. Still, give me them carrying a little less weight for age.

"Well, it is all your fault," Judge Henry G. Blake says. "You go and marry that chile con carne guy, and look what happens!"

I can see there is no sense in me horning in on Madame La Gimp and Judge Henry G. Blake while they are cutting up old touches in this manner, so I think I will just say good-by to the young people and let it go at that, but while I am looking for Madame La Gimp's baby, and her guy, I run into Dave the Dude.

"You will not find them here," Dave says. "By this time they are being married over at Saint Malachy's with my ever-loving wife and Big Nig standing up with them. We get the license for them yesterday afternoon. Can you imagine a couple of young saps wishing to wait until they go plumb around the world before getting married?"

Well, of course this elopement creates much excitement for a few minutes, but by Monday Mr. and Mrs. Conde and the young folks and Madame La Gimp's sister take a train for California to keep on going around the world, leaving us nothing to talk about but about old Judge Henry G. Blake and Madame La Gimp getting themselves married too, and going to Detroit where Judge Henry G. Blake claims he has a brother in the plumbing business who will give him a job, although personally I think Judge Henry G. Blake figures to do a little booting on his own hook in and out of Canada. It is not like Judge Henry G. Blake to tie himself up to the plumbing business.

So there is nothing more to the story, except that Dave the Dude is around a few days later with a big sheet of paper in his duke and very, very indignant.

"If every single article listed here is not kicked back to the owners of the different joints in the Marberry that they are taken from by next Tuesday night, I will bust a lot of noses around this town," Dave says. "I am greatly mortified by such happenings at my social affairs, and everything must be returned at once. Especially," Dave says, "the baby grand piano that is removed from Apartment 9-D."

What changes does Madame La Gimp undergo? What other characters in the story are also changed? How are they changed? What forces are responsible for these changes in Madame and her friends?

How do Madame and her friends overcome the social restrictions that block the marriage of Madame La Gimp's daughter? What other stock situations and characters found in the selections in the first three units are in this story as well?

The Beautiful Changes

One wading a Fall meadow finds on all sides
The Queen Anne's Lace lying like lilies
On water; it glides
So from the walker, it turns
Dry grass to a lake, as the slightest shade of you
Valleys my mind in fabulous blue Lucernes.

The beautiful changes as a forest is changed
By a chameleon's tuning his skin to it;
As a mantis, arranged
On a green leaf, grows
Into it, makes the leaf leafier, and proves
Any greenness is deeper than anyone knows.

Your hands hold roses always in a way that says
They are not only yours; the beautiful changes
In such kind ways,
Wishing ever to sunder
Things and things' selves for a second finding, to lose
For a moment all that it touches back to wonder.

RICHARD WILBUR

What effect does the poet's imagination have on his vision of nature? How does love affect his imagination? What transformation does the poet achieve?

her in his arms — she remained a cold and passive form. For a time he tried to pretend, as children do with their toys. He would dress her in rich robes, trying the effect of one delicate or glowing color after another, and imagine she was pleased. He would bring her the gifts real maidens love, little birds and gay flowers and the shining tears of amber Phaëthon's sisters, weep, and then dream that she thanked him with eager affection. He put her to bed at night, and tucked her in all soft and warm, as little girls do their dolls. But he was not a child; he could not keep on pretending. In the end he gave up. He loved a lifeless thing and he was utterly and hopelessly wretched.

This singular passion did not long remain concealed from the goddess of passionate love. Venus was interested in something that seldom came her way, a new kind of lover, and she determined to help a young man who could be enamored and yet original.

The feast day of Venus was, of course, especially honored in Cyprus, the island which first received the goddess after she rose from the foam. Snow-white heifers whose horns had been gilded were offered in numbers to her; the heavenly odor of incense was spread through the island from her many altars; crowds thronged her temples; not an unhappy lover but was there with his gift, praying that his love might turn kind. There too, of course, was Pygmalion. He dared to ask the goddess only that he might find a maiden like his statue, but Venus knew what he really wanted and as a sign that she favored his prayer the flame on the altar he stood before leaped up three times, blazing into the air.

Very thoughtful at this good omen Pygmalion sought his house and his love, the thing he had created and given his heart to. There she stood on her pedestal, entrancingly beautiful. He caressed her and then he started back. Was it self-deception or did she really feel warm to his touch? He kissed her lips, a long lingering kiss, and felt them grow soft beneath his. He touched her arms, her shoulders; their hardness vanished. It was like watching wax soften in the sun. He clasped her wrist; blood was pulsing there. Venus, he thought. This is the goddess's doing. And with unutterable gratitude and joy he put his arms around his love and saw her smile into his eyes and blush.

Venus herself graced their marriage with her presence, but what happened after that we do not know, except that Pygmalion named the maiden Galatea, and that their son, Paphos, gave his name to Venus's favorite city.

What transformation does Pygmalion bring about? What force is responsible for the change?

Why does the goddess bestow life on the statue? In what sense do artists and poets share in the powers of the gods?

If possible, read the play *Pygmalion* by George Bernard Shaw upon which *My Fair Lady* was based. Why do you think the author called the play "Pygmalion"? What beautiful changes take place in the play?

A Blessing

Just off the highway to Rochester, Minnesota,
Twilight bounds softly forth on the grass.
And the eyes of those two Indian ponies
Darken with kindness.
They have come gladly out of the willows
To welcome my friend and me.
We step over the barbed wire into the pasture
Where they have been grazing all day, alone.
They ripple tensely, they can hardly contain their happiness
That we have come.
They bow shyly as wet swans. They love each other.
There is no loneliness like theirs.
At home once more,
They begin munching the young tufts of spring in the darkness.
I would like to hold the slenderer one in my arms,
For she has walked over to me
And nuzzled my left hand.
She is black and white,
Her mane falls wild on her forehead,
And the light breeze moves me to caress her long ear
That is delicate as the skin over a girl's wrist.
Suddenly I realize
That if I stepped out of my body I would break
Into blossom.

JAMES WRIGHT

What does the word "blessing" suggest? How did the encounter with the
ponies "bless" the poet? What barriers has the experience helped the poet
to conquer or go beyond?

The Key

ISAAC BASHEVIS SINGER

At about three o'clock in the afternoon, Bessie Popkin began to prepare to go down to the street. Going out was connected with many difficulties, especially on a hot summer day: first, forcing her fat body into a corset, squeezing her swollen feet into shoes, and combing her hair, which Bessie dyed at home and which grew wild and was streaked in all colors — yellow, black, gray, red; then making sure that while she was out her neighbors would not break into her apartment and steal linen, clothes, documents, or just disarrange things and make them disappear.

Besides human tormentors, Bessie suffered from demons, imps, Evil Powers. She hid her eyeglasses in the night table and found them in a slipper. She placed her bottle of hair dye in the medicine chest; days later she discovered it under the pillow. Once, she left a pot of borscht in the refrigerator, but the Unseen took it from there and after long searching Bessie came upon it in her clothes closet. On its surface was a thick layer of fat that gave off the smell of rancid tallow.

What she went through, how many tricks were played on her and how much she had to wrangle in order not to perish or fall into insanity, only God knew. She had given up the telephone because racketeers and degenerates called her day and night, trying to get secrets out of her. The Puerto Rican milkman once tried to rape her. The errand boy from the grocery store attempted to burn her belongings with a cigarette. To evict her from the rent-controlled apartment where she had lived for thirty-five years, the company and the superintendent infested her rooms with rats, mice, cockroaches.

Bessie had long ago realized that no means were adequate against those determined to be spiteful — not the metal door, the special lock, her letters to the police, the mayor, the FBI, and even the president in Washington. But while one breathed one had to eat. It all took time:

checking the windows, the gas vents, securing the drawers. Her paper money she kept in volumes of the encyclopedia, in back copies of the *National Geographic,* and in Sam Popkin's old ledgers. Her stocks and bonds Bessie had hidden among the logs in the fireplace, which was never used, as well as under the seats of the easy chairs. Her jewels she had sewn into the mattress. There was a time when Bessie had safe-deposit boxes at the bank, but she long ago convinced herself that the guards there had passkeys.

At about five o'clock, Bessie was ready to go out. She gave a last look at herself in the mirror—small, broad, with a narrow forehead, a flat nose, and eyes slanting and half-closed, like a Chinaman's. Her chin sprouted a little white beard. She wore a faded dress in a flowered print, a misshapen straw hat trimmed with wooden cherries and grapes, and shabby shoes. Before she left, she made a final inspection of the three rooms and the kitchen. Everywhere there were clothes, shoes, and piles of letters that Bessie had not opened. Her husband, Sam Popkin, who had died almost twenty years ago, had liquidated his real-estate business before his death, because he was about to retire to Florida. He left her stocks, bonds, and a number of passbooks from savings banks, as well as some mortgages. To this day, firms wrote to Bessie, sent her reports, checks. The Internal Revenue Service claimed taxes from her. Every few weeks she received announcements from a funeral company that sold plots in an "airy cemetery." In former years, Bessie used to answer letters, deposit her checks, keep track of her income and expenses. Lately she had neglected it all. She even stopped buying the newspaper and reading the financial section.

In the corridor, Bessie tucked cards with signs on them that only she could recognize between the door and the door frame. The keyhole she stuffed with putty. What else could she do—a widow without children, relatives, or friends? There was a time when the neighbors used to open their doors, look out, and laugh at her exaggerated care; others teased her. That had long passed. Bessie spoke to no one. She didn't see well, either. The glasses she had worn for years were of no use. To go to an eye doctor and be fitted for new ones was too much of an effort. Everything was difficult—even entering and leaving the elevator, whose door always closed with a slam.

Bessie seldom went farther than two blocks from her building. The street between Broadway and Riverside Drive became noisier and filthier from day to day. Hordes of urchins ran around half-naked. Dark men with curly hair and wild eyes quarreled in Spanish with little women whose bellies were always swollen in pregnancy. They talked back in rattling voices. Dogs barked, cats meowed. Fires broke out and fire engines, ambulances, and police cars drove up. On Broadway, the old groceries had been replaced by supermarkets, where food must be picked out and put in a wagon and one had to stand in line before the cashier.

God in Heaven, since Sam died, New York, America—perhaps the whole world—was falling apart. All the decent people had left the neighborhood and it was overrun by a mob of thieves, robbers, whores. Three times Bessie's pocketbook had been stolen. When she reported it to the police, they just laughed. Every time one crossed the street, one risked one's life. Bessie took a step and stopped. Someone had advised her to use a cane, but she was far from considering herself an old woman or a cripple. Every few weeks she painted her nails red. At times, when the rheumatism left her in peace, she took clothes she used to wear from the closets, tried them on, and studied herself in the mirror.

Opening the door of the supermarket was impossible. She had to wait till someone held it for her. The supermarket itself was a place that only the Devil could have invented. The lamps burned with a glaring light. People pushing wagons were likely to knock down anyone in their path. The shelves were either too high or too low. The noise was deafening, and the contrast between the heat outside and the freezing temperature inside! It was miracle that she didn't get pneumonia. More than anything else, Bessie was tortured by indecision. She picked up each item with a trembling hand and read the label. This was not the greed of youth but the uncertainty of age. According to Bessie's figuring, today's shopping should not have taken longer than three-quarters of an hour, but two hours passed and Bessie was still not finished. When she finally brought the wagon to the cashier, it occurred to her that she had forgotten the box of oatmeal. She went back and a woman took her place in line. Later, when she paid, there was new trouble. Bessie had put the bill in the right side of her bag, but it was not there. After long rummaging, she found it in a small change purse on the opposite side. Yes, who could believe that such things were possible? If she told someone, he would think she was ready for the madhouse.

When Bessie went into the supermarket, the day was still bright;

now it was drawing to a close. The sun, yellow and golden, was sinking toward the Hudson, to the hazy hills of New Jersey. The buildings on Broadway radiated the heat they had absorbed. From under gratings where the subway trains rumbled, evil-smelling fumes arose. Bessie held the heavy bag of food in one hand, and in the other she grasped her pocketbook tightly. Never had Broadway seemed to her so wild, so dirty. It stank of softened asphalt, gasoline, rotten fruit, the excrement of dogs. On the sidewalk, among torn newspapers and the butts of cigarettes, pigeons hopped about. It was difficult to understand how these creatures avoided being stepped on in the crush of passers-by. From the blazing sky a golden dust was falling. Before a storefront hung with artificial grass, men in sweated shirts poured papaya juice and pineapple juice into themselves with haste, as if trying to extinguish a fire that consumed their insides. Above their heads hung coconuts carved in the shapes of Indians. On a side street, black and white children had opened a hydrant and were splashing naked in the gutter. In the midst of that heat wave, a truck with microphones drove around blaring out shrill songs and deafening blasts about a candidate for political office. From the rear of the truck, a girl with hair that stood up like wires threw out leaflets.

It was all beyond Bessie's strength—crossing the street, waiting for the elevator, and then getting out on the fifth floor before the door slammed. Bessie put the groceries down at the threshold and searched for her keys. She used her nail file to dig the putty out of the keyhole. She put in the key and turned it. But woe, the key broke. Only the handle remained in her hand. Bessie fully grasped the catastrophe. The other people in the building had copies of their keys hanging in the superintendent's apartment, but she trusted no one—some time ago, she had ordered a new combination lock, which she was sure no master key could open. She had a duplicate key somewhere in a drawer, but with her she carried only this one. "Well, this is the end," Bessie said aloud.

There was nobody to turn to for help. The neighbors were her blood enemies. The super only waited for her downfall. Bessie's throat was so constricted that she could not even cry. She looked around, expecting to see the fiend who had delivered this latest blow. Bessie had long since made peace with death, but to die on the steps or in the streets was too harsh. And who knows how long such agony could last? She began to ponder. Was there still open somewhere a store where they fitted keys? Even if there were, what could the locksmith copy from?

He would have to come up here with his tools. For that, one needed a mechanic associated with the firm which produced these special locks. If at least she had money with her. But she never carried more than she needed to spend. The cashier in the supermarket had given her back only some twenty-odd cents. "O dear Momma, I don't want to live anymore!" Bessie spoke Yiddish, amazed that she suddenly reverted to that half-forgotten tongue.

After many hesitations, Bessie decided to go back down to the street. Perhaps a hardware store or one of those tiny shops that specialize in keys was still open. She remembered that there used to be such a key stand in the neighborhood. After all, other people's keys must get broken. But what should she do with the food? It was too heavy to carry with her. There was no choice. She would have to leave the bag at the door. "They steal anyhow," Bessie said to herself. Who knows, perhaps the neighbors intentionally manipulated her lock so that she would not be able to enter the apartment while they robbed her or vandalized her belongings.

Before Bessie went down to the street, she put her ear to the door.

She heard nothing except a murmur that never stopped, the cause and origin of which Bessie could not figure out. Sometimes it ticked like a clock; other times it buzzed, or groaned—an entity imprisoned in the walls or the water pipes. In her mind Bessie said goodbye to the food, which should have been in the refrigerator, not standing here in the heat. The butter would melt, the milk would turn sour. "It's a punishment! I am cursed, cursed," Bessie muttered. A neighbor was about to go down in the elevator and Bessie signaled to him to hold the door for her. Perhaps he was one of the thieves. He might try to hold her up, assault her. The elevator went down and the man opened the door for her. She wanted to thank him, but remained silent. Why thank her enemies? These were all sly tricks.

When Bessie stepped out into the street, night had fallen. The gutter was flooded with water. The streetlamps were reflected in the black pool as in a lake. Again there was a fire in the neighborhood. She heard the wailing of a siren, the clang of fire engines. Her shoes were wet. She came out on Broadway, and the heat slapped her like a sheet of tin. She had difficulty seeing in daytime; at night she was almost blind. There was light in the stores, but what they displayed Bessie could not make out. Passers-by bumped into her, and Bessie regretted that she didn't have a cane. Nevertheless, she began to walk along, close to the windows. She passed a drugstore, a bakery, a shop of rugs, a funeral parlor, but nowhere was there a sign of a hardware store. Bessie continued on her way. Her strength was ebbing, but she was determined not to give up. What should a person do when her key was broken off—die? Perhaps apply to the police. There might be some institution that took care of such cases. But where?

There must have been an accident. The sidewalk was crowded with spectators. Police cars and an ambulance blocked the street. Someone sprayed the asphalt with a hose, probably cleaning away the blood. It occurred to Bessie that the eyes of the onlookers gleamed with an uncanny satisfaction. They enjoy other people's misfortunes, she thought. It is their only comfort in this miserable city. No, she wouldn't find anybody to help her.

She had come to a church. A few steps led to the closed door, which was protected by an overhang and darkened by shadows. Bessie was barely able to sit down. Her knees wobbled. Her shoes had begun to pinch in the toes and above the heels. A bone in her corset broke and cut into her flesh. "Well, all the Powers of Evil are upon me tonight." Hunger mixed with nausea gnawed at her. An acid fluid came up to her mouth. "Father in Heaven, it's my end." She remembered the Yiddish proverb "If one lives without a reckoning, one dies without confession." She had even neglected to write her will.

Bessie must have dozed off, because when she opened her eyes there was a late-night stillness, the street half-empty and darkened. Store windows were no longer lit. The heat had evaporated and she felt chilly under her dress. For a moment she thought that her pocketbook had been stolen, but it lay on a step below her, where it had probably slipped. Bessie tried to stretch out her hand for it; her arm was numb. Her head, which rested against the wall, felt as heavy as a stone. Her legs had become wooden. Her ears seemed to be filled with water. She lifted one of her eyelids and saw the moon. It hovered low in the sky over a flat roof, and near it twinkled a greenish star. Bessie gaped. She had almost forgotten that there was a sky, a moon, stars. Years had passed and she never looked up—always down. Her windows were hung with draperies so that the spies across the street could not see her. Well, if there was a sky, perhaps there was also a God, angels, Paradise. Where else did the souls of her parents rest? And where was Sam now? She, Bessie, had abandoned all her duties. She never visited Sam's grave in the cemetery. She didn't even light a candle on the anniversary of his death. She was so steeped in wrangling with the lower powers that she did not remember the higher ones.

For the first time in years, Bessie felt the need to recite a prayer. The Almighty would have mercy on her even though she did not deserve it. Father and Mother might intercede for her on high. Some Hebrew words hung on the tip of her tongue, but she could not recall them. Then she remembered. "Hear, O Israel." But what followed? "God forgive me," Bessie said. "I deserve everything that falls on me."

It became even quieter and cooler. Traffic lights changed from red to green, but a car rarely passed. From somewhere a Negro appeared. He staggered. He stopped not far from Bessie and turned his eyes to her. Then he walked on. Bessie knew that her bag was full of important documents, but for the first time she did not care about her property. Sam had left a fortune; it all had gone for naught. She continued to save for her old age as if she were still young. "How old am I?" Bessie asked herself. "What have I accomplished in all these years? Why didn't I go somewhere, enjoy my money, help somebody?" Something in her laughed. "I was possessed, completely not myself. How else can it be explained?" Bessie was astounded. She felt as if she had awakened from a long sleep. The broken key had opened a door in her brain that had shut when Sam died.

The moon had shifted to the other side of the roof—unusually large, red, its face obliterated. It was almost cold now. Bessie shivered. She realized that she could easily get pneumonia, but the fear of death was gone, along with her fear of being homeless. Fresh breezes drifted from the Hudson River. New stars appeared in the sky. A black cat approached from the other side of the street. For a while, it stood on the edge of the sidewalk and its green eyes looked straight at Bessie. Then slowly and cautiously it drew near. For years Bessie had hated all animals—dogs, cats, pigeons, even sparrows. They carried sicknesses. They made everything filthy. Bessie believed that there was a demon in every cat. She especially dreaded an encounter with a black cat, which was always an omen of evil. But now Bessie felt love for this creature that had no home, no possessions, no doors or keys, and lived on God's bounty. Before the cat neared Bessie, it smelled her bag. Then it began to rub its back on her leg, lifting up its tail and meowing. The poor thing is hungry. I wish I could give her something. How can one hate a creature like this, Bessie wondered. O Mother of mine, I was bewitched, bewitched. I'll begin a new life. A treacherous thought ran through her mind: perhaps remarry?

The night did not pass without adventure. Once, Bessie saw a white butterfly in the air. It hovered for a while over a parked car and then took off. Bessie knew it was a soul of a newborn baby, since real butter-flies do not fly after dark. Another time, she wakened to see a ball of fire, a kind of lit-up soap bubble, soar from one roof to another and sink behind it. She was aware that what she saw was the spirit of someone who had just died.

Bessie had fallen asleep. She woke up with a start. It was daybreak. From the side of Central Park the sun rose. Bessie could not see it from here, but on Broadway the sky became pink and reddish. On the building to the left, flames kindled in the windows; the panes ran and blinked like the portholes of a ship. A pigeon landed nearby. It hopped on its little red feet and pecked into something that might have been a dirty piece of stale bread or dried mud. Bessie was baffled. How do these birds live? Where do they sleep at night? And how can they survive the rains, the cold, the snow? I will go home, Bessie decided. People will not leave me in the streets.

Getting up was a torment. Her body seemed glued to the step on which she sat. Her back ached and her legs tingled. Nevertheless, she began to walk slowly toward home. She inhaled the moist morning air. It smelled of grass and coffee. She was no longer alone. From the side streets men and women emerged. They were going to work. They bought newspapers at the stand and went down into the subway. They were silent and strangely peaceful, as if they, too, had gone through a night of soul-searching and come out of it cleansed. When do they get up if they are already on their way to work now, Bessie marveled. No, not all in this neighborhood were gangsters and murderers. One young man even nodded good morning to Bessie. She tried to smile at him, realizing she had forgotten that feminine gesture she knew so well in her youth; it was almost the first lesson her mother had taught her.

She reached her building, and outside stood the Irish super, her deadly enemy. He was talking to the garbage collectors. He was a giant of a man, with a short nose, a long upper lip, sunken cheeks, and a pointed chin. His yellow hair covered a bald spot. He gave Bessie a startled look. "What's the matter, Grandma?"

Stuttering, Bessie told him what had happened to her. She showed him the handle of the key she had clutched in her hand all night.

"Mother of God!" he called out.

"What shall I do?" Bessie asked.

"I will open your door."

"But you don't have a passkey."

"We have to be able to open all doors in case of fire."

The super disappeared into his own apartment for a few minutes, then he came out with some tools and a bunch of keys on a large ring. He went up in the elevator with Bessie. The bag of food still stood on the threshold, but it looked depleted. The super busied himself at the lock. He asked, "What are these cards?"

Bessie did not answer.

"Why didn't you come to me and tell me what happened? To be roaming around all night at your age—my God!" As he poked with his tools, a door opened and a little woman in a housecoat and slippers, her hair bleached and done up in curlers, came out. She said, "What happened to you? Every time I opened the door, I saw this bag. I took out your butter and milk and put them in my refrigerator."

Bessie could barely restrain her tears. "O my good people," she said. "I didn't know that . . ."

The super pulled out the other half of Bessie's key. He worked a little longer. He turned a key and the door opened. The cards fell down. He entered the hallway with Bessie and she sensed the musty odor of an apartment that has not been lived in for a long time. The super said, "Next time, if something like this happens call me. That's what I'm here for."

Bessie wanted to give him a tip, but her hands were too weak to open her bag. The neighbor woman brought in the milk and butter. Bessie went into her bedroom and lay down on the bed. There was a pressure on her breast and she felt like vomiting. Something heavy vibrated up from her feet to her chest. Bessie listened to it without alarm, only curious about the whims of the body; the super and the neighbor talked, and Bessie could not make out what they were saying. The same thing had happened to her over thirty years ago when she had been given anesthesia in the hospital before an operation—the doctor and the nurse were talking but their voices seemed to come from far away and in a strange language.

Soon there was silence, and Sam appeared. It was neither day nor night—a strange twilight. In her dream, Bessie knew that Sam was dead but that in some clandestine way he had managed to get away from the grave and visit her. He was feeble and embarrassed. He could not speak. They wandered through a space without a sky, without earth, a tunnel full of debris—the wreckage of a nameless structure —a corridor dark and winding, yet somehow familiar. They came to a region where two mountains met, and the passage between shone like sunset or sunrise. They stood there hesitating and even a little ashamed. It was like that night of their honeymoon when they went to Ellenville in the Catskills and were led by the hotel owner into their bridal suite. She heard the same words he had said to them then, in the same voice and intonation: "You don't need no key here. Just enter—and *mazel tov.*"

In what ways did Bessie Popkin change as a result of the breaking of her house key? What experiences contributed to this change in Bessie? How is she similar to Madame La Gimp?

What is the significance of the butterfly and the floating ball of fire which Bessie sees?

In what ways is the ending of this story a comic one?

*For a century Earth has been ruled
by a race of beings from another
world. On Earth they are called the
Overlords and Karellen is their chief.
In this passage, Karellen speaks to
all the men of earth from his vast
spaceship which hovers over earth.*

A New Race

From Childhood's End
ARTHUR C. CLARKE

"My work here is nearly ended," said Karellen's voice from a million radios. "At last, after a hundred years, I can tell you what it was.

"There are many things we have had to hide from you, as we hid ourselves for half our stay on Earth. Some of you, I know, thought that concealment unnecessary. You are accustomed to our presence: you can no longer imagine how your ancestors would have reacted to us. But at least you can understand the purpose of our concealment, and know we had a reason for what we did.

"The supreme secret we kept from you was our purpose in coming to Earth—that purpose about which you have speculated so endlessly. We could not tell you until now, for the secret was not ours to reveal.

"A century ago we came to your world and saved you from self-destruction. I do not believe that anyone would deny that fact—but what that self-destruction was, you never guessed.

"Because we banned nuclear weapons and all the other deadly toys you were accumulating in your armories, the danger of physical annihilation was removed. You thought that was the only danger. We wanted you to believe that, but it was never true. The greatest danger that confronted you was of a different character altogether—and it did not concern your race alone.

"Many worlds have come to the crossroads of nuclear power, have avoided disaster, have gone on to build peaceful and happy civilizations—and have then been utterly destroyed by forces of which they knew nothing. In the twentieth century, you first began to tamper seriously with those forces. That was why it became necessary to act.

"All through that century, the human race was drawing slowly nearer to the abyss—never even suspecting its existence. Across that abyss, there is only one bridge. Few races, unaided, have ever found it. Some have turned back while there was still time, avoiding both the danger and the achievement. Their worlds have become Elysian islands of effortless content, playing no further part in the story of the universe. That would never have been your fate—or your fortune. Your race was too vital for that. It would have plunged into ruin and taken others with it, for you would never have found the bridge.

"I am afraid that almost all I have to say now must be by means of such analogies. You have no words, no conceptions, for many of the things I wish to tell you—and our own knowledge of them is also sadly imperfect.

"To understand, you must go back into the past and recover much that your ancestors would have found familiar, but which you have forgotten—which, in fact, we deliberately helped you to forget. For all our sojourn here has been based on a vast deception, a concealment of truths which you were not ready to face.

"In the centuries before our coming, your scientists uncovered the secrets of the physical world and led you from the energy of steam to the energy of the atom. You had put superstition behind you: Science was the only real religion of mankind. It was the gift of the Western minority to the remainder of mankind, and it had destroyed all other faiths. Those that still existed when we came were already dying. Science, it was felt, could explain everything: there were no forces which did not come within its scope, no events for which it could not ultimately account. The origin of the universe might be forever unknown, but all that had happened since obeyed the laws of physics.

"Yet your mystics, though they were lost in their own delusions, had seen part of the truth. There are powers of the mind, and powers beyond the mind, which your science could never have brought within its framework without shattering it entirely. All down the ages there have been countless reports of strange phenomena—poltergeists, telepathy, precognition—which you had named but never explained. At first science ignored them, even denied their existence, despite the testimony of five thousand years. But they exist, and, if it is to be complete, any theory of the universe must account for them.

"During the first half of the twentieth century, a few of your scientists began to investigate these matters. They did not know it, but they were tampering with the lock of Pandora's box. The forces they might have unleashed transcended any perils that the atom could have brought. For the physicists could only have ruined the earth: the paraphysicists could have spread havoc to the stars.

"That could not be allowed. I cannot explain the full nature of the threat you represented. It would not have been a threat to us, and therefore we do not comprehend it. Let us say that you might have become a telepathic cancer, a malignant mentality which in its inevitable dissolution would have poisoned other and greater minds.

"And so we came—we were *sent*—to Earth. We interrupted your development on every cultural level, but in particular we checked all serious work on paranormal phenomena. I am well aware of the fact that we have also inhibited, by the contrast between our civilizations, all other forms of creative achievement as well. But that was a secondary effect, and it is of no importance.

"Now I must tell you something which you may find very surprising, perhaps almost incredible. All these potentialities, all these latent powers—we do not possess them, nor do we understand them. Our intellects are far more powerful than yours, but there is something in your minds that has always eluded us. Ever since we came to Earth we have been studying you; we have learned a great deal, and will learn more, yet I doubt if we shall discover all the truth.

"Our races have much in common—that is why we were chosen for this task. But in other respects, we represent the ends of two different evolutions. Our minds have reached the end of their development. So, in their present form, have yours. Yet you can make the jump to the next stage, and therein lies the difference between us. Our potentialities are exhausted, but yours are still untapped. They are linked, in ways we do not understand, with the powers I have mentioned—the powers that are now awakening on your world.

"We held the clock back, we made you mark time while those powers developed, until they could come flooding out into the channels that were being prepared for them. What we did to improve your planet, to raise your standards of living, to bring justice and peace— those things we should have done in any event, once we were forced to intervene in your affairs. But all that vast transformation diverted you from the truth, and therefore helped to serve our purpose.

"We are your guardians—no more. Often you must have wondered what position my race held in the hierarchy of the universe. As we are above you, so there is something above us, using us for its own purposes. We have never discovered what it is, though we have been its tool for ages and dare not disobey it. Again and again we have received our orders, have gone to some world in the early flower of its civilization, and have guided it along the road that we can never follow—the road that you are traveling now.

"Again and again we have studied the process we have been sent to foster, hoping that we might learn to escape from our own limitations. But we have glimpsed only the vague outlines of the truth. You called us the Overlords, now knowing the irony of that title. Let us say that above us is the *Overmind,* using us as the potter uses his wheel.

"And your race is the clay that is being shaped on that wheel.

"We believe—it is only a theory—that the Overmind is trying to grow, to extend its powers and its awareness of the universe. By now it must be the sum of many races, and long ago it left the tyranny of matter behind. It is conscious of intelligence, everywhere. When it knew that you were almost ready, it sent us here to do its bidding, to prepare you for the transformation that is now at hand.

"All the earlier changes your race has known took countless ages. But this is a transformation of the mind, not of the body. By the standards of evolution, it will be cataclysmic—instantaneous. It has already begun. You must face the fact that yours is the last generation of *Homo sapiens.*

"As to the nature of that change, we can tell you very little. We do not know how it is produced—what trigger impulse the Overmind employs when it judges that the time is ripe. All we have discovered is that it starts with a single individual—always a child—and then spreads explosively, like the formation of crystals round the first nucleus in a saturated solution. Adults will not be affected, for their minds are already set in an unalterable mold.

"In a few years, it will all be over, and the human race will have divided in twain. There is no way back, and no future for the world you know. All the hopes and dreams of your race are ended now. You have given birth to your successors, and it is your tragedy that you will never understand them—will never even be able to communicate with their minds. Indeed, they will not possess minds as you know them. They will be a single entity, as you yourselves are the sums of your myriad cells. You will not think them human, and you will be right.

"I have told you these things so that you will know what faces you.

In a few hours, the crisis will be upon us. My task and my duty is to protect those I have been sent here to guard. Despite their wakening powers, they could be destroyed by the multitudes around them—yes, even by their parents, when they realized the truth. I must take them away and isolate them, for their protection, and for yours. Tomorrow my ships will begin the evacuation. I shall not blame you if you try to interfere, but it will be useless. Greater powers than mine are wakening now; I am only one of their instruments.

"And then—what am I to do with you, the survivors, when your purpose has been fulfilled? It would be simplest, and perhaps most merciful, to destroy you—as you yourselves would destroy a mortally wounded pet you loved. But this I cannot do. Your future will be your own to choose in the years that are left to you. It is my hope that humanity will go to its rest in peace, knowing that it has not lived in vain.

"For what you will have brought into the world may be utterly alien, it may share none of your desires or hopes, it may look upon your greatest achievements as childish toys—yet it is something wonderful, and you will have created it.

"When our race is forgotten, part of yours will still exist. Do not, therefore, condemn us for what we were compelled to do. And remember this—we shall always envy you."

How would you describe the peculiar powers which Karellen attributes to human beings?

What transformation is described in this story? How is the role of the Overmind similar to the role of the gods in "Pygmalion and Galatea"?

Do you consider the ending of this story comic or tragic? Why? Write an imaginative sequel to this story in which you tell how the survivors reacted to their fate.

It was said earlier that the form of comedy is related to the power of nature to renew itself. Perhaps at no time is that power more spectacular than when spring triumphs over winter each year. In early agricultural societies, nature's return to life was often celebrated by a ritual battle between two actors, called by titles like "King of Winter" and "King of Summer." In this battle, the Summer King often symbolically killed the Winter King and claimed the May Queen as his bride. The outlines of this ancient ritual can be seen in the pattern of the poem "Putting Winter to Bed."

But besides the ritual battle of the seasons, there is another pattern suggested by spring that even more strongly shapes the form of comic writing—transformation. In the spring the face of nature is completely transformed by the power of life. Dry, pale, seemingly dead seeds turn, almost before our eyes, into lush plants, as if some inner power were forcing them to break open their shells and create new forms. Soon the whole appearance of the earth is transformed into a green world.

In comic writing this pattern of transformation in the natural world is extended into the human world. If all of nature can change and blend its form and appearance, why must the boundaries that seem to separate parts of human experience be so rigidly fixed? Why should the mysterious and supernatural be always separate from the everyday? Is what goes on inside the human mind doomed to be cut off from what goes on outside it? Must each human person be always individual, isolated, and unable to merge with other living things?

It is by our imagination that we can break down the barriers which separate man from nature and man from man. Imagination can take anything in the natural world around us and transform it into an image of desire. This is the point of the poem "The Beautiful Changes," which tells us that "a mantis, arranged on a green leaf, grows into it, makes the leaf leafier, and proves any greenness is deeper than anyone knows." In "Pygmalion and Galatea," Pygmalion, an artist, a creator, uses his imagination to transform rough stone into the image of a beautiful woman.

The myth of Pygmalion shows too that the power of the imagination is very close to the power of love. Love, in fact, seems to work hand in hand with the imagination. As Pygmalion's imagination helps him shape a formless piece of stone into the statue of a beautiful woman, so his love is responsible for the transformation of that lifeless statue into a living human being. So too, in "A Blessing," the speaker's exhilaration at the horse's affection for him breaks down his sense of the normal boundaries between man and nature and lets him "realize that if I stepped out of my body I would break into blossom."

The power of the imagination to transform and go beyond the boundaries of space and time is not restricted to individual experience only. It can take hold of whole segments of society, as it does in "Madame La Gimp." Madame has been battered and beaten by life, and in her later years, she seems to be "an old haybag," lame in one leg, and reduced to selling out-of-date newspapers. Yet with the help of the imagination of her friends who care about her, she is transformed into an attractive woman again. In the process, her friends also transform her surroundings to fit the romantic dream she has kept alive for so many years in her letters to her daughter. All this ends in breaking down the artificial social barriers that stand in the way of her daughter's marriage. And at the same time the years seem to fall away from Madame.

The human imagination is the part of man not subject to time and space, and its power to transform the image of nature and of man keeps working to repair the ravages wrought by time and life. By the power of the imagination, man retains an almost endless promise of vitality and potential for renewal.

5
FROM THE MOUNTAIN TOP

Jeannine Guertin

New Life at Kyerefaso

EFUA THEODORA SUTHERLAND

Shall we say,

Shall we put it this way.

Shall we say that the maid of Kyerefaso, Foruwa, daughter of the Queen Mother, was as a young deer, graceful in limb? Such was she, with head held high, eyes soft and wide with wonder. And she was light of foot, light in all her moving.

Stepping springily along the water path like a deer that had strayed from the thicket, springily stepping along the water path, she was a picture to give the eye a feast. And nobody passed her by but turned to look at her again.

Those of her village said that her voice in speech was like the murmur of a river quietly flowing beneath shadows of bamboo leaves. They said her smile would sometimes blossom like a lily on her lips and sometimes rise like sunrise.

The butterflies do not fly away from the flowers, they draw near. Foruwa was the flower of her village.

So shall we say,

Shall we put it this way, that all the village butterflies, the men, tried to draw near her at every turn, crossed and crossed her path? Men said of her, "She shall be my wife, and mine, and mine and mine."

But suns rose and set, moons silvered and died and as the days passed Foruwa grew more lovesome, yet she became no one's wife. She smiled at the butterflies and waved her hand lightly to greet them as she went swiftly about her daily work:

"Morning, Kweku

Morning, Kwesi

Morning, Kodwo"

but that was all.

And so they said, even while their hearts thumped for her:

"Proud!

Foruwa is proud . . . and very strange."

And so the men when they gathered would say:

"There goes a strange girl. She is not just stiff-in-the-neck proud, not just breasts-stuck-out-I-am-the-only-girl-in-the-village proud. What kind of pride is hers?"

The end of the year came round again, bringing the season of festivals. For the gathering in of corn, yams and cocoa there were harvest celebrations. There were bride-meetings too. And it came to the time when the Asafo companies should hold their festival. The village was full of manly sounds, loud musketry, and swelling choruses.

The pathfinding, path-clearing ceremony came to an end. The Asafo marched on toward the Queen Mother's house, the women fussing round them, prancing round them, spreading their cloths in their way.

"Osee!" rang the cry. "Osee!" to the manly men of old. They crouched like leopards upon the branches.

Before the drums beat

Before the danger drums beat, beware!

Before the horns moaned

Before the wailing horns moaned, beware!

They were upright, they sprang. They sprang. They sprang upon the enemy. But now, blood no more! No more thundershot on thundershot.

But still we are the leopards on the branches. We are those who roar and cannot be answered back. Beware, we are they who cannot be answered back.

There was excitement outside the Queen Mother's courtyard gate.

"Gently, gently," warned the Asafo leader. "Here comes the Queen Mother.

Spread skins of the gentle sheep in her way.

Lightly, lightly walks our Mother Queen.

Shower her with silver,

Shower her with silver for she is peace."

And the Queen Mother stood there, tall, beautiful, before the men and there was silence.

"What news, what news do you bring?" she quietly asked.

"We come with dusty brows from our pathfinding, Mother. We come with tired, thorn-pricked feet. We come to bathe in the coolness of your peaceful stream. We come to offer our manliness to new life."

The Queen Mother stood there, tall and beautiful and quiet. Her fanbearers stood by her and all the women clustered near. One by one the men laid their guns at her feet and then she said:

"It is well. The gun is laid aside. The gun's rage is silenced in the stream. Let your weapons from now on be your minds and your hands' toil.

"Come maidens, women all, join the men in dance for they offer themselves to new life."

There was one girl who did not dance.

"What, Foruwa!" urged the Queen Mother, "Will you not dance? The men are tired of parading in the ashes of their grandfathers' glorious deeds. That should make you smile. They are tired of the empty croak: 'We are men, we are men.'

"They are tired of sitting like vultures upon the rubbish heaps they have piled upon the half-built walls of their grandfathers. Smile, then, Foruwa, smile.

"Their brows shall now indeed be dusty, their feet thorn-pricked, and 'I love my land' shall cease to be the empty croaking of a vulture upon the rubbish heap. Dance, Foruwa, dance!"

Foruwa opened her lips and this was all she said: "Mother, I do not find him here."

"Who? Who do you not find here?"

"He with whom this new life shall be built. He is not here, Mother. These men's faces are empty; there is nothing in them, nothing at all."

"Alas, Foruwa, alas, alas! What will become of you, my daughter?"

"The day I find him, Mother, the day I find the man, I shall come running to you, and your worries will come to an end."

"But, Foruwa, Foruwa," argued the Queen Mother, although in her heart she understood her daughter, "five years ago your rites were fulfilled. Where is the child of your womb? Your friend Maanan married. Your friend Esi married. Both had their rites with you."

"Yes, Mother, they married and see how their steps once lively now drag in the dust. The sparkle has died out of their eyes. Their husbands drink palm wine the day long under the mango trees, drink palm wine and push counters across the draughtboards all the day, and are they not already looking for other wives? Mother, the man I say is not here."

This conversation had been overheard by one of the men and soon others heard what Foruwa had said. That evening there was heard a new song in the village.

> "There was a woman long ago,
> Tell that maid, tell that maid,
> There was a woman long ago,
> She would not marry Kwesi,
> She would not marry Kwaw,
> She would not, would not, would not.
> One day she came home with hurrying feet,
> I've found the man, the man, the man,
> Tell that maid, tell that maid,
> Her man looked like a chief,
> Tell that maid, tell that maid,
> Her man looked like a chief,
> Most splendid to see,
> But he turned into a python,
> He turned into a python
> *And swallowed her up.*"

From that time onward there were some in the village who turned their backs on Foruwa when she passed.

Shall we say,

Shall we put it this way.

Shall we say that a day came when Foruwa with hurrying feet came running to her mother? She burst through the courtyard gate; and there she stood in the courtyard, joy all over. And a stranger walked in after her and stood in the courtyard beside her, stood tall and strong as a pillar. Foruwa said to the astonished Queen Mother:

"Here he is, Mother, here is the man."

The Queen Mother took a slow look at the stranger standing there strong as a forest tree, and she said:

"You carry the light of wisdom on your face, my son. Greetings, you are welcome. But who are you, my son?"

"Greetings, Mother," replied the stranger quietly, "I am a worker. My hands are all I have to offer your daughter, for they are all my riches. I have traveled to see how men work in other lands. I have that knowledge and my strength. That is all my story."

Shall we say,

Shall we put it this way,

strange as the story is, that Foruwa was given in marriage to the stranger.

There was a rage in the village and many openly mocked saying, "Now the proud ones eat the dust."

Yet shall we say,

Shall we put it this way

that soon, quite soon, the people of Kyerefaso began to take notice of the stranger in quite a different way.

"Who," some said, "is this who has come among us? He who mingles sweat and song, he for whom toil is joy and life is full and abundant?"

"See," said others, "what a harvest the land yields under his ceaseless care."

"He has taken the earth and molded it into bricks. See what a home he has built, how it graces the village where it stands."

"Look at the craft of his fingers, baskets or kente, stool or mat, the man makes them all."

"And our children swarm about him, gazing at him with wonder and delight."

Then it did not satisfy them any more to sit all day at their draughtboards under the mango trees.

"See what Foruwa's husband has done," they declared; "shall the sons of the land not do the same?"

And soon they began to seek out the stranger to talk with him. Soon they too were toiling, their fields began to yield as never before, and the women labored joyfully to bring in the harvest. A new spirit stirred the village. As the carelessly built houses disappeared one by one, and new homes built after the fashion of the stranger's grew up, it seemed as if the village of Kyerefaso had been born afresh.

The people themselves became more alive and new pride possessed them. They were no longer just grabbing from the land what they desired for their stomachs' present hunger and for their present comfort. They were looking at the land with new eyes, feeling it in their blood, and thoughtfully building a permanent and beautiful place for themselves and their children.

"Osee!" It was festival-time again. "Osee! Blood no more. Our fathers found for us the paths. We are the roadmakers. They bought for us the land with their blood. We shall build it with our strength. We shall create it with our minds."

Following the men were the women and children. On their heads they carried every kind of produce that the land had yielded and crafts that their fingers had created. Green plantains and yellow bananas were carried by the bunch in large white wooden trays. Garden eggs, tomatoes, red oil-palm nuts warmed by the sun were piled high in black earthen vessels. Oranges, yams, maize filled shining brass trays and golden calabashes. Here and there were children proudly carrying colorful mats, baskets, and toys which they themselves had made.

The Queen Mother watched the procession gathering on the new village playground now richly green from recent rains. She watched the people palpitating in a massive dance toward her where she stood with her fanbearers outside the royal house. She caught sight of Foruwa. Her load of charcoal in a large brass tray which she had adorned with red hibiscus danced with her body. Happiness filled the Queen Mother when she saw her daughter thus.

Then she caught sight of Foruwa's husband. He was carrying a white lamb in his arms, and he was singing happily with the men. She looked on with pride. The procession had approached the royal house.

"See!" rang the cry of the Asafo leader. "See how the best in all the lands stands. See how she stands waiting, our Queen Mother. Waiting to wash the dust from our brow in the coolness of her peaceful stream. Spread skins of the gentle sheep in her way, gently, gently. Spread the yield of the land before her. Spread the craft of your hands before her, gently, gently.

"Lightly, lightly walks our Queen Mother, for she is peace."

What effects did the marriage between Foruwa and the stranger have on the village of the Asafo? What transforming power is at work?

The villagers say they will create the land "with their minds." What could this mean?

How are the animal, vegetable, and human worlds identified or associated with one another in this story?

The Vision of Odin

A Scandinavian myth
Retold by A. and E. KEARY

Then all mankind forsook the earth, and the earth itself sank down slowly into the ocean. Water swelled over the mountains, rivers gurgled through thick trees, deep currents swept down the valleys—nothing was to be seen on the earth but a wide flood. The stars fell from the sky, and flew about hither and thither. At last, smoky clouds drifted upward from the infinite deep, encircling the earth and the water; fire burst forth from the midst of them, red flames wrapped the world, roared through the branches of Yggdrasil, and played against heaven itself. The flood swelled, the fire raged; there was now nothing but flood and fire.

"Then," said Odin, in his dream, "I see the end of all things. The end is like the beginning, and it will now be forever as if nothing had ever been."

But, as he spoke, the fire ceased suddenly; the clouds rolled away, a new and brighter sun looked out of heaven, and he saw arise a second time the earth from ocean. It rose slowly as it had sunk. First, the waters fell back from the tops of new hills that rose up fresh and verdant; raindrops like pearls dripped from the freshly budding trees, and fell into the sea with a sweet sound; waterfalls splashed glittering from the high rocks; eagles flew over the mountain streams; earth arose springlike; unsown fields bore fruit; there was no evil, and all nature smiled. Then from Memory's Forest came forth a new race of men, who spread over the whole earth, and who fed on the dew of the dawn. There was also a new city on Asgard's Hill—a city of gems, and Odin saw a new hall standing in it, fairer than the sun, and roofed with gold. Above all, the wide blue expanded, and into that fair city came Modi and Magni, Thor's two sons, holding Miölnir between them. Vali and Vidar came, and the deathless Hœnir; Baldur came up from the deep, leading his blind brother Hödur peacefully by the hand; there was no longer any strife between them. Two brothers' sons inhabited the spacious Wind-Home.

Then Odin watched how the Æsir sat on the green plain, and talked of many things. "Garm is dead," said Hödur to Baldur, "and so are Loki and Jörmungand, and Fenrir, and the world rejoices, but did our dead brothers rejoice who fell in slaying them?

"They did, Hödur," answered Baldur, "they gave their lives willingly for the life of the world," and, as he listened, Odin felt that this was true; for, when he looked upon that beautiful and happy age, it gave him no pain to think that he must die before it came—that, though for many, it was not for him.

By and bye Hœnir came up to Hödur and Baldur with something glittering in his hand—something that he had found in the grass, and as he approached he said, "Behold the golden tablets, my brothers, which in the beginning of time were given to the Æsir's Father, and were lost in the Old World."

Then they all looked eagerly at the tablets, and, as they bent over them, their faces became even brighter than before.

"There is no longer any evil thing," said Odin, "not an evil sight, nor an evil sound."

How would you describe the new earth that is born from the ruins of the old in Odin's vision? What details about Odin's dream relate to Karellen's speech in "A New Race"?

Read the account of Noah and the Flood in the Old Testament. What similarities and differences do you see between the Biblical story and the Scandinavian myth?

How will the new race of men in this vision differ from the old?

If you enjoy drawing or painting, you might find ideas for a picture in the description of the new earth rising in this myth.

"And I saw a new heaven and a new earth . . ."

And I saw a new heaven and a new earth: for the first heaven and the first earth were passed away; and there was no more sea.

And I, John, saw the holy city, new Jerusalem, coming down from God out of heaven, prepared as a bride adorned for her husband.

And I heard a great voice out of heaven saying, "Behold, the tabernacle of God is with men, and he will dwell with them, and they shall be his people, and God himself shall be with them, and be their God.

"And God shall wipe away all tears from their eyes; and there shall be no more death, neither sorrow, nor crying, neither shall there be any more pain: for the former things are passed away."

And he that sat upon the throne said, "Behold, I make all things new."

REVELATION 21 : 1–5

How is John's vision of a new world similar to Odin's vision? Who, in John's vision, will bring about this new and more perfect order?

Weddings are often used to conclude comedies. Why are they appropriate endings for comic stories? How is wedding imagery used in this vision?

The Rose-Beetle Man

From My Family and Other Animals
GERALD DURRELL

In the morning, when I woke, the bedroom shutters were luminous and barred with gold from the rising sun. The morning air was full of the scent of charcoal from the kitchen fire, full of eager cock-crows, the distant yap of dogs, and the unsteady, melancholy tune of the goat bells as the flocks were driven out to pasture.

We ate breakfast out in the garden, under the small tangerine trees. The sky was fresh and shining, not yet the fierce blue of noon, but a clear milky opal. The flowers were half asleep, roses dew-crumpled, marigolds still tightly shut. Breakfast was, on the whole, a leisurely and silent meal, for no member of the family was very talkative at that hour. By the end of the meal the influence of the coffee, toast, and eggs made itself felt, and we started to revive, to tell each other what we intended to do, why we intended to do it, and then argue earnestly as to whether each had made a wise decision. I never joined in these discussions, for I knew perfectly well what I intended to do, and would concentrate on finishing my food as rapidly as possible.

"*Must* you gulp and slush your food like that?" Larry would inquire in a pained voice, delicately picking his teeth with a matchstick.

"Eat it slowly, dear," Mother would murmur; "there's no hurry."

No hurry? With Roger waiting at the garden gate, an alert black shape, watching for me with eager brown eyes? No hurry, with the first sleepy cicadas starting to fiddle experimentally among the olives? No hurry, with the island waiting, morning cool, bright as a star, to be explored? I could hardly expect the family to understand this point of view, however, so I would slow down until I felt that their attention had been attracted elsewhere, and then stuff my mouth again.

Finishing at last, I would slip from the table and saunter toward the gate, where Roger sat gazing at me with a questioning air. Together we would peer through the wrought-iron gates into the olive groves beyond. I would suggest to Roger that perhaps it wasn't worth going out today. He would wag his stump in hasty denial, and his nose would butt my hand. No, I would say, I really didn't think we ought to go out. It looked as though it was going to rain, and I would peer up into the clear, burnished sky with a worried expression. Roger, ears cocked, would peer into the sky too, and then look at me imploringly. Anyway, I would go on, if it didn't look like rain now it was almost certain to rain later, and so it would be much safer just to sit in the garden with a book. Roger, in desperation, would place a large black paw on the gate, and then look at me, lifting one side of his upper lip, displaying his white teeth in a lopsided, ingratiating grin, his stump working itself into a blur of excitement. This was his trump card, for he knew I could never resist his ridiculous grin. So I would stop teasing him, fetch my matchboxes and my butterfly net, the garden gate would creak open and clang shut, and Roger would be off through the olive groves swiftly as a cloud-shadow, his deep bark welcoming the new day.

In those early days of exploration Roger was my constant companion. Together we ventured farther and farther afield, discovering quiet, remote olive groves which had to be investigated and remembered, working our way through a maze of blackbird-haunted myrtles, venturing into narrow valleys where the cypress trees cast a cloak of mysterious, inky shadow. He was the perfect companion for an adventure, affectionate without exuberance, brave without being belligerent, intelligent and full of good-humored tolerance for my eccentricities. If I slipped when climbing a dew-shiny bank, Roger appeared suddenly, gave a snort that sounded like suppressed laughter, a quick look over, a rapid lick of commiseration, shook himself, sneezed, and gave me his lopsided grin. If I found something that interested me — an ant's nest, a caterpillar on a leaf, a spider wrapping up a fly in swaddling clothes of silk — Roger sat down and waited until I had finished examining it. If he thought I was taking too long, he shifted nearer, gave a gentle, whiny yawn, and then sighed deeply and started to wag his tail. If the matter was of no great importance, we would move on, but if it was something absorbing that had to be pored over, I had only to frown at Roger and he would realize it was going to be a long job. His ears would drop, his tail slow down and stop, and he would slouch off to the near-est bush and fling himself down in the shade, giving me a martyred look as he did so.

During these trips Roger and I came to know and be known by a great number of people in various parts of the surrounding country-side. There was, for example, a strange, mentally defective youth with a round face as expressionless as a puffball. He was always dressed in tattered shirt, shiny blue serge trousers that were rolled up to the knee, and on his head the elderly remains of a bowler hat without a brim. Whenever he saw us he came hurrying through the olives, raised his absurd hat politely, and wished us good day in a voice as childish and sweet as a flute. He would stand, watching us without expression, nodding at any remark I happened to make, for ten minutes or so. Then, raising his hat politely, he would go off through the trees. And there was the immensely fat and cheerful Agathi, who lived in a tiny tumble-down cottage high up the hill. She was always sitting outside her house with a spindle of sheep's wool, twining and pulling it into coarse thread. She must have been well over seventy, but her hair was still black and lustrous, plaited carefully and wound round a pair of pol-ished cow's horns, an ornament that some of the older peasant women adopted. As she sat in the sun, like a great black toad with a scarlet headdress draped over the cow's horns, the bobbin of wool would rise and fall, twisting like a top, her fingers busy unraveling and plucking, and her drooping mouth with its hedge of broken and discolored teeth wide open as she sang, loudly and harshly, but with great vigor.

It was from Agathi that I learned some of the most beautiful and haunting of the peasant songs. Sitting on an old tin in the sun, eating grapes or pomegranates from her garden, I would sing with her, and she would break off now and then to correct my pronunciation. We sang, verse by verse, the gay, rousing song of the river, *Vangelió*, and of how it dropped from the mountains, making the gardens rich, the fields fertile, and the trees heavy with fruit. We sang, rolling our eyes at each other in exaggerated coquetry, the funny little love song called "Falsehood." "Lies, lies," we warbled, shaking our heads, "all lies, but it is my fault for teaching you to go round the countryside telling people I love you." Then we would strike a mournful note and sing, perhaps, the slow, lilting song called "Why Are You Leaving Me?" We were almost overcome by this one, and would wail out the long, soulful lyrics, our voices quavering. When we came to the last bit, the most heart-rending of all, Agathi would clasp her hands to her great breasts, her black eyes would become misty and sad, and her chins would tremble with emotion. As the last discordant notes of our duet faded away, she would turn to me, wiping her nose on the corner of her headdress.

"What fools we are, eh? What fools, sitting here in the sun, singing. And of love, too! I am too old for it and you are too young, and yet we waste our time singing about it. Ah, well, let's have a glass of wine, eh?"

Apart from Agathi, the person I liked best was the old shepherd Yani, a tall, slouching man with a great hooked nose like an eagle's, and incredible moustaches. I first met him one hot afternoon when Roger and I had spent an exhausting hour trying to dig a large green lizard out of its hole in a stone wall. At length, unsuccessful, sweaty and tired, we had flung ourselves down beneath five little cypress trees that cast a neat square of shadow on the sun-bleached grass. Lying there, I heard the gentle, drowsy tinkling of a goat bell, and presently the herds wandered past us, pausing to stare with vacant yellow eyes, bleat sneeringly, and then move on. The soft sound of their bells, and of their mouths ripping and tearing at the undergrowth, had a soothing effect on me, and by the time they had drifted slowly past and the shepherd appeared I was nearly asleep. He stopped and looked at me, leaning heavily on his brown olive-wood stick, his little black eyes fierce under his shaggy brows, his big boots planted firmly in the heather.

"Good afternoon," he greeted me gruffly; "you are the foreigner . . . the little English lord?"

By then I was used to the curious peasant idea that all English people were lords, and I admitted that that's who I was. He turned and roared at a goat which had reared onto its hind legs and was tearing at a young olive, and then turned back.

"I will tell you something, little lord," he said; "it is dangerous for you to lie here, beneath these trees."

I glanced up at the cypresses, but they seemed safe enough to me, and so I asked why he thought they were dangerous.

"Ah, you may *sit* under them yes. They cast a good shadow, cold as well-water; but that's the trouble, they tempt you to sleep. And you must never, for any reason, sleep beneath a cypress."

He paused, stroked his moustache, waited for me to ask why, and then went on:

"Why? Why? Because if you did you would be changed when you woke. Yes, the black cypresses, they are dangerous. While you sleep, their roots grow into your brains and steal them, and when you wake up you are mad, head as empty as a whistle."

I asked whether it was only the cypress that could do this, or did it apply to other trees.

"No, only the cypress," said the old man, peering up fiercely at the trees above me as though to see whether they were listening; "only the cypress is the thief of intelligence. So be warned, little lord, and don't sleep here."

He nodded briefly, gave another fierce glance at the dark blades of the cypress, as if daring them to make some comment, and then picked his way carefully through the myrtle bushes to where his goats grazed scattered about the hill, their great udders swinging like bagpipes beneath their bellies.

I got to know Yani very well, for I was always meeting him during my explorations, and occasionally I visited him in his little house, when he would ply me with fruit, and give me advice and warnings to keep me safe on my walks.

Perhaps one of the most weird and fascinating characters I met during my travels was the Rose-Beetle Man. He had a fairy-tale air about him that was impossible to resist, and I used to look forward eagerly to my infrequent meetings with him. I first saw him on a high, lonely road leading to one of the remote mountain villages. I could hear him long before I could see him, for he was playing a rippling tune on a shepherd's pipe, breaking off now and then to sing a few words in a curious nasal voice. As he rounded the corner both Roger and I stopped and stared at him in amazement.

He had a sharp, foxlike face with large, slanting eyes of such a dark brown that they appeared black. They had a weird, vacant look about them, and a sort of bloom such as one finds on a plum, a pearly covering almost like a cataract. He was short and slight, with a thinness about his wrists and neck that argued a lack of food. His dress was fantastic, and on his head was a shapeless hat with a very wide, floppy brim. It had once been bottle green, but was now speckled and smeared with dust, wine stains, and cigarette burns. In the band were stuck a fluttering forest of feathers: cock feathers, hoopoe feathers, owl feathers, the wing of a kingfisher, the claw of a hawk, and a large dirty white feather that may have come from a swan. His shirt was worn and frayed, gray with sweat, and round the neck dangled an enormous cravat of the most startling blue satin. His coat was dark and shapeless, with patches of different hues here and there; on the sleeve a bit of white cloth with the

design of rosebuds; on the shoulder a triangular patch of wine-red and white spots. The pockets of this garment bulged, the contents almost spilling out: combs, balloons, little highly colored pictures of the saints, olive-wood carvings of snakes, camels, dogs, and horses, cheap mirrors, a riot of handkerchiefs, and long twisted rolls of bread decorated with seeds. His trousers, patched like his coat, drooped over a pair of scarlet *charouhias*, leather shoes with upturned toes decorated with a large black-and-white pompon. This extraordinary character carried on his back bamboo cages full of pigeons and young chickens, several mysterious sacks, and a large bunch of fresh green leeks. With one hand he held his pipe to his mouth, and in the other a number of lengths of cotton, to each of which was tied an almond-size rose-beetle, glittering golden green in the sun, all of them flying round his hat with desperate, deep buzzings, trying to escape from the threads tied firmly round their waists. Occasionally, tired of circling round and round without success, one of the beetles would settle for a moment on his hat, before launching itself off once more on its endless merry-go-round.

When he saw us the Rose-Beetle Man stopped, gave a very exaggerated start, doffed his ridiculous hat, and swept us a low bow. Roger was so overcome by this unlooked-for attention that he let out a volley of surprised barks. The man smiled at us, put on his hat again, raised his hands, and waggled his long, bony fingers at me. Amused and rather startled by this apparition, I politely bade him good day. He gave another courtly bow. I asked him if he had been to some fiesta. He nodded his head vigorously, raised his pipe to his lips and played a lilting little tune on it, pranced a few steps in the dust of the road, and then stopped and jerked his thumb over his shoulder, pointing back the way he had come. He smiled, patted his pockets, and rubbed his forefinger and thumb together in the Greek way of expressing money. I suddenly realized that he must be dumb. So, standing in the middle of the road, I carried on a conversation with him and he replied with a varied and very clever pantomime. I asked what the rose-beetles were for, and why he had them tied with pieces of cotton. He held his hand out to denote small boys, took one of the lengths of cotton from which a beetle hung, and whirled it rapidly round his head. Immediately the insect came to life and started on its planet-like circling of his hat, and he beamed at me. Pointing up at the sky, he stretched his arms out and gave a deep nasal buzzing, while he banked and swooped across the road. Airplane, any fool could see that. Then he pointed to the beetles, held out his hand to denote children and whirled his stock of beetles round his head so that they all started to buzz peevishly.

Exhausted by his explanation, he sat down by the edge of the road, played a short tune on his flute, breaking off to sing in his curious nasal voice. They were not articulate words he used, but a series of strange gruntings and tenor squeaks, that appeared to be formed at the back of his throat and expelled through his nose. He produced them, however, with such verve and such wonderful facial expressions that you were convinced the curious sounds really meant something. Presently he stuffed his flute into his bulging pocket, gazed at me reflectively for a moment, and then swung a small sack off his shoulder, undid it, and, to my delight and astonishment, tumbled half a dozen tortoises into the dusty road. Their shells had been polished with oil until they shone, and by some means or other he had managed to decorate their front legs with little red bows. Slowly and ponderously they unpacked their heads and legs from their gleaming shells and set off down the road, doggedly and without enthusiasm. I watched them, fascinated; the one that particularly took my fancy was quite a small one with a shell about the size of a tea-cup. It seemed more sprightly than the others, and its shell was a paler color—chestnut, caramel, and amber. Its eyes were bright and its walk was as alert as any tortoise's could be. I sat contemplating it for a long time. I convinced myself that the family would greet its arrival at the villa with tremendous enthusiasm, even, perhaps, congratulating me on finding such an elegant specimen. The fact that I had no money on me did not worry me in the slightest, for I would simply tell the man to call at the villa for payment the next day. It never occurred to me that he might not trust me. The fact that I was English was sufficient, for the islanders had a love and respect for the Englishman out of all proportion to his worth. They would trust an Englishman where they would not trust each other. I asked the Rose-Beetle Man the price of the little tortoise. He held up both hands, fingers spread out. However, I hadn't watched the peasants transacting business for nothing. I shook my head firmly and held up two fingers, unconsciously imitating the man. He closed his eyes in horror at the thought, and held up nine fingers; I held up three; he shook his head, and after some thought held up six fingers; I, in return, shook my head and held up five. The Rose-Beetle Man shook his head, and sighed deeply and sorrowfully, so we sat in silence and stared at the tortoises crawling heavily and uncertainly about the road, with the curious graceless determination of babies. Presently the Rose-Beetle Man indicated the little tortoise and held up six fingers again. I shook my head and held up five. Roger yawned loudly; he was thoroughly bored by this silent bargaining. The Rose-Beetle Man picked up the reptile and showed me in pantomime how smooth and lovely its shell was, how erect its head, how pointed its nails. I remained implacable. He shrugged, handed me the tortoise, and held up five fingers.

Then I told him I had no money, and that he would have to come the next day to the villa, and he nodded as if it were the most natural thing in the world. Excited by owning this new pet, I wanted to get back home as quickly as possible in order to show it to everyone, so I said good-by, thanked him, and hurried off along the road. When I reached the place where I had to cut down through the olive groves, I stopped and examined my acquisition carefully. He was undoubtedly the finest tortoise I had ever seen, and worth, in my opinion, at least twice what I had paid for him. I patted his scaly head with my finger and placed him carefully in my pocket. Before diving down the hillside I glanced back. The Rose-Beetle Man was still in the same place on the road, but he was doing a little jig, prancing and swaying, his flute warbling, while in the road at his feet the tortoises ambled to and fro, dimly and heavily. . . .

For some time the Rose-Beetle Man would turn up at the villa fairly regularly with some new addition to my menagerie: a frog, perhaps, or a sparrow with a broken wing. One afternoon Mother and I, in a fit of extravagant sentimentalism, bought up his entire stock of rose-beetles and, when he had left, let them all go in the garden. For days the villa was full of rose-beetles, crawling on the beds, lurking in the bathroom, banging against the lights at night, and falling like emeralds into our laps.

The last time I saw the Rose-Beetle Man was one evening when I was sitting on a hilltop overlooking the road. He had obviously been to some fiesta and had been plied with much wine, for he swayed to and fro across the road, piping a melancholy tune on his flute. I shouted a greeting, and he waved extravagantly without looking back. As he rounded the corner he was silhouetted for a moment against the pale lavender evening sky. I could see his battered hat with the fluttering feathers, the bulging pockets of his coat, the bamboo cages full of sleepy pigeons on his back, and above his head, circling drowsily round and round, I could see the dim specks that were the rose-beetles. Then he rounded the curve of the road and there was only the pale sky with a new moon floating in it like a silver feather, and the soft twittering of his flute dying away in the dusk.

What is the boy's attitude toward the natural world? What images does he use that make his world seem innocent, untouched by evil?

What kind of life do the young, the old, the uneducated, and the weak have in this island society?

How would you describe the relationship between the natural and the human worlds on this island? Can you find examples in this story of people who are identified or compared with animals or flowers?

What other images of a desirable, innocent world have you encountered in this unit? How do these worlds contrast with the blocking societies that triumph in the first unit?

"The wolf also shall dwell
with the lamb . . ."

The wolf also shall dwell with the lamb, and the leopard shall lie down with the kid; and the calf and the young lion and the fatling together; and a little child shall lead them.

And the cow and the bear shall feed; their young ones shall lie down together: and the lion shall eat straw like the ox.

And the sucking child shall play on the hole of the asp, and the weaned child shall put his hand on the cockatrice's den.

They shall not hurt nor destroy in all my holy mountain: for the earth shall be full of the knowledge of the Lord, as the waters cover the sea.

ISAIAH 11: 6–9

What is the relationship between man and nature described in this Biblical passage? Why do you think it is a child who shall lead man to this better way of life?

How is the way of life envisioned here similar to the life described in Odin's vision and in "The Rose-Beetle Man"? How is it different?

Happiness

From the Dhammapada
A Buddhist scripture
Translated by F. MAX MULLER

We live happily indeed, not hating those who hate us! among men who hate us we dwell free from hatred!

We live happily indeed, free from ailments among the ailing! among men who are ailing let us dwell free from ailments!

We live happily indeed, free from greed among the greedy! among men who are greedy let us dwell free from greed!

We live happily indeed, though we call nothing our own! We shall be like the bright gods, feeding on happiness!

Victory breeds hatred, for the conquered is unhappy. He who has given up both victory and defeat, he, the contented, is happy.

There is no fire like passion; there is no losing throw like hatred; there is no pain like this body; there is no happiness higher than rest.

Hunger is the worst of diseases, the elements of the body the greatest evil; if one knows this truly, that is Nirvâna, the highest happiness.

Health is the greatest of gifts, contentedness the best riches; trust is the best of relationships, Nirvâna the highest happiness.

He who has tasted the sweetness of solitude and tranquility is free from fear and free from sin, while he tastes the sweetness of drinking in the law.

The sight of the elect is good, to live with them is always happiness; if a man does not see fools, he will be truly happy.

He who walks in the company of fools suffers a long way; company with fools, as with an enemy, is always painful; company with the wise is pleasure, like meeting with kinsfolk.

Therefore, one ought to follow the wise, the intelligent, the learned, the much enduring, the dutiful, the elect; one ought to follow such a good and wise man, as the moon follows the path of the stars.

Changes IV

Words and music by CAT STEVENS

Woah . . .   Yeah . . .

Woah . . .   Yeah . . .

Don't you feel a change a - com -
Don't you feel the day is com -
Don't you feel the day is com -

in'   from an - oth - er   side   of time ___   Break - ing
in'   that will stay   and   re - main ___   When your
in'   and it won't   be   too soon ___   When the

down the walls   of si - lence   lift - ing sha-dows from   your mind
chil - dren see   the an-swers   that you   saw   the same
peo - ple of ___ the world ___   can   all   live   in   one room

___   Plac - ing back the miss-ing mir - rors   that be
___   When the clouds have all ___ gone ___   there will
___   When we shake   off the an - cient   the

fore   you could - n't find ___   Fill - ing   my - ster - ies ___ of
be   no more   rain ___   And the   beau - ty of ___ all
an - cient chains of   our tomb   We will   all   be born a - gain

emp - ti - ness ___ that yes - ter-day left ___ be - hind ___
things   is   un - cov - ered a - gain ___
___   of   the   e - ter - nal   womb ___

And   we   all   know it's bet - ter   Yes - ter-day has

234   *From the Mountain Top*

in'   liv - in'   liv - in' liv - in' for the

one that's going to last Woah . . .

What changes will take place when the day comes "that's going to last"?

What other visions of a better transformed world does this description resemble?

What do you think "the ancient chains of our tomb" might be?

To envision or to live in a better world, we must free ourselves from old, limiting habits and embrace new freeing ways. What according to the excerpt from the *Dhammapada* must we leave behind to live happily?

Mecca

From The Autobiography of Malcolm X

MALCOLM X

The pilgrimage to Mecca, known as Hajj, is a religious obligation that every orthodox Muslim fulfills, if humanly able, at least once in his or her lifetime.

The Holy Quran says it, "Pilgrimage to the Ka'ba is a duty men owe to God; those who are able, make the journey."

Allah said: "And proclaim the pilgrimage among men; they will come to you on foot and upon each lean camel, they will come from every deep ravine. . . ."

The literal meaning of Hajj in Arabic is to set out toward a definite objective. In Islamic law, it means to set out for Ka'ba, the Sacred House, and to fulfill the pilgrimage rites. The Cairo airport was where scores of Hajj groups were becoming *Muhrim*, pilgrims, upon entering the state of Ihram, the assumption of a spiritual and physical state of consecration. Upon advice, I arranged to leave in Cairo all of my luggage and four cameras, one a movie camera. I had bought in Cairo a small valise, just big enough to carry one suit, shirt, a pair of underwear sets and a pair of shoes into Arabia. Driving to the airport with our Hajj group, I began to get nervous, knowing that from there in, it was going to be watching others who knew what they were doing, and trying to do what they did.

Entering the state of Ihram, we took off our clothes and put on two white towels. One, the *Izar*, was folded around the loins. The other, the *Rida*, was thrown over the neck and shoulders, leaving the right shoulder and arm bare. A pair of simple sandals, the *na'l*, left the ankle bones bare. Over the *Izar* waist-wrapper, a money belt was worn, and a bag, something like a woman's big handbag, with a long strap, was for carrying the passport and other valuable papers, such as the letter I had from Dr. Shawarbi.

Every one of the thousands at the airport, about to leave for Jedda, was dressed this way. You could be a king or a peasant and no one would know. Some powerful personages, who were discreetly pointed out to me, had on the same thing I had on. Once thus dressed, we all had begun intermittently calling out *"Labbayka! Labbayka!"* (Here I come, O Lord!) The airport sounded with the din of *Muhrim* expressing their intention to perform the journey of the Hajj.

Planeloads of pilgrims were taking off every few minutes, but the airport was jammed with more, and their friends and relatives waiting to see them off. Those not going were asking others to pray for them at Mecca. We were on our plane, in the air, when I learned for the first time that with the crush, there was not supposed to have been space for me, but strings had been pulled, and someone had been put off because they didn't want to disappoint an American Muslim. I felt mingled emotions of regret that I had inconvenienced and discomfited whoever was bumped off the plane for me, and, with that, an utter humility and gratefulness that I had been paid such an honor and respect.

Packed in the plane were white, black, brown, red, and yellow people, blue eyes and blond hair, and my kinky red hair—all together, brothers! All honoring the same God Allah, all in turn giving equal honor to each other.

From some in our group, the word was spreading from seat to seat that I was a Muslim from America. Faces turned, smiling toward me in greeting. A box lunch was passed out and as we ate that, the word that a Muslim from America was aboard got up into the cockpit.

The captain of the plane came back to meet me. He was an Egyptian, his complexion was darker than mine; he could have walked in Harlem and no one would have given him a second glance. He was delighted to meet an American Muslim. When he invited me to visit the cockpit, I jumped at the chance.

The co-pilot was darker than he was. I can't tell you the feeling it gave me. I had never seen a black man flying a jet. That instrument panel: no one ever could know what all of those dials meant! Both of the pilots were smiling at me, treating me with the same honor and respect I had received ever since I left America. I stood there looking through the glass at the sky ahead of us. In America, I had ridden in more planes than probably any other Negro, and I never had been invited up into the cockpit. And there I was, with two Muslim seat-mates, one from Egypt, the other from Arabia, all of us bound for

Mecca, with me up in the pilots' cabin. Brother, I *knew* Allah was with me.

I got back to my seat. All of the way, about an hour's flight, we pilgrims were loudly crying out, *"Labbayka! Labbayka!"* The plane landed at Jedda. It's a seaport town on the Red Sea, the arrival or disembarkation point for all pilgrims who come to Arabia to go to Mecca. Mecca is about forty miles to the east, inland.

The Jedda airport seemed even more crowded than Cairo's had been. Our party became another shuffling unit in the shifting mass with every race on earth represented. Each party was making its way toward the long line waiting to go through Customs. Before reaching Customs, each Hajj party was assigned a *Mutawaf,* who would be responsible for transferring that party from Jedda to Mecca. Some pilgrims cried *"Labbayka!"* Others, sometimes large groups, were chanting in unison a prayer that I will translate, "I submit to no one but Thee, O Allah, I submit to no one but Thee. I submit to Thee because Thou hast no partner. All praise and blessings come from Thee, and Thou art alone in Thy kingdom." The essence of the prayer is the Oneness of God.

Only officials were not wearing the *Ihram* garb, or the white skull caps, long, white, nightshirt-looking gown and the little slippers of the *Mutawaf,* those who guided each pilgrim party, and their helpers. In Arabic, an *mmmm* sound before a verb makes a verbal noun, so *"Mutawaf"* meant "the one who guides" the pilgrims on the "*Tawaf,*" which is the circumambulation of the Ka'ba in Mecca.

I was nervous, shuffling in the center of our group in the line waiting to have our passports inspected. I had an apprehensive feeling. Look what I'm handing them. I'm in the Muslim world, right at The Fountain. I'm handing them the American passport which signifies the exact opposite of what Islam stands for.

The judge in our group sensed my strain. He patted my shoulder. Love, humility, and true brotherhood was almost a physical feeling wherever I turned. Then our group reached the clerks who examined each passport and suitcase carefully and nodded to the pilgrim to move on.

I was so nervous that when I turned the key in my bag, and it didn't work, I broke open the bag, fearing that they might think I had something in the bag that I shouldn't have. Then the clerk saw that I was handing him an American passport. He held it, he looked at me and said something in Arabic. My friends around me began speaking rapid

Arabic, gesturing and pointing, trying to intercede for me. The judge asked me in English for my letter from Dr. Shawarbi, and he thrust it at the clerk, who read it. He gave the letter back, protesting—I could tell that. An argument was going on, *about* me. I felt like a stupid fool, unable to say a word, I couldn't even understand what was being said. But, finally, sadly, the judge turned to me.

I had to go before the *Mahgama Sharia,* he explained. It was the Muslim high court which examined all possibly nonauthentic converts to the Islamic religion seeking to enter Mecca. It was absolute that no non-Muslim could enter Mecca.

My friends were going to have to go on to Mecca without me. They seemed stricken with concern for me. And *I* was stricken. I found the words to tell them, "Don't worry, I'll be fine. Allah guides me." They said they would pray hourly in my behalf. The white-garbed *Mutawaf* was urging them on, to keep schedule in the airport's human crush. With all of us waving, I watched them go.

It was then about three in the morning, a Friday morning. I never had been in such a jammed mass of people, but I never had felt more alone, and helpless, since I was a baby. Worse, Friday in the Muslim world is a rough counterpart of Sunday in the Christian world. On Friday, all the members of a Muslim community gather, to pray together. The event is called *yaum al-jumu'a*—"the day of gathering." It meant that no courts were held on Friday. I would have to wait until Saturday, at least.

An official beckoned a young Arab *Mutawaf's* aide. In broken English, the official explained that I would be taken to a place right at the airport. My passport was kept at Customs. I wanted to object, because it is a traveler's first law never to get separated from his passport, but I didn't. In my wrapped towels and sandals, I followed the aid in his skull cap, long white gown, and slippers. I guess we were quite a sight. People passing us were speaking all kinds of languages. I couldn't speak anybody's language. I was in bad shape.

Right outside the airport was a mosque, and above the airport was a huge, dormitory-like building, four tiers high. It was semi-dark, not long before dawn, and planes were regularly taking off and landing, their landing lights sweeping the runways, or their wing and tail lights blinking in the sky. Pilgrims from Ghana, Indonesia, Japan, and Russia, to mention some, were moving to and from the dormitory where I was being taken. I don't believe that motion picture cameras ever have filmed a human spectacle more colorful than my eyes took in. We reached the dormitory and began climbing, up to the fourth, top, tier, passing members of every race on earth. Chinese, Indonesians, Afghanistanians. Many, not yet changed into the *Ihram* garb, still wore their national dress. It was like pages out of the *National Geographic* magazine.

My guide, on the fourth tier, gestured me into a compartment that contained about fifteen people. Most lay curled up on their rugs asleep. I could tell that some were women, covered head and foot. An old Russian Muslim and his wife were not asleep. They stared frankly at me. Two Egyptian Muslims and a Persian roused and also stared as my guide moved us over into a corner. With gestures, he indicated that he would demonstrate to me the proper prayer ritual postures. Imagine, being a Muslim minister, a leader in Elijah Muhammad's Nation of Islam, and not knowing the prayer ritual.

I tried to do what he did. I knew I wasn't doing it right. I could feel the other Muslims' eyes on me. Western ankles won't do what Muslim ankles have done for a lifetime. Asians squat when they sit, Westerners sit upright in chairs. When my guide was down in a posture, I tried everything I could to get down as he was, but there I was, sticking up. After about an hour, my guide left, indicating that he would return later.

I never even thought about sleeping. Watched by the Muslims, I kept practicing prayer posture. I refused to let myself think how ridiculous I must have looked to them. After a while, though, I learned a little trick that would let me get down closer to the floor. But after two or three days, my ankle was going to swell.

As the sleeping Muslims woke up, when dawn had broken, they almost instantly became aware of me, and we watched each other while they went about their business. I began to see what an important role the rug played in the overall cultural life of the Muslims. Each individual had a small prayer rug, and each man and wife, or large group, had a larger communal rug. These Muslims prayed on their rugs there in the compartment. Then they spread a tablecloth over the rug and ate, so the rug became the dining room. Removing the dishes and cloth, they sat on the rug—a living room. Then they curl up and sleep on the rug—a bedroom. In that compartment, before I was to leave it, it dawned on me for the first time why the fence had paid such a high price for Oriental rugs when I had been a burglar in Boston. It was because so much intricate care was taken to weave fine rugs in countries where rugs were so culturally versatile. Later, in Mecca, I would see yet another use of the rug. When any kind of a dispute arose, someone who was respected highly and who was not involved would sit on a rug with the disputers around him, which made the rug a courtroom. In other instances it was a classroom.

One of the Egyptian Muslims, particularly, kept watching me out of the corner of his eye. I smiled at him. He got up and came over to me. "Hel-lo—" he said. It sounded like the Gettysburg Address. I beamed at him, "Hello!" I asked his name. "Name? Name?" He was trying hard, but he didn't get it. We tried some words on each other. I'd guess his English vocabulary spanned maybe twenty words. Just enough to frustrate me. I was trying to get him to comprehend anything. "Sky." I'd point. He'd smile. "Sky," I'd say again, gesturing for him to repeat it after me. He would. "Airplane . . . rug . . . foot . . . sandal . . . eyes. . . ." Like that. Then an amazing thing happened. I was so glad I had some communication with a human being, I was just saying whatever came to mind. I said "Muhammad Ali Clay—" All of the Muslims listening lighted up like a Christmas tree. "You? You?" My friend was pointing at me. I shook my head, "No, no. Muhammad Ali Clay my friend—*friend!*" They half understood me. Some of them didn't understand, and that's how it began to get around that I was Cassius Clay, world heavyweight champion. I was later to learn that apparently every man, woman and child in the Muslim world had heard how Sonny Liston (who in the Muslim world had the image of a man-eating ogre) had been beaten in Goliath-David fashion by Cassius Clay, who then had told the world that his name was Muhammad Ali and his religion was Islam and Allah had given him his victory.

Establishing the rapport was the best thing that could have happened in the compartment. My being an American Muslim changed the attitudes from merely watching me to wanting to look out for me. Now, the others began smiling steadily. They came closer, they were frankly looking me up and down. Inspecting me. Very friendly. I was like a man from Mars.

The *Mutawaf's* aide returned, indicating that I should go with him. He pointed from our tier down at the mosque and I knew that he had come to take me to make the morning prayer, *El Sobh,* always before sunrise. I followed him down, and we passed pilgrims by the thousands, babbling languages, everything but English. I was angry with myself for not having taken the time to learn more of the orthodox prayer rituals before leaving America. In Elijah Muhammad's Nation of Islam, we hadn't prayed in Arabic. About a dozen or more years before, when I was in prison, a member of the orthodox Muslim movement in Boston, named Abdul Hameed, had visited me and had later sent me prayers in Arabic. At that time, I had learned those prayers phonetically. But I hadn't used them since.

I made up my mind to let the guide do everything first and I would watch him. It wasn't hard to get him to do things first. He wanted to anyway. Just outside the mosque there was a long trough with rows of faucets. Ablutions had to precede praying. I knew that. Even watching the *Mutawaf's* helper, I didn't get it right. There's an exact way that an orthodox Muslim washes, and the exact way is very important.

I followed him into the mosque, just a step behind, watching. He did his prostration, his head to the ground. I did mine. *"Bi-smi-llahi-r-Rahmain-r-Rahim—"* ("In the name of Allah, the Beneficent, the Merciful—") All Muslim prayers began that way. After that, I may not have been mumbling the right thing, but I was mumbling.

I don't mean to have any of this sound joking. It was far from a joke with me. No one who happened to be watching could tell that I wasn't saying what the others said.

After that Sunrise Prayer, my guide accompanied me back up to the fourth tier. By sign language, he said he would return within three hours, then he left.

Our tier gave an excellent daylight view of the whole airport area. I stood at the railing, watching. Planes were landing and taking off like clockwork. Thousands upon thousands of people from all over the world made colorful patterns of movement. I saw groups leaving for Mecca, in buses, trucks, cars. I saw some setting out to walk the forty miles. I wished that I could start walking. At least, I knew how to do that.

I was afraid to think what might lie ahead. Would I be rejected as a Mecca pilgrim? I wondered what the test would consist of, and when I would face the Muslim high court.

The Persian Muslim in our compartment came up to me at the rail. He greeted me, hesitantly, "Amer . . . America?" He indicated that he wanted me to come and have breakfast with him and his wife, on their rug. I knew that it was an immense offer he was making. You don't have tea with a Muslim's wife. I didn't want to impose, I don't know if the Persian understood or not when I shook my head and smiled, meaning "No, thanks." He brought me some tea and cookies, anyway. Until then, I hadn't even thought about eating.

Others made gestures. They would just come up and smile and nod at me. My first friend, the one who had spoken a little English, was gone. I didn't know it, but he was spreading the word of an American Muslim on the fourth tier. Traffic had begun to pick up, going past our compartment. Muslims in the *Ihram* garb, or still in their national dress, walked slowly past smiling. It would go on for as long as I was there to be seen. But I hadn't yet learned that I was the attraction.

I have always been restless, and curious. The *Mutawaf's* aide didn't return in the three hours he had said, and that made me nervous. I feared that he had given up on me as beyond help. By then, too, I was really getting hungry. All of the Muslims in the compartment had offered me food, and I had refused. The trouble was, I have to admit it, at that point I didn't know if I could go for their manner of eating. Everything was in one pot on the dining-room rug, and I saw them just fall right in, using their hands.

I kept standing at the tier railing observing the courtyard below, and I decided to explore a bit on my own. I went down to the first tier. I thought, then, that maybe I shouldn't get too far, someone might come for me. So I went back up to our compartment. In about forty-five minutes, I went back down. I went further this time, feeling my way. I saw a little restaurant in the courtyard. I went straight in there. It was jammed, and babbling with languages. Using gestures, I bought a whole roasted chicken and something like thick potato chips. I got back out in the courtyard and I tore up that chicken, using my hands. Muslims were doing the same thing all around me. I saw men at least seventy years old bringing both legs up under them, until they made a human knot of themselves, eating with as much aplomb and satisfaction as though they had been in a fine restaurant with waiters all over the place. All ate as One, and slept as One. Everything about the pilgrimage atmosphere accented the Oneness of Man under One God.

I made, during the day, several trips up to the compartment and back out in the courtyard, each time exploring a little further than before. Once, I nodded at two black men standing together. I nearly shouted when one spoke to me in British-accented English. Before their party approached, ready to leave for Mecca, we were able to talk enough to exchange that I was American and they were Ethiopians. I was heartsick. I had found two English-speaking Muslims at last—and they were leaving. The Ethiopians had both been schooled in Cairo, and they were living in Ryadh, the political capital of Arabia. I was later going to learn to my surprise that in Ethiopia, with eighteen million people, ten million are Muslims. Most people think Ethiopia is Christian. But only its government is Christian. The West has always helped to keep the Christian government in power.

I had just said my Sunset Prayer, *El Maghrib;* I was lying on my cot in the fourth-tier compartment, feeling blue and alone, when out of the darkness came a sudden light!

It was actually a sudden thought. On one of my venturings in the yard full of activity below, I had noticed four men, officials, seated at a table with a telephone. Now, I thought about seeing them there, and with *telephone,* my mind flashed to the connection that Dr. Shawarbi in New York had given me, the telephone number of the son of the author of the book which had been given to me. Omar Azzam lived right there in Jedda!

In a matter of a few minutes, I was downstairs and rushing to where I had seen the four officials. One of them spoke functional English. I excitedly showed him the letter from Dr. Shawarbi. He read it. Then he read it aloud to the other three officials. "A Muslim from America!" I could almost see it capture their imaginations and curiosity. They were very impressed. I asked the English-speaking one if the would please do me the favor of telephoning Dr. Omar Azzam at the number I had. He was glad to do it. He got someone on the phone and conversed in Arabic.

Dr. Omar Azzam came straight to the airport. With the four officials beaming, he wrung my hand in welcome, a young, tall, powerfully built man. I'd say he was six foot three. He had an extremely polished manner. In America, he would have been called a white man, but — it struck me, hard and instantly — from the way he acted, I had no *feeling* of him being a white man. "Why didn't you call before?" he demanded of me. He showed some identification to the four officials, and he used their phone. Speaking in Arabic, he was talking with some airport officials. "Come!" he said.

In something less than half an hour, he had gotten me released, my suitcase and passport had been retrieved from Customs, and we were in Dr. Azzam's car, driving through the city of Jedda, with me dressed in the *Ihram* two towels and sandals. I was speechless at the man's attitude, and at my own physical feeling of no difference between us as human beings. I had heard for years of Muslim hospitality, but one couldn't quite imagine such warmth. I asked questions. Dr. Azzam was a Swiss-trained engineer. His field was city planning. The Saudi Arabian government had borrowed him from the United Nations to direct all of the reconstruction work being done on Arabian holy places. And Dr. Azzam's sister was the wife of Prince Faisal's son. I was in a car with the brother-in-law of the son of the ruler of Arabia. Nor was that all that Allah had done. "My father will be so happy to meet you," said Dr. Azzam. The author who had sent me the book!

I asked questions about his father. Abd ir-Rahman Azzam was known as Azzam Pasha, or Lord Azzam, until the Egyptian revolution, when President Nasser eliminated all "Lord" and "Noble" titles. "He should be at my home when we get there," Dr. Azzam said. "He spends much time in New York with his United Nations work, and he has followed you with great interest."

I was speechless.

It was early in the morning when we reached Dr. Azzam's home. His father was there, his father's brother, a chemist, and another friend —all up that early, waiting. Each of them embraced me as though I were a long-lost child. I had never seen these men before in my life, and they treated me so good! I am going to tell you that I had never been so honored in my life, nor had I ever received such true hospitality.

A servant brought tea and coffee, and disappeared. I was urged to make myself comfortable. No women were anywhere in view. In Arabia, you could easily think there were no females.

Dr. Abd ir-Rahman Azzam dominated the conversation. Why hadn't I called before? They couldn't understand why I hadn't. Was I comfortable? They seemed embarrassed that I had spent the time at the airport; that I had been delayed in getting to Mecca. No matter how I protested that I felt no inconvenience, that I was fine, they would not hear it. "You must rest," Dr. Azzam said. He went to use the telephone.

I didn't know what this distinguished man was doing. I had no dream. When I was told that I would be brought back for dinner that evening, and that, meanwhile, I should get back in the car, how could I have realized that I was about to see the epitome of Muslim hospitality?

Abd ir-Rahman Azzam, when at home, lived in a suite at the Jedda Palace Hotel. Because I had come to them with a letter from a friend, he was going to stay at his son's home, and let me use his suite, until I could get on to Mecca.

When I found out, there was no use protesting: I was in the suite; young Dr. Azzam was gone; there was no one to protest to. The three-room suite had a bathroom that was as big as a double at the New York Hilton. It was suite number 214. There was even a porch outside, affording a beautiful view of the ancient Red Sea city.

There had never before been in my emotions such an impulse to pray — and I did, prostrating myself on the living-room rug.

Nothing in either of my two careers as a black man in America had served to give me any idealistic tendencies. My instincts automatically examined the reasons, the motives, of anyone who did anything they didn't have to do for me. Always in my life, if it was any white person, I could see a selfish motive.

But there in that hotel that morning, a telephone call and a few hours away from the cot on the fourth-floor tier of the dormitory, was one of the few times I had been so awed that I was totally without resistance. That white man — at least he would have been considered "white" in America — related to Arabia's ruler, to whom he was a close adviser, truly an international man, with nothing in the world to gain, had given up his suite to me, for my transient comfort. He had *nothing* to gain. He didn't need me. He had everything. In fact, he had more to lose than gain. He had followed the American press about me. If he did that, he knew there was only stigma attached to me. I was supposed to have horns. I was a "racist." I was "anti-white" — and he from all appearances was white. I was supposed to be a criminal; not only that, but everyone was even accusing me of using his religion of Islam as a cloak for my criminal practices and philosophies. Even if he had had some motive to use me, he knew that I was separated from Elijah Muhammad and the Nation of Islam, my "power base," according to the press in America. The only organization that I had was just a few weeks old. I had no job. I had no money. Just to get over there, I had had to borrow money from my sister.

That morning was when I first began to reappraise the "white man." It was when I first began to perceive that "white man," as commonly used, means complexion only secondarily; primarily it described attitudes and actions. In America, "white man" meant specific attitudes and actions toward the black man, and toward all other non-white men. But in the Muslim world, I had seen that men with white complexions were more genuinely brotherly than anyone else had ever been.

That morning was the start of a radical alteration in my whole outlook about "white" men. . . .

I will never forget the dinner at the Azzam home. I quote my notebook again: "I couldn't say in my mind that these were 'white' men. Why, the men acted as if they were brothers of mine, the elder Dr. Azzam as if he were my father. His fatherly, scholarly speech. I *felt* like he was my father. He was, you could tell, a highly skilled diplomat, with a broad range of mind. His knowledge was so worldly. He was as current on world affairs as some people are to what's going on in their living room.

"The more we talked, the more his vast reservoir of knowledge and its variety seemed unlimited. He spoke of the racial lineage of the descendants of Muhammad the Prophet, and he showed how they were both black and white. He also pointed out how color, the complexities of color, and the problems of color which exist in the Muslim world, exist only where, and to the extent that, that area of the Muslim world has been influenced by the West. He said that if one encountered any differences based on attitude toward color, this directly reflected the degree of Western influence."

I learned during dinner that while I was at the hotel, the Hajj Committee Court had been notified about my case, and that in the morning I should be there. And I was.

The Judge was Sheikh Muhammad Harkon. The Court was empty except for me and a sister from India, formerly a Protestant, who had converted to Islam, and was, like me, trying to make the Hajj. She was brown-skinned, with a small face that was mostly covered. Judge Harkon was a kind, impressive man. We talked. He asked me some questions, having to do with my sincerity. I answered him as truly as I could. He not only recognized me as a true Muslim, but he gave me two books, one in English, the other in Arabic. He recorded my name in the Holy Register of true Muslims, and we were ready to part. He told me, "I hope you will become a great preacher of Islam in America." I said that I shared that hope, and I would try to fulfill it.

The Azzam family were very elated that I was qualified and accepted to go to Mecca. I had lunch at the Jedda Palace. Then I slept again for several hours, until the telephone awakened me.

It was Muhammad Abdul Azziz Maged, the Deputy Chief of Protocol for Prince Faisal. "A special car will be waiting to take you to Mecca, right after your dinner," he told me. He advised me to eat heartily, as the Hajj rituals require plenty of strength.

I was beyond astonishment by then.

Two young Arabs accompanied me to Mecca. A well-lighted, modern turnpike highway made the trip easy. Guards at intervals along the way took one look at the car, and the driver made a sign, and we were passed through, never even having to slow down. I was, all at once, thrilled, important, humble, and thankful.

Mecca, when we entered, seemed as ancient as time itself. Our car slowed through the winding streets, lined by shops on both sides and with buses, cars, and trucks, and tens of thousands of pilgrims from all over the earth were everywhere.

The car halted briefly at a place where a *Mutawaf* was waiting for me. He wore the white skullcap and long nightshirt garb that I had seen at the airport. He was a short, dark-skinned Arab, named Muhammad. He spoke no English whatever.

We parked near the Great Mosque. We performed our ablution and entered. Pilgrims seemed to be on top of each other, there were so many, lying, sitting, sleeping, praying, walking.

My vocabulary cannot describe the new mosque that was being built around the Ka'ba. I was thrilled to realize that it was only one of the tremendous rebuilding tasks under the direction of young Dr. Azzam, who had just been my host. The Great Mosque of Mecca, when it is finished, will surpass the architectural beauty of India's Taj Mahal.

Carrying my sandals, I followed the *Mutawaf*. Then I saw the Ka'ba, a huge black stone house in the middle of the Great Mosque. It was being circumambulated by thousands upon thousands of praying pilgrims, both sexes, and every size, shape, color, and race in the world. I knew the prayer to be uttered when the pilgrim's eyes first perceive the Ka'ba. Translated, it is "O God, You are peace, and peace derives from You. So greet us, O Lord, with peace." Upon entering the Mosque, the pilgrim should try to kiss the Ka'ba if possible, but if the crowds prevent him getting that close, he touches it, and if the crowds prevent that, he raises his hand and cries out "Takbir!" ("God is great!") I could not get within yards. "Takbir!"

My feeling there in the House of God was a numbness. My *Mutawaf* led me in the crowd of praying, chanting pilgrims, moving seven times around the Ka'ba. Some were bent and wizened with age; it was a sight that stamped itself on the brain. I saw incapacitated pilgrims being carried by others. Faces were enraptured in their faith. The seventh time around, I prayed two *Rak'a*, prostrating myself, my head on the floor. The first prostration, I prayed the Quran verse "Say He is God, the one and only"; the second prostration: "Say O you who are unbelievers, I worship not that which you worship. . . ."

As I prostrated, the *Mutawaf* fended pilgrims off to keep me from being trampled.

The *Mutawaf* and I next drank water from the well of Zem Zem. Then we ran between the two hills, Safa and Marwa, where Hajar wandered over the same earth searching for water for her child Ishmael.

Three separate times, after that, I visited the Great Mosque and circumambulated the Ka'ba. The next day we set out after sunrise toward Mount Arafat, thousands of us, crying in unison: *"Labbayka! Labbayka!"* and *"Allah Akbar!"* Mecca is surrounded by the crudest-looking mountains I have ever seen; they seem to be made of the slag from a blast furnace. No vegetation is on them at all. Arriving about noon, we prayed and chanted from noon until sunset, and the *asr* (afternoon) and *Maghrib* (sunset) special prayers were performed.

Finally, we lifted our hands in prayer and thanksgiving, repeating Allah's words: "There is no God but Allah. He has no partner. His are authority and praise. Good emanates from Him, and He has power over all things."

Standing on Mount Arafat had concluded the essential rites of being a pilgrim to Mecca. No one who missed it could consider himself a pilgrim.

The *Ihram* had ended. We cast the traditional seven stones at the devil. Some had their hair and beards cut. I decided that I was going to let my beard remain. I wondered what my wife Betty, and our little daughters, were going to say when they saw me with a beard, when I got back to New York. New York seemed a million miles away. I hadn't seen a newspaper that I could read since I left New York. I had no idea what was happening there. A Negro rifle club that had been in existence for over twelve years in Harlem had been "discovered" by the police; it was being trumpeted that I was "behind it." Elijah Muhammad's Nation of Islam had a lawsuit going against me, to force me and my family to vacate the house in which we lived on Long Island.

The major press, radio, and television media in America had representatives in Cairo hunting all over, trying to locate me, to interview me about the furor in New York that I had allegedly caused—when I knew nothing about any of it.

I only knew what I had left in America, and how it contrasted with what I had found in the Muslim world. About twenty of us Muslims who had finished the Hajj were sitting in a huge tent on Mount Arafat. As a Muslim from America, I was the center of attention. They asked me what about the Hajj had impressed me the most. One of the several who spoke English asked; they translated my answers for the others. My answer to that question was not the one they expected, but it drove home my point.

I said, "The *brotherhood!* The people of all races, colors, from all over the world coming together as *one!* It has proved to me the power of the One God."

What is the one, most important quality of the pilgrimage that helped Malcolm X realize what an ideal society would be like?

What happens to Malcolm X as result of his pilgrimage to Mecca? Do you think he underwent a transformation? Why or why not?

Try writing a description of an ideal human society. Write as if you are viewing this society from a point high above the earth.

The Steeple-Jack

Dürer would have seen a reason for living
    in a town like this, with eight stranded whales
to look at; with the sweet air coming into your house
on a fine day, from water etched
    with waves as formal as the scales
on a fish.

One by one in two's and three's, the seagulls keep
    flying back and forth over the town clock,
or sailing around the lighthouse without moving their wings—
rising steadily with a slight
    quiver of the body—or flock
mewing where

a sea the purple of the peacock's neck is
    paled to greenish azure as Dürer changed
the pine green of the Tyrol to peacock blue and guinea
gray. You can see a twenty-five-
    pound lobster; and fishnets arranged
to dry. The

whirlwind fife-and-drum of the storm bends the salt
    marsh grass, disturbs stars in the sky and the
star on the steeple; it is a privilege to see so
much confusion. Disguised by what
    might seem the opposite, the sea-
side flowers and

trees are favored by the fog so that you have
    the tropics at first hand: the trumpet-vine,

fox-glove, giant snap-dragon, a salpiglossis that has
spots and stripes; morning-glories, gourds,
        or moon-vines trained on fishing-twine
at the back

door; cat-tails, flags, blueberries and spiderwort,
        stripped grass, lichens, sunflowers, asters, daisies—
yellow and crab-claw ragged sailors with green bracts—toad-plant,
petunias, ferns; pink lilies, blue
        ones, tigers; poppies; black sweet-peas.
The climate

is not right for the banyan, frangipani, or
        jack-fruit trees; or an exotic serpent
life. King lizard and snake-skin for the foot, if you see fit;
but here they've cats, not cobras, to
        keep down the rats. The diffident
little newt

with white pin-dots on black horizontal spaced
        out bands lives here; yet there is nothing that
ambition can buy or take away. The college student
named Ambrose sits on the hillside
        with his not-native books and hat
and sees boats

at sea progress white and rigid as if in
        a groove. Liking an elegance of which
the source is not bravado, he knows by heart the antique
sugar-bowl shaped summer-house of
        interlacing slats, and the pitch
of the church

spire, not true, from which a man in scarlet lets
        down a rope as a spider spins a thread;
he might be part of a novel, but on the sidewalk a
sign says C. J. Poole, Steeple-Jack,
        in black and white; and one in red
and white says

Danger. The church portico has four fluted
     columns, each a single piece of stone, made
modester by white-wash. This would be a fit haven for
waifs, children, animals, prisoners,
     and presidents who have repaid
sin-driven

senators by not thinking about them. The
     place has a school-house, a post-office in a
store, fish-houses, hen-houses, a three-masted
     schooner on
the stocks. The hero, the student,
     the steeple-jack, each in his way,
is at home.

It could not be dangerous to be living
     in a town like this, of simple people,
who have a steeple-jack placing danger-signs by the church
while he is gilding the solid-
     pointed star, which on a steeple
stands for hope.

MARIANNE MOORE

The speaker in the poem is painting a word picture of a happy community.
What are its characteristics? How are these characteristics similar to those
of Odin's vision or of the island world described in "The Rose-Beetle Man"?

In this community everyone in his own way is "at home." In light of what
you have read in this book and from your own experience, what do you
think makes an individual feel at home?

A Human World

From Black Skin, White Masks
FRANTZ FANON
Translated by CHARLES LAM MARKMANN

I as a man of color do not have the right to seek to know in what respect my race is superior or inferior to another race.

I as a man of color do not have the right to hope that in the white man there will be a crystallization of guilt toward the past of my race.

I as a man of color do not have the right to seek ways of stamping down the pride of my former master.

I have neither the right nor the duty to claim reparation for the domestication of my ancestors.

There is no Negro mission; there is no white burden.

I find myself suddenly in a world in which things do evil; a world in which I am summoned into battle; a world in which it is always a question of annihilation or triumph.

I find myself—I, a man—in a world where words wrap themselves in silence; in a world where the other endlessly hardens himself.

No, I do not have the right to go and cry out my hatred at the white man. I do not have the duty to murmur my gratitude to the white man.

My life is caught in the lasso of existence. My freedom turns me back on myself. No, I do not have the right to be a Negro.

I do not have the duty to be this or that. . . .

If the white man challenges my humanity, I will impose my whole weight as a man on his life and show him that I am not that "sho' good eatin' " that he persists in imagining.

I find myself suddenly in the world and I recognize that I have one right alone: That of demanding human behavior from the other.

One duty alone: That of not renouncing my freedom through my choices.

I have no wish to be the victim of the *Fraud* of a black world.

My life should not be devoted to drawing up the balance sheet of Negro values.

There is no white world, there is no white ethic, any more than there is a white intelligence.

There are in every part of the world men who search.

I am not a prisoner of history. I should not seek there for the meaning of my destiny.

I should constantly remind myself that the real *leap* consists in introducing invention into existence.

In the world through which I travel, I am endlessly creating myself.

I am a part of Being to the degree that I go beyond it.

And, through a private problem, we see the outline of the problem of Action. Placed in this world, in a situation, "embarked," as Pascal would have it, am I going to gather weapons?

Am I going to ask the contemporary white man to answer for the slave-ships of the seventeenth century?

Am I going to try by every possible means to cause Guilt to be born in minds?

Moral anguish in the face of the massiveness of the Past? I am a Negro, and tons of chains, storms of blows, rivers of expectoration flow down my shoulders.

But I do not have the right to allow myself to bog down. I do not have the right to allow the slightest fragment to remain in my existence. I do not have the right to allow myself to be mired in what the past has determined.

I am not the slave of the Slavery that dehumanized my ancestors.

To many colored intellectuals European culture has a quality of exteriority. What is more, in human relationships, the Negro may feel himself a stranger to the Western world. Not wanting to live the part of a poor relative, of an adopted son, of a bastard child, shall he feverishly seek to discover a Negro civilization?

Let us be clearly understood. I am convinced that it would be of the greatest interest to be able to have contact with a Negro literature or architecture of the third century before Christ. I should be very happy to know that a correspondence had flourished between some Negro philosopher and Plato. But I can absolutely not see how this fact would change anything in the lives of the eight-year-old children who labor in the cane fields of Martinique or Guadeloupe.

No attempt must be made to encase man, for it is his destiny to be set free.

The body of history does not determine a single one of my actions. I am my own foundation.

And it is by going beyond the historical, instrumental hypothesis that I will initiate the cycle of my freedom.

The disaster of the man of color lies in the fact that he was enslaved.

The disaster and the inhumanity of the white man lie in the fact that somewhere he has killed man.

And even today they subsist, to organize this dehumanization rationally. But I as a man of color, to the extent that it becomes possible for me to exist absolutely, do not have the right to lock myself into a world of retroactive reparations.

I, the man of color, want only this:

That the tool never possess the man. That the enslavement of man by man cease forever. That is, of one by another. That it be possible for me to discover and to love man, wherever he may be.

The Negro is not. Any more than the white man.

Both must turn their backs on the inhuman voices which were those of their respective ancestors in order that authentic communication be possible. Before it can adopt a positive voice, freedom requires an effort at disalienation. At the beginning of his life a man is always clotted, he is drowned in contingency. The tragedy of the man is that he was once a child.

It is through the effort to recapture the self and to scrutinize the self, it is through the lasting tension of their freedom that men will be able to create the ideal conditions of existence for a human world.

Superiority? Inferiority?

Why not the quite simple attempt to touch the other, to feel the other, to explain the other to myself?

Was my freedom not given to me then in order to build the world of the *You?*

At the conclusion of this study, I want the world to recognize, with me, the open door of every consciousness.

My final prayer:

O my body, make of me always a man who questions!

Explain what Fanon means by: "The Negro is not. Any more than the white man." What does this tell us about the truly human society he calls for?

In the stories in the first four phases of comedy, we watched a young hero or heroine struggling to free himself from bondage to others or to something in himself. We have seen how the hero's fight for freedom to grow and to create can have an effect on the world around him. In the first two phases, he is mostly concerned with making room for himself, while those around him remain relatively unchanged. But the goal of the characters in the third phase is marriage, and that promises a new family, a society in miniature that will follow the hero's lead. In the fourth phase we see more and more people around the hero being caught up in his imaginative world and changed accordingly. In the fifth phase we reach a point where society itself might be said to be the hero. The foreground is now taken over by the vision of a whole society freed from bondage to fear, hatred, jealousy, division, and strife—all the forces that bind men and strangle their creative powers.

Now we discover that in order to survive, society, like the individual, must become flexible and adaptable. It must resist both the rigidity of its institutions and the attempts to divide and tear it apart. A comic society must be a tolerant society, one that welcomes all, or almost all, on equal terms. Its features look very much like those of the world of childhood that the narrator of "The Rose-Beetle Man" recreates for us, where all is delight in a fresh new world and in the free men and women who inhabit it.

It might even be said that American society has always had a comic model—the idea of democracy, though this may be more of an ideal than a reality. But even if it is not always a reality here and now, each person seeks to find or build a better society. Malcolm X believed that he found a more open society in Mecca.

This vision of a reborn society brings a sense of exaltation, as though we have been privileged to see a little further beyond the horizon than less fortunate men and women who are still bound to fear or hatred. It is the kind of exhilaration we might feel if, like Noah, we had miraculously survived a great flood, and now from a high place watched the waters recede and land reappear. From this perspective Odin's dream of the destruction of the human race resembles the way a nightmare seems when we awake in the sunshine of a bright morning. It is with that feeling that Odin sees a new race of men founding a beautiful city on Asgard's hill. Or like the steeple-jack in the poem, we gaze down serenely on the peacefulness of the little sea village and see that it is "a fit haven for waifs, children, animals, prisoners and presidents," where there is "nothing that ambition can buy or take away."

It is this sense of elevation, of release, that allows us to feel "free from greed among the greedy," and live "happily indeed though we call nothing our own," as the *Dhammapada* puts it. Looking out, by chance, upon the city from a high hotel window, Malcolm X feels this sense of exhileration. But it is not by chance that the concluding rites that admit him into the Muslim world take place on Mount Arafat. For from there he can see beyond the boundaries that, as Frantz Fanon puts it, "encase" man. From the vantage point of height it becomes clear that the happy ending of comedy has always been with us, and that sorrow, hatred, and tragedy are all like Odin's dream—a nightmare of destruction from which we will awake into reality.

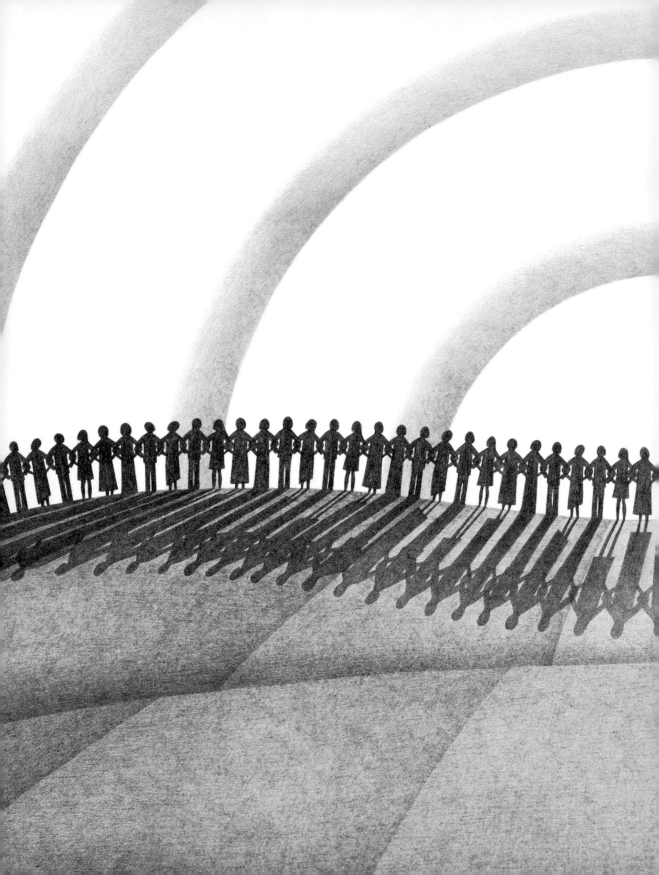

6
THE PEOPLE WILL LIVE ON

Jeannine Guertin

Carry On

One morning I woke up and I knew you were really gone.
A new day, a new way,
And new eyes to see the dawn.
Gone your way
I'll go mine and carry on.

The sky is clearing and the night has cried enough.
The sun he comes the world to soften up.
Rejoice, rejoice, we have no choice but to carry on.
The fortunes of fables are able to see the stars,
Now witness the quickness with which we carry on.
To sing the blues, you've got to live the dues
And carry on.

Carry on love is coming,
Love is coming to us all.

Where are you going now my love?
Where will you be tomorrow?
Will you bring me happiness?
Will you bring me sorrow?
Are the questions of a thousand dreams
What you do and what you see
Lover, can you talk to me?

Girl, when I was on my own
Chasing you down
What was it made you run
Tryin' your best just to get around
The questions of a thousand dreams
What you do and what you see
Lover, can you talk to me?

STEPHEN STILLS

Just One More Time

JOHN CHEEVER

There is no sense in looking for trouble, but in any big, true picture of the city where we all live there is surely room for one more word on the diehards, the hangers-on, the people who never got along and who never gave up, the insatiables that we have all known at one time or another. I mean the shoestring aristocrats of the upper East Side—the elegant, charming, and shabby men who work for brokerage houses, and their high-flown wives, with their thrift-shop minks and their ash-can fur pieces, their alligator shoes and their snotty ways with doormen and with the cashiers in supermarkets, their gold jewelry and their dregs of Je Reviens and Chanel. I'm thinking of the Beers now—Alfreda and Bob—who lived in the East Side apartment house that Bob's father used to own, surrounded by sailing trophies, autographed photographs of President Hoover, Spanish furniture, and other relics of the golden age. It wasn't much of a place, really—large and dark—but it was more than they could afford; you could tell by the faces of the doormen and the elevator operators when you told them where you were going. I suppose they were always two or three months behind with the rent and had nothing to spare for tips. Of course, Alfreda had been to school in Fiesole. Her father, like Bob's had lost millions and millions and millions of dollars. All her memories were thickly inlaid with patinas of bright gold: yesteryear's high bridge stakes, and how difficult it was to get the Daimler started on a rainy day, and picnics on the Brandy-wine with the du Pont girls.

She was a good-looking woman—long-faced and with that New England fairness that seems to state a tenuous racial claim to privilege.

She looked imperturbable. When they were on their uppers, she worked—first at the Steuben glass store, on Fifth Avenue, and then she went to Jensen's, where she got into trouble by insisting on her right to smoke. She went from there to Bonwit's, and from Bonwit's to Bendel's. Schwarz's took her on one Christmas, and she was on the street-floor glove counter at Saks the next Easter. She had a couple of children between jobs and she used to leave them in the care of an old Scotchwoman—an old family retainer from the good days—who seemed just as unable as the Beers to make an advantageous adjustment to change.

They were the kind of people that you met continually at railroad stations and cocktail parties. I mean Sunday-night railroad stations; weekend and season's-end places like the junction at Hyannis or Flemington; places like the station at Lake George, or Aiken and Greenville in the early spring; places like Westhampton, the Nantucket steamer, Stonington, and Bar Harbor; or, to go farther afield, places like Paddington Station, Rome, and the Antwerp night boat. "Hello! Hello!" they called across the crowd of travelers, and there he would be, in his white raincoat, with his stick and his Homburg, and there she was, in her mink or her ash-can fur piece. And in some ways the cocktail parties where your paths crossed were not so different, after all, from the depots, junctions, and boat trains where you met. They were the kind of party where the company is never very numerous and the liquor is never very good—parties where, as you drink and talk, you feel a palpable lassitude overtaking any natural social ardor, as if the ties of family, society, school, and place that held the group together were dissolving like the ice in your drink. But the atmosphere is not so much one of social dissolution as of social change, realignment—in effect, the atmosphere of travel. The guests seem to be gathered in a boat shed or at a railroad junction, waiting for the boat or the train to depart. Past the maid who takes the wraps, past the foyer and the fireproof door, there seems to lie a stretch of dark water, stormy water sometimes—the cry of the wind, the creak of iron sign hinges and the lights, the deckhand voices, and the soulful whistling of an approaching Channel boat.

One reason you always saw the Beers at cocktail parties and railroad stations was that they were always looking for somebody. They weren't looking for somebody like you or me—they were looking for the Marchioness of Bath—but any port in a storm. The way they used to come in to a party and stare around them is understandable—we all do it—but the way they used to peer at their fellow travelers on a station platform was something else. In any place where those two had to wait fifteen minutes or longer for a public conveyance they would turn the crowd inside out, peering under hatbrims and behind newspapers for somebody they might happen to know.

I'm speaking of the thirties and the forties now, the years—before and after the Big War—years when the Beers' financial problems must have been complicated by the fact that their children were old enough to go to expensive schools. They did some unsavory things; they kited checks, and, borrowing someone's car for a weekend, they ran it into a ditch and walked away, washing their hands of the whole thing. These tricks brought some precariousness to their social as well as their economic status, but they continued to operate on a margin of charm and expectation—there was Aunt Margaret in Philadelphia and Aunt Laura in Boston—and, to tell the truth, they were charming. People were always glad to see them, for, if they were the pathetic grasshoppers of some gorgeous economic summer, they somehow had it in their power to remind one of good things—good places, games, food, and company —and the ardor with which they looked for friends on railroad platforms could perhaps be accounted for by the fact that they were only looking for a world that they understood.

Then Aunt Margaret died, and this is how I discovered that interesting fact. It was in the spring, and my boss and his wife were sailing for England, and I went down to the boat one morning with a box of cigars and a historical romance. The ship was new, as I recall, with lots of drifters looking at the sets of Edna Ferber under lock and key in the library and admiring the dry swimming pools and the dry bars. The passageways were crowded, and every cabin in first class was full of flowers and of well-wishers drinking champagne at eleven o'clock on a gloomy morning, with the rich green soup of New York Harbor sending its tragic smell up to the clouds, I gave my boss and his wife their presents, and then, looking for the main deck, passed a cabin or suite where I heard Alfreda's boarding-school laugh. The place was jammed, and a waiter was pouring champagne, and when I had greeted my friends, Alfreda took me aside. "Aunt Margaret has departed this life," she said, "and we're *loaded* again. . . ." I had some champagne, and then the all-ashore whistle blew—vehement, deafening, the hoarse summons of life itself, and somehow, like the smell of harbor water, tragic, too; for, watching the party break up, I wondered how long Aunt

Margaret's fortune would last those two. Their debts were enormous, and their habits were foolish, and even a hundred thousand wouldn't take them far.

This idea seems to have stayed at the back of my mind, for at a heavyweight fight at Yankee Stadium that fall I thought I saw Bob wandering around with a tray of binoculars to rent. I called his name — I shouted — and it wasn't he, but the resemblance was so striking that I felt as if I *had* seen him, or had at least seen the scope of the vivid social and economic contrasts in store for such a couple.

I wish I could say that, leaving the theater one snowy evening, I saw Alfreda selling pencils on Forty-sixth Street and that she would return to some basement on the West Side where Bob lay dying on a pallet, but this would only reflect on the poverty of my imagination.

In saying that the Beers were the kind of people you met at railroad stations and cocktail parties, I overlooked the beaches. They were *very* aquatic. You know how it is. In the summer months, the northeastern coast up from Long Island and deep into Maine, including all the sea islands, seems to be transformed into a vast social clearinghouse, and as you sit on the sand listening to the heavy furniture of the North Atlantic, figures from your social past appear in the surf, as thick as raisins in a cake. A wave takes form, accelerates its ride over the shallows, boils, and breaks, revealing Consuelo Roosevelt and Mr. and Mrs. Dundas Vanderbilt, with the children of both marriages. Then a wave comes in from the right like a cavalry charge, bearing landward on the rubber raft Lathrope Macy with Emerson Crane's second wife, and the Bishop of Pittsburgh in an inner tube. Then a wave breaks at your feet with the noise of a slammed trunk lid and there are the Beers. "How nice to see you, how very *nice* to see you. . . ."

So the summer and the sea will be the setting for their last appearance — their last appearance for our purposes here, at any rate. We are in a small town in Maine — let's say — and decide to take the family for a sail and a picnic. The man at the inn tells us where there is a boat livery, and we pack our sandwiches and follow his directions to a wharf. We find an old man in a shack with a catboat to rent, and we make a deposit and sign a dirty paper, noticing that the old man, at ten in the morning, is drunk. He rows us out to the mooring in a skiff, and we say good-by, and then, seeing how dilapidated his catboat is, we call after him, but he has already headed for the mainland and is out of hearing.

The floor boards are floating, the rudder pin is bent, and one of the bolts in the rudder has rusted away. The blocks are broken, and when we pump her dry and hoist the sail, it is rotted and torn. We get under way at last—urged by the children—and sail out to an island and eat our picnic. Then we start home. But now the wind has freshened; it has backed around to the southwest; and when we have left the island our port stay snaps, and the wire flies upward and coils itself around the mast. We take down the sail and repair the stay with rope. Then we see that we are on an ebb tide and traveling rapidly out to sea. With the repaired stay we sail for ten minutes before the starboard stay gives. Now we are in trouble. We think of the old man in the shack, who holds the only knowledge of our whereabouts in his drunken head. We try to paddle with the floor boards, but we can make no headway against the sweep of the tide. Who will save us? The Beers!

They come over the horizon at dusk in one of those bulky cabin cruisers, with a banquette on the bridge and shaded lamps and bowls of roses in the cabin. A hired hand is at the helm, and Bob throws us a line. This is more than a chance reunion of old friends—our lives have been saved. We are nearly delirious. The hired hand is settled in the catboat, and ten minutes after we have been snatched from the jaws of death we are drinking Martinis on the bridge. They will take us back to their house, they say. We can spend the night there. And while the background and the appointments are not so different, their relationship to them has been revolutionized. It is *their* house, *their* boat. We wonder how—we gape—and Bob is civil enough to give us an explanation, in a low voice, a mumble, nearly, as if the facts were parenthetical. "We took most of Aunt Margaret's money and all of Aunt Laura's and a little something Uncle Ralph left us and invested it all in the market, you know, and it's more than tripled in the last two years. I've bought back everything Dad lost—everything I wanted, that is. That's my schooner over there. Of course, the house is new. Those are our lights." The afternoon and the ocean, which seemed so menacing in the catboat, now spread out around us with a miraculous tranquillity, and we settle back to enjoy our company, for the Beers are charming—they always were—and now they appear to be smart, for what else was it but smart of them to know that summertime would come again?

What personal qualities do the Beers possess that make them comic rather than tragic figures? How are the Beers like the speaker in "Carry On"?

Holiday Memory

DYLAN THOMAS

August Bank Holiday—a tune on an ice-cream cornet. A slap of sea and a tickle of sand. A fanfare of sunshades opening. A wince and whinny of bathers dancing into deceptive water. A tuck of dresses. A rolling of trousers. A compromise of paddlers. A sunburn of girls and a lark of boys. A silent hullabaloo of balloons.

I remember the sea telling lies in a shell held to my ear for a whole harmonious, hollow minute by a small, wet girl in an enormous bathing suit marked Corporation Property.

I remember sharing the last of my moist buns with a boy and a lion. Tawny and savage, with cruel nails and capacious mouth, the little boy tore and devoured. Wild as seedcake, ferocious as a hearthrug, the depressed and verminous lion nibbled like a mouse at his half a bun and hiccupped in the sad dusk of his cage.

I remember a man like an alderman or a bailiff, bowlered and collarless, with a bag of monkeynuts in his hand, crying "Ride 'em, cowboy!" time and again as he whirled in his chairaplane giddily above the upturned laughing faces of the town girls bold as brass and the boys with padded shoulders and shoes sharp as knives; and the monkeynuts flew through the air like salty hail.

Children all day capered or squealed by the glazed or bashing sea, and the steam-organ wheezed its waltzes in the threadbare playground and the waste lot, where the dodgems dodged, behind the pickle factory.

And mothers loudly warned their proud pink daughters or sons to put that jellyfish down; and fathers spread newspapers over their faces; and sandfleas hopped on the picnic lettuce; and someone had forgotten the salt.

In those always radiant, rainless, lazily rowdy and skyblue summers departed, I remember August Monday from the rising of the sun over the stained and royal town to the husky hushing of the roundabout music and the dowsing of the naphtha jets in the seaside fair: from bubble-and-squeak to the last of the sandy sandwiches.

There was no need, that holiday morning, for the sluggardly boys to be shouted down to breakfast; out of their jumbled beds they tumbled, and scrambled into their rumpled clothes; quickly at the bathroom basin they catlicked their hands and faces, but never forgot to run the water loud and long as though they washed like colliers; in front of the cracked looking glass, bordered with cigarette cards, in their treasure-trove bedrooms, they whisked a gap-tooth comb through their surly hair; and with shining cheeks and noses and tidemarked necks, they took the stairs three at a time.

But for all their scramble and scamper, clamor on the landing, catlick and toothbrush flick, hair-whisk and stair-jump, their sisters were always there before them. Up with the lady lark, they had prinked and frizzed and hot-ironed; and smug in their blossoming dresses, ribboned for the sun, in gymshoes white as the blanco'd snow, neat and silly with doilies and tomatoes they helped in the higgledy kitchen. They were calm; they were virtuous; they had washed their necks; they did not romp, or fidget; and only the smallest sister put out her tongue at the noisy boys.

And the woman who lived next door came into the kitchen and said that her mother, an ancient uncertain body who wore a hat with cherries, was having one of her days and had insisted, that very holiday morning, in carrying, all the way to the tramstop, a photograph album and the cutglass fruitbowl from the front room.

This was the morning when father, mending one hole in the thermos-flask, made three; when the sun declared war on the butter, and the butter ran; when dogs, with all the sweet-binned backyards to wag and sniff and bicker in, chased their tails in the jostling kitchen, worried sandshoes, snapped at flies, writhed between legs, scratched among towels, sat smiling on hampers.

And if you could have listened at some of the open doors of some of the houses in the street you might have heard:—

"Uncle Owen says he can't find the bottleopener—"

"Has he looked under the hallstand?"

"Willy's cut his finger—"

"Got your spade?"

"If somebody doesn't kill that dog—"

"Uncle Owen says why should the bottle-opener be under the hall-stand?"

   "Never again, never again—"

"I know I put the pepper somewhere—"

   "Willy's bleeding—"

"Look, there's a bootlace in my bucket—"

   "Oh come *on*, come *on*—"

"Let's have a look at the bootlace in your bucket—"

   "If I lay my hands on that dog—"

"Uncle Owen's found the bottle-opener—"

   "Willy's bleeding over the cheese—"

And the trams that hissed like ganders took us all to the beautiful beach.

There was cricket on the sand, and sand in the spongecake, sand-flies in the watercress, and foolish, mulish, religious donkeys on the unwilling trot. Girls undressed in slipping tents of propriety; under invisible umbrellas, stout ladies dressed for the male and immoral sea. Little naked navvies dug canals; children with spades and no ambition built fleeting castles; wispy young men, outside the bathing-huts, whistled at substantial young women and dogs who desired thrown stones more than the bones of elephants. Recalcitrant uncles huddled, over luke ale, in the tiger-striped marquees. Mothers in black, like wobbling mountains, gasped under the discarded dresses of daughters who shrilly braved the gobbling waves. And fathers, in the once-a-year sun, took fifty winks. Oh, think of all the fifty winks along the paper-bagged sand.

Licorice allsorts, and Welsh hearts, were melting. And the sticks of rock, that we all sucked, were like barbers' poles made of rhubarb.

In the distance, surrounded by disappointed theoreticians and an ironmonger with a drum, a cross man on an orange-box shouted that holidays were wrong. And the waves rolled in, with rubber ducks and clerks upon them.

I remember the patient, laborious, and enamoring hobby, or profession, of burying relatives in sand.

I remember the princely pastime of pouring sand, from cupped hands or bucket, down collars of tops of dresses; the shriek, the shake, the slap.

I can remember the boy by himself, the beachcombing lone-wolf, hungrily waiting at the edge of family cricket; the friendless fielder, the boy uninvited to bat or to tea.

I remember the smell of sea and seaweed, wet flesh, wet hair, wet bathing-dresses, the warm smell as of a rabbity field after rain, the smell of pop and splashed sunshades and toffee, the stable-and-straw smell of hot, tossed, tumbled, dug and trodden sand, the swill-and-gaslamp smell of Saturday night, though the sun shone strong, from the bellying beet-tents, the smell of the vinegar on shelled cockles, winkle-smell, shrimp-smell, the dripping-oily backstreet winter-smell of chips in newspapers, the smell of ships from the sundazed docks round the corner of the sandhills, the smell of the known and paddled-in sea moving, full of the drowned and herrings, out and away and beyond and further still toward the antipodes that hung their koala-bears and Maoris, kangaroos and boomerangs, upside down over the backs of the stars.

And the noise of pummeling Punch and Judy falling, and a clock tolling or telling no time in the tenantless town; now and again a bell from a lost tower or a train on the lines behind us clearing its throat, and always the hopeless, ravenous swearing and pleading of the gulls, donkey-bray and hawker-cry, harmonicas and toy trumpets, shouting and laughing and singing, hooting of tugs and tramps, the clip of the chair-attendant's puncher, the motorboat coughing in the bay, and the same hymn and washing of the sea that was heard in the Bible.

"If it could only just, if it could only just," your lips said again and again as you scooped, in the hob-hot sand, dungeons, garages, torture-chambers, train tunnels, arsenals, hangars for zeppelins, witches' kitchens, vampires' parlors, smugglers' cellars, trolls' grog-shops, sewers, under the ponderous and cracking castle, "If it could only just be like this for ever and ever amen." August Monday all over the earth, from Mumbles where the aunties grew like ladies on a seaside tree to brown, bear-hugging Henty-land and the turtled Ballantyne Islands.

"Could donkeys go on the ice?"

"Only if they got snowshoes."

We snowshoed a meek, complaining donkey and galloped him off in the wake of the ten-foot-tall and Atlas-muscled Mounties, rifled and pemmicaned, who always, in the white Gold Rush wastes, got their black-oathed-and-bearded Man.

"Are there donkeys on desert islands?"

"Only sort-of donkeys."

"What d'you mean, sort-of donkeys?"

"Native donkeys. They hunt things on them!"

"Sort-of walruses and seals and things?"

"Donkeys can't swim!"

"These donkeys can. They swim like whales, they swim like anything, they swim like—"

"Liar."

"Liar yourself."

And two small boys fought fiercely and silently in the sand, rolling
together in a ball of legs and bottoms. Then they went and saw the
pierrots, or bought vanilla ices.

Lolling or larriking that unsoiled, boiling beauty of a common day,
great gods with their braces over their vests sang, spat pips, puffed
smoke at wasps, gulped and ogled, forgot the rent, embraced, posed
for the dicky-bird, were coarse, had rainbow-colored armpits, winked,
belched, blamed the radishes, looked at Ilfracombe, played hymns on
paper and comb, peeled bananas, scratched, found seaweed in their
panamas, blew up paper bags and banged them, wished for nothing.
But over all the beautiful beach I remember most the children playing,
boys and girls tumbling, moving jewels, who might never be happy
again. And "happy as a sandboy" is true as the heat of the sun.

Dusk came down; or grew up out of the sands and the sea; or curled
around us from the calling docks and the bloodily smoking sun. The
day was done, the sands brushed and ruffled suddenly with a sea-
broom of cold wind. And we gathered together all the spades and
buckets and towels, empty hampers and bottles, umbrellas and fish-
frails, bats and balls and knitting, and went—oh, listen, Dad!—to the
Fair in the dusk on the bald seaside field.

Fairs were no good in the day; then they were shoddy and tired;
the voices of hoopla girls were crimped as elocutionists; no cannon-
ball could shake the roosting coconuts; the gondolas mechanically
repeated their sober lurch; the Wall of Death was safe as a governess-
cart; the wooden animals were waiting for the night.

But in the night, the hoopla girls, like operatic crows, croaked at
the coming moon; whizz, whirl, and ten for a tanner, the coconuts
rained from their sawdust like grouse from the Highland sky; tipsy
the griffon-prowed gondolas weaved on dizzy rails, and the Wall of
Death was a spinning rim of ruin, and the neighing wooden horses
took, to a haunting hunting tune, a thousand Beecher's Brooks as
easily and breezily as hooved swallows.

Approaching, at dusk, the Fair-field from the beach, we scorched
and gritty boys heard above the belaboring of the batherless sea the
siren voices of the raucous, horsy barkers.

"Roll up, roll up!"

In her tent and her rolls of flesh the Fattest Woman in the World sat sewing her winter frock, another tent, and fixed her little eyes, black-currants in blancmange, on the skeletons who filed and sniggered by.

"Roll up, roll up, roll up to see the Largest Rat on the Earth, the Rover or Bonzo of vermin."

Here scampered the smallest pony, like a Shetland shrew. And here the Most Intelligent Fleas, trained, reined, bridled, and bitted, minutely cavorted in their glass corral.

Round galleries and shies and stalls, pennies were burning holes in a hundred pockets. Pale young men with larded hair and Valentino-black sidewhiskers, fags stuck to their lower lips, squinted along their swivel-sighted rifles and aimed at ping-pong balls dancing on fountains. In knife-creased, silver-gray, skirt-like Oxford bags, and a sleeve-less, scarlet, zip-fastened shirt with yellow horizontal stripes, a collier at the strength-machine spat on his hands, raised the hammer, and brought it Thor-ing down. The bell rang for Blaina.

Outside his booth stood a bitten-eared and barndoor-chested pug with a nose like a twisted swede and hair that startled from his eye-brows and three teeth yellow as a camel's, inviting any sportsman to a sudden and sickening basting in the sandy ring or a quid if he lasted a round; and wiry, cocky, bowlegged, coal-scarred, boozed sportsmen by the dozen strutted in and reeled out; and still those three teeth re-mained, chipped and camel-yellow in the bored, teak face.

Draggled and stout-wanting mothers, with haphazard hats, hostile hatpins, buns awry, bursting bags, and children at their skirts like pop-filled and jam-smeared limpets, screamed, before distorting mirrors, at their suddenly tapering or tubular bodies and huge bal-looning heads, and the children gaily bellowed at their own reflected bogies withering and bulging in the glass.

Old men, smelling of Milford Haven in the rain, shuffled, badgering and cadging, round the edges of the swaggering crowd, their only wares a handful of damp confetti. A daring dash of schoolboys, safely, shoulder to shoulder, with their fathers' trilbies cocked at a desperate angle over one eye, winked at and whistled after the procession past the swings of two girls arm-in-arm: always one pert and pretty, and always one with glasses. Girls in skulled and crossboned tunnels shrieked, and were comforted. Young men, heroic after pints, stood up on the flying chairaplanes, tousled, crimson, and against the rules. Jaunty girls gave sailors sauce.

All the Fun of the Fair in the hot, bubbling night. The Man in the sand-yellow Moon over the hurdy of gurdies. The swingboats swimming to and fro like slices of the moon. Dragons and hippogriffs at the prows of the gondolas breathing fire and Sousa. Midnight roundabout riders tantivying under the fairy-lights, huntsmen on billygoats and zebras hallooing under a circle of glowworms.

And as we climbed home, up the gas-lit hill, to the still house over the mumbling bay, we heard the music die and the voices drift like sand. And we saw the lights of the Fair fade. And, at the far end of seaside field, they lit their lamps, one by one, in the caravans.

The writer is recalling a family holiday at the seaside in Wales. Does he describe a completely happy day? Do you think the actual day was as he described it? Why or why not? How does memory transform events in the past?

Why do you think recalling happy events of the past brings pleasure to the author in the present? How can memory conquer time? How can literature conquer time? Explain.

How do holidays transform certain days of the year in your own cultural tradition? How are holidays and their rituals related to the cycles of nature? What does the observance of holidays provide for the community?

The First Jasmines

Ah, these jasmines, these white jasmines!

I seem to remember the first day when I filled my hands with these jasmines, these white jasmines.

I have loved the sunlight, the sky and the green earth;

I have heard the liquid murmur of the river through the darkness of midnight;

Autumn sunsets have come to me at the bend of a road in the lonely waste, like a bride raising her veil to accept her lover.

Yet my memory is still sweet with the first white jasmines that I held in my hands when I was a child.

Many a glad day has come in my life, and I have laughed with merrymakers on festival nights.

On gray mornings of rain I have crooned many an idle song.

I have worn round my neck the evening wreath of *bakulas* woven by the hand of love.

Yet my heart is sweet with the memory of the first fresh jasmines that filled my hands when I was a child.

RABINDRANATH TAGORE

Try to recall, as this poet does, things and events from the past that make your "memory sweet." Combine them in a poem or collage of your own.

A Refusal to Mourn the Death, by Fire, of a Child in London

Never until the mankind making
Bird beast and flower
Fathering and all humbling darkness
Tells with silence the last light breaking
And the still hour
Is come of the sea tumbling in harness

And I must enter again the round
Zion of the water bead
And the synagogue of the ear of corn
Shall I let pray the shadow of a sound
Or sow my salt seed
In the least valley of sackcloth to mourn

The majesty and burning of the child's death.
I shall not murder
The mankind of her going with a grave truth
Nor blaspheme down the stations of the breath
With any further
Elegy of innocence and youth.

Deep with the first dead lies London's daughter,
Robed in the long friends,
The grains beyond age, the dark veins of her mother,
Secret by the unmourning water
Of the riding Thames.
After the first death, there is no other.

DYLAN THOMAS

Why does the poet refuse to mourn the dead girl?

Report on the Barnhouse Effect

KURT VONNEGUT, JR.

Let me begin by saying that I don't know any more about where Professor Arthur Barnhouse is hiding than anyone else does. Save for one short, enigmatic message left in my mailbox on Christmas Eve, I have not heard from him since his disappearance a year and a half ago.

What's more, readers of this article will be disappointed if they expect to learn how *they* can bring about the so-called "Barnhouse Effect." If I were able and willing to give away that secret, I would certainly be something more important than a psychology instructor.

I have been urged to write this report because I did research under the professor's direction and because I was the first to learn of his astonishing discovery. But while I was his student I was never entrusted with knowledge of how the mental forces could be released and directed. He was unwilling to trust anyone with that information.

I would like to point out that the term "Barnhouse Effect" is a creation of the popular press, and was never used by Professor Barnhouse. The name he chose for the phenomenon was *"dynamopsychism,"* or *force of the mind.*

I cannot believe that there is a civilized person yet to be convinced that such a force exists, what with its destructive effects on display in every national capital. I think humanity has always had an inkling that this sort of force does exist. It has been common knowledge that some people are luckier than others with inanimate objects like dice. What Professor Barnhouse did was to show that such "luck" was a measurable force, which in his case could be enormous.

By my calculations, the professor was about fifty-five times more powerful than a Nagasaki-type atomic bomb at the time he went into hiding. He was not bluffing when, on the eve of "Operation Brainstorm," he told General Honus Barker: "Sitting here at the dinner table, I'm pretty sure I can flatten anything on earth—from Joe Louis to the Great Wall of China."

There is an understandable tendency to look upon Professor Barnhouse as a supernatural visitation. The First Church of Barnhouse in Los Angeles has a congregation numbering in the thousands. He is godlike in neither appearance nor intellect. The man who disarms the world is single, shorter than the average American male, stout, and averse to exercise. His I.Q. is 143, which is good but certainly not sensational. He is quite mortal, about to celebrate his fortieth birthday, and in good health. If he is alone now, the isolation won't bother him too much. He was quiet and shy when I knew him, and seemed to find more companionship in books and music than in his associations at the college.

Neither he nor his powers fall outside the sphere of Nature. His dynamopsychic radiations are subject to many known physical laws that apply in the field of radio. Hardly a person has not now heard the snarl of "Barnhouse static" on his home receiver. The radiations are affected by sunspots and variations in the ionosphere.

However, they differ from ordinary broadcast waves in several important ways. Their total energy can be brought to bear on any single point the professor chooses, and that energy is undiminished by distance. As a weapon, then, dynamopsychism has an impressive advantage over bacteria and atomic bombs, beyond the fact that it costs nothing to use: it enables the professor to single out critical individuals and objects instead of slaughtering whole populations in the process of maintaining international equilibrium.

As General Honus Barker told the House Military Affairs Committee: "Until someone finds Barnhouse, there is no defense against the Barnhouse Effect." Efforts to "jam" or block the radiations have failed. Premier Slezak could have saved himself the fantastic expense of his "Barnhouseproof" shelter. Despite the shelter's twelve-foot-thick lead armor, the premier has been floored twice while in it.

There is talk of screening the population for men potentially as powerful dynamopsychically as the professor. Senator Warren Foust demanded funds for this purpose last month, with the passionate declaration: "He who rules the Barnhouse Effect rules the world!"

Commissar Kropotnik said much the same thing, so another costly armaments race, with a new twist, has begun.

This race at least has its comical aspects. The world's best gamblers are being coddled by governments like so many nuclear physicists. There may be several hundred persons with dynamopsychic talent on earth, myself included. But, without knowledge of the professor's technique, they can never be anything but dice-table despots. With the secret, it would probably take them ten years to become dangerous weapons. It took the professor that long. He who rules the Barnhouse Effect is Barnhouse and will be for some time.

Popularly, the "Age of Barnhouse" is said to have begun a year and a half ago, on the day of Operation Brainstorm. That was when dynamopsychism became significant politically. Actually, the phenomenon was discovered in May, 1942, shortly after the professor turned down a direct commission in the Army and enlisted as an artillery private. Like X-rays and vulcanized rubber, dynamopsychism was discovered by accident.

From time to time Private Barnhouse was invited to take part in games of chance by his barrack mates. He knew nothing about the games, and usually begged off. But one evening, out of social grace, he agreed to shoot craps. It was a terrible or wonderful game that he played, depending upon whether or not you like the world as it now is.

"Shoot sevens, Pop," someone said.

So "Pop" shot sevens—ten in a row to bankrupt the barracks. He retired to his bunk and, as a mathematical exercise, calculated the odds against his feat on the back of a laundry slip. His chances of doing it, he found, were one in almost ten million! Bewildered, he borrowed a pair of dice from the man in the bunk next to his. He tried to roll sevens again, but got only the usual assortment of numbers. He lay back for a moment, then resumed his toying with the dice. He rolled ten more sevens in a row.

He might have dismissed the phenomenon with a low whistle. But the professor instead mulled over the circumstances surrounding his two lucky streaks. There was one single factor in common: on both occasions, *the same thought train had flashed through his mind just before he threw the dice.* It was that thought train which aligned the professor's brain cells into what has since become the most powerful weapon on earth.

The soldier in the next bunk gave dynamopsychism its first token of respect. In an understatement certain to bring wry smiles to the faces of the world's dejected demagogues, the soldier said, "You're hotter'n a two-dollar pistol, Pop." Professor Barnhouse was all of that. The dice that did his bidding weighed but a few grams, so the forces involved were minute; but the unmistakable fact that there were such forces was earth-shaking.

Professional caution kept him from revealing his discovery immediately. He wanted more facts and a body of theory to go with them. Later, when the atomic bomb was dropped on Hiroshima, it was fear that made him hold his peace. At no time were his experiments, as Premier Slezak called them, "a bourgeois plot to shackle the true democracies of the world." The professor didn't know where they were leading.

In time, he came to recognize another startling feature of dynamopsychism: *its strength increased with use.* Within six months, he was able to govern dice thrown by men the length of a barracks distant. By the time of his discharge in 1945, he could knock bricks loose from chimneys three miles away.

Charges that Professor Barnhouse could have won the last war in a minute, but did not care to do so, are perfectly senseless. When the war ended, he had the range and power of a 37-millimeter cannon, perhaps —certainly no more. His dynamopsychic powers graduated from the small-arms class only after his discharge and return to Wyandotte College.

I enrolled in the Wyandotte Graduate School two years after the professor had rejoined the faculty. By chance, he was assigned as my thesis adviser. I was unhappy about the assignment, for the professor was, in the eyes of both colleagues and students, a somewhat ridiculous figure. He missed classes or had lapses of memory during lectures. When I arrived, in fact, his shortcomings had passed from the ridiculous to the intolerable.

"We're assigning you to Barnhouse as a sort of temporary thing," the dean of social studies told me. He looked apologetic and perplexed. "Brilliant man, Barnhouse, I guess. Difficult to know since his return, perhaps, but his work before the war brought a great deal of credit to our little school."

When I reported to the professor's laboratory for the first time, what I saw was more distressing than the gossip. Every surface in the room was covered with dust; books and apparatus had not been disturbed for months. The professor sat napping at his desk when I entered. The only signs of recent activity were three overflowing ashtrays, a pair of scissors, and a morning paper with several items clipped from its front page.

As he raised his head to look at me, I saw that his eyes were clouded with fatigue. "Hi," he said, "just can't seem to get my sleeping done at night." He lighted a cigarette, his hands trembling slightly. "You are the young man I'm supposed to help with a thesis?"

"Yes, sir," I said. In minutes he converted my misgivings to alarm.

"You an overseas veteran?" he asked.

"Yes, sir."

"Not much left over there, is there?" He frowned. "Enjoy the last war?"

"No, sir."

"Look like another war to you?"

"Kind of, sir."

"What can be done about it?"

I shrugged. "Looks pretty hopeless."

He peered at me intently. "Know anything about international law, the U.N., and all that?"

"Only what I pick up from the papers."

"Same here," he sighed. He showed me a fat scrapbook packed with newspaper clippings. "Never used to pay any attention to international politics. Now I study them the way I used to study rats in mazes. Everybody tells me the same thing—'Looks hopeless.'"

"Nothing short of a miracle—" I began.

"Believe in magic?" he asked sharply. The professor fished two dice from his vest pocket. "I will try to roll twos," he said. He rolled twos three times in a row. "One chance in about 47,000 of that happening. There's a miracle for you." He beamed for an instant, then brought the interview to an end, remarking that he had a class which had begun ten minutes ago.

He was not quick to take me into his confidence, and he said no more about his trick with the dice. I assumed they were loaded, and forgot about them. He set me the task of watching male rats cross electrified metal strips to get to food or female rats—an experiment that had been done to everyone's satisfaction in the nineteen-thirties. As though the pointlessness of my work were not bad enough, the professor annoyed me further with irrelevant questions. His favorites were: "Think we should have dropped the atomic bomb on Hiroshima?" and "Think every new piece of scientific information is a good thing for humanity?"

However, I did not feel put upon for long. "Give those poor animals a holiday," he said one morning, after I had been with him only a month. "I wish you'd help me look into a more interesting problem—namely, my sanity."

I returned the rats to their cages.

"What you must do is simple," he said, speaking softly. "Watch the inkwell on my desk. If you see nothing happen to it, say so, and I'll go quietly—relieved, I might add—to the nearest sanitarium."

I nodded uncertainly.

He locked the laboratory door and drew the blinds, so that we were in twilight for a moment. "I'm odd, I know," he said. "It's fear of myself that's made me odd."

"I've found you somewhat eccentric, perhaps, but certainly not—"

"If nothing happens to that inkwell, 'crazy as a bedbug' is the only description of me that will do," he interrupted, turning on the overhead lights. His eyes narrowed. "To give you an idea of how crazy, I'll tell you what's been running through my mind when I should have been sleeping. I think maybe I can save the world. I think maybe I can make every nation a *have* nation, and do away with war for good. I think maybe I can clear roads through jungles, irrigate deserts, build dams overnight."

"Yes, sir."

"Watch the inkwell!"

Dutifully and fearfully I watched. A high-pitched humming seemed to come from the inkwell; then it began to vibrate alarmingly, and finally to bound about the top of the desk, making two noisy circuits. It stopped, hummed again, glowed red, then popped in splinters with a blue-green flash.

Perhaps my hair stood on end. The professor laughed gently. "Magnets?" I managed to say at last.

"Wish to heaven it were magnets," he murmured. It was then that he told me of dynamopsychism. He knew only that there was such a force; he could not explain it. "It's me and me alone—and it's awful."

"I'd say it was amazing and wonderful!" I cried.

"If all I could do was make inkwells dance, I'd be tickled silly with the whole business." He shrugged disconsolately. "But I'm no toy, my boy. If you like, we can drive around the neighborhood, and I'll show you what I mean." He told me about pulverized boulders, shattered oaks, and abandoned farm buildings demolished within a fifty-mile radius of the campus. "Did every bit of it sitting right here, just think-ing—not even thinking hard."

He scratched his head nervously. "I have never dared to concentrate as hard as I can for fear of the damage I might do. I'm to the point where a mere whim is a blockbuster." There was a depressing pause. "Up until a few days ago, I've thought it best to keep my secret for fear of what use it might be put to," he continued. "Now I realize that I haven't any more right to it than a man has a right to own an atomic bomb."

He fumbled through a heap of papers. "This says about all that needs to be said, I think." He handed me a draft of a letter to the Secre-tary of State.

Dear Sir:

I have discovered a new force which costs nothing to use, and which is probably more important than atomic energy. I should like to see it used most effectively in the cause of peace, and am, therefore, requesting your advice as to how this might best be done.

Yours truly,
A. Barnhouse.

"I have no idea what will happen next," said the professor.

There followed three months of perpetual nightmare, wherein the nation's political and military great came at all hours to watch the pro-fessor's tricks.

We were quartered in an old mansion near Charlottesville, Vir-ginia, to which we had been whisked five days after the letter was mailed. Surrounded by barbed wire and twenty guards, we were la-beled "Project Wishing Well," and were classified as Top Secret.

For companionship we had General Honus Barker and the State De-partment's William K. Cuthrell. For the professor's talk of peace-through-plenty they had indulgent smiles and much discourse on practical measures and realistic thinking. So treated, the professor, who had at first been almost meek, progressed in a matter of weeks toward stubbornness.

He had agreed to reveal the thought train by means of which he aligned his mind into a dynamopsychic transmitter. But, under Cuth-rell's and Barker's nagging to do so, he began to hedge. At first he de-

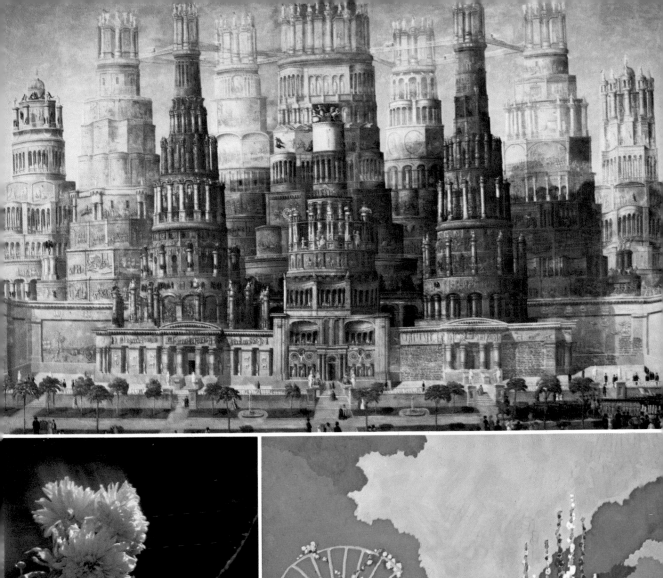

"Bombers sighted!" cried the Aleutian observers.

"Rockets away!" barked the New Mexico radio operator.

All of us looked quickly at the big electric clock over the mantel, while the professor, a half-smile on his face, continued to watch the television sets. In hollow tones, the general counted away the seconds remaining. "Five . . . four . . . three . . . two . . . one . . . *Concentrate!*"

Professor Barnhouse closed his eyes, pursed his lips, and stroked his temples. He held the position for a minute. The television images were scrambled, and the radio signals were drowned in the din of Barnhouse static. The professor sighed, opened his eyes, and smiled confidently.

"Did you give it everything you had?" asked the general dubiously.

"I was wide open," the professor replied.

The television images pulled themselves together, and mingled cries of amazement came over the radios tuned to the observers. The Aleutian sky was streaked with the smoke trails of bombers screaming down in flames. Simultaneously, there appeared high over the rocket target a cluster of white puffs, followed by faint thunder.

General Barker shook his head happily. "By George!" he crowed. "Well, sir, by George, by George, by George!"

"Look!" shouted the admiral seated next to me. "The fleet—it wasn't touched!"

"The guns seem to be drooping," said Mr. Cuthrell.

We left the bench and clustered about the television sets to examine the damage more closely. What Mr. Cuthrell had said was true. The ships' guns curved downward, their muzzles resting on the steel decks. We in Virginia were making such a hullabaloo that it was impossible to hear the radio reports. We were so engrossed, in fact, that we didn't miss the professor until two short snarls of Barnhouse static shocked us into sudden silence. The radios went dead.

We looked around apprehensively. The professor was gone. A harassed guard threw open the front door from the outside to yell that the professor had escaped. He brandished his pistol in the direction of the gates, which hung open, limp and twisted. In the distance, a speeding government station wagon topped a ridge and dropped from sight into the valley beyond. The air was filled with choking smoke, for every vehicle on the grounds was ablaze. Pursuit was impossible.

"What in God's name got into him?" bellowed the general.

Mr. Cuthrell, who had rushed out onto the front porch, now slouched back into the room, reading a penciled note as he came. He thrust the note into my hands. "The good man left this billet-doux under the door knocker. Perhaps our young friend here will be kind enough to read it to you gentlemen, while I take a restful walk through the woods."

"Gentlemen," I read aloud, "*As the first superweapon with a conscience, I am removing myself from your national defense stockpile. Setting a new precedent in the behavior of ordnance, I have humane reasons for going off. A. Barnhouse.*"

Since that day, of course, the professor has been systematically destroying the world's armaments, until there is now little with which to equip an army other than rocks and sharp sticks. His activities haven't exactly resulted in peace, but have, rather, precipitated a bloodless and entertaining sort of war that might be called the "War of the Tattletales." Every nation is flooded with enemy agents whose sole mission is to locate military equipment, which is promptly wrecked when it is brought to the professor's attention in the press.

Just as every day brings news of more armaments pulverized by dynamopsychism, so has it brought rumors of the professor's whereabouts. During last week alone, three publications carried articles proving variously that he was hiding in an Inca ruin in the Andes, in the sewers of Paris, and in the unexplored lower chambers of Carlsbad Caverns. Knowing the man, I am inclined to regard such hiding places as unnecessarily romantic and uncomfortable. While there are numerous persons eager to kill him, there must be millions who would care for him and hide him. I like to think that he is in the home of such a person.

One thing is certain: at this writing, Professor Barnhouse is not dead, Barnhouse static jammed broadcasts not ten minutes ago. In the eighteen months since his disappearance, he has been reported dead some half-dozen times. Each report has stemmed from the death of an unidentified man resembling the professor, during a period free of the static. The first three reports were followed at once by renewed talk of rearmament and recourse to war. The saber-rattlers have learned how imprudent premature celebrations for the professor's demise can be.

Many a stout-hearted patriot has found himself prone in the tangled bunting and timbers of a smashed reviewing stand, seconds after having announced that the arch-tyranny of Barnhouse was at an end. But those who would make war if they could, in every country in the world, wait in sullen silence for what must come—the passing of Professor Barnhouse.

To ask how much longer the professor will live is to ask how much longer we must wait for the blessings of another world war. He is of short-lived stock: his mother lived to be fifty-three, his father to be forty-nine, and the life-spans of his grandparents on both sides were of the same order. He might be expected to live, then, for perhaps fifteen years more, if he can remain hidden from his enemies. When one considers the number and vigor of these enemies, however, fifteen years seems an extraordinary length of time, which might better be revised to fifteen days, hours, or minutes.

The professor knows that he cannot live much longer. I say this because of the message left in my mailbox on Christmas Eve. Unsigned, typewritten on a soiled scrap of paper, the note consisted of ten sentences. The first nine of these, each a bewildering tangle of psychological jargon and references to obscure texts, made no sense to me at first reading. The tenth, unlike the rest, was simply constructed and contained no large words—but its irrational content made it the most puzzling and bizarre sentence of all. I nearly threw the note away, thinking it a colleague's warped notion of a practical joke. For some reason, though, I added it to the clutter on top of my desk, which included, among other mementos, the professor's dice.

It took me several weeks to realize that the message really meant something, that the first nine sentences, when unsnarled, could be taken as instructions. The tenth still told me nothing. It was only last night that I discovered how it fitted in with the rest. The sentence appeared in my thoughts last night, while I was toying absently with the professor's dice.

I promised to have this report on its way to the publishers today. In view of what has happened, I am obliged to break that promise, or release the report incomplete. The delay will not be a long one, for one of the few blessings accorded a bachelor like myself is the ability to move quickly from one abode to another, or from one way of life to another. What property I want to take with me can be packed in a few hours. Fortunately, I am not without substantial private means, which may take as long as a week to realize in liquid and anonymous form. When this is done, I shall mail the report.

I have just returned from a visit to my doctor, who tells me my health is excellent. I am young, and, with any luck at all, I shall live to a ripe old age indeed, for my family on both sides is noted for longevity.

Briefly, I propose to vanish.

Sooner or later, Professor Barnhouse must die. But long before then

I shall be ready. So, to the saber-rattlers of today—and even, I hope, of tomorrow—I say: Be advised. Barnhouse will die. But not the Barnhouse Effect.

Last night, I tried once more to follow the oblique instructions on the scrap of paper. I took the professor's dice, and then, with the last, nightmarish sentence flitting through my mind, I rolled fifty consecutive sevens.

Good-by.

How does the writer see the human race as having two conflicting kinds of impulses and desires? Which kind of influence does he think will eventually win out?

Personal death is not the end of all hope in comedy. In what way will Professor Barnhouse live on after his death?

since feeling is first

since feeling is first
who pays any attention
to the syntax of things
will never wholly kiss you;

wholly to be a fool
while Spring is in the world
my blood approves,
and kisses are a better fate
than wisdom
lady i swear by all flowers. Don't cry
—the best gesture of my brain is less than
your eyelid's flutter which says

we are for each other: then
laugh, leaning back in my arms
for life's not a paragraph

And death i think is no parenthesis

E. E. CUMMINGS

What does parenthesis imply? Why is death no parenthesis? What force, according to the poet, defeats death?

Ballad of the Clairvoyant Widow

A kindly Widow Lady, who lived upon a hill,
Climbed to her attic window and gazed across the sill.

    "O tell me, Widow Lady, what is it that you see,
    As you look across my city, in God's country?"

"I see ten million windows, I see ten thousand streets,
I see the traffic doing miraculous feats.

The lawyers all are cunning, the business men are fat,
Their wives go out on Sunday beneath the latest hat.

The kids play cops and robbers, the kids play mumbley-peg,
Some learn the art of thieving, and some grow up to beg;

The rich can play at polo, the poor can do the shag,
Professors are condoning the cultural lag.

I see a banker's mansion with twenty wood-grate fires,
Alone, his wife is grieving for what her heart desires.

Next door there is a love-nest of plaster board and tin,
The rats soon will be leaving, the snow will come in."

    "Clairvoyant Widow Lady, with an eye like a telescope,
    Do you see any sign or semblance of that thing called 'Hope'?"

"I see the river harbor, alive with men and ships,
A surgeon guides a scalpel with thumb and finger-tips.

I see grandpa surviving a series of seven strokes,
The unemployed are telling stale unemployment jokes.

The gulls ride on the water, the gulls have come and gone,
The men on rail and roadway keep moving on and on.

The salmon climb the rivers, the rivers nudge the sea,
The green comes up forever in the fields of our country."

THEODORE ROETHKE

Does the widow see anything that gives her hope? What does she see?
What do these things tell her about the nature of human life?

How is hope symbolized in the poem "The Steeple-Jack"? What other
symbols or images can you think of that might suggest "hope" to the human imagination?

The People Will Live On

The people will live on.
The learning and blundering people will live on.
They will be tricked and sold and again sold
And go back to the nourishing earth for rootholds,
The people so peculiar in renewal and comeback,
You can't laugh off their capacity to take it.
The mammoth rests between his cyclonic dramas.

The people so often sleepy, weary, enigmatic,
is a vast huddle with many units saying:
"I earn my living.
I make enough to get by
and it takes all my time.
If I had more time
I could do more for myself
and maybe for others.
I could read and study
and talk things over
and find out about things.
It takes time.
I wish I had the time."

The people is a tragic and comic two-face:
hero and hoodlum: phantom and gorilla twisting to moan with a gargoyle mouth: "They
buy me and sell me . . . it's a game . . .
sometime I'll break loose . . ."

Once having marched
Over the margins of animal necessity,

Over the grim line of sheer subsistence
    Then man came
To the deeper rituals of his bones,
To the lights lighter than any bones,
To the time for thinking things over,
To the dance, the song, the story,
Or the hours given over to dreaming,
    Once having so marched.

Between the finite limitations of the five senses
and the endless yearnings of man for the beyond
the people hold to the humdrum bidding of work and food
while reaching out when it comes their way
for lights beyond the prism of the five senses,
for keepsakes lasting beyond any hunger or death.
    This reaching is alive.
The panderers and liars have violated and smutted it.
    Yet this reaching is alive yet
    for lights and keepsakes.

        The people know the salt of the sea
        and the strength of the winds
        lashing the corners of the earth.
        The people take the earth
        as a tomb of rest and a cradle of hope.
        Who else speaks for the Family of Man?
        They are in tune and step
        with constellations of universal law.

        The people is a polychrome,
        a spectrum and a prism
        held in a moving monolith,
        a console organ of changing themes,
        a clavilux of color poems
        wherein the sea offers fog
        and the fog moves off in rain
        and the labrador sunset shortens
        to a nocturne of clear stars
        serene over the shot spray
        of northern lights.

The steel mill sky is alive.
The fire breaks white and zigzag
shot on a gun-metal gloaming.
Man is a long time coming.
Man will yet win.
Brother may yet line up with brother:

This old anvil laughs at many broken hammers.
There are men who can't be bought.
The fireborn are at home in fire.
The stars make no noise.
You can't hinder the wind from blowing.
Time is a great teacher.
Who can live without hope?

In the darkness with a great bundle of grief
the people march.
In the night, and overhead a shovel of stars for
keeps, the people march:
"Where to? what next?"

CARL SANDBURG

The people in this poem have many of the same qualities the Beers possess. What are these qualities?

Does the poet see the people as perfect heroes? What does he consider their greatest quality?

Do you think the story of the human race is a hopeful or comic story or a hopeless and tragic one? What makes you feel this way?

The comic view of life is essentially a long-term view. The ideas of destruction and death limit the tragic view. But comedy can conceive of death as something that, though it may be the end of an individual life, fits into the larger scheme of the history of the whole human race. And the history of mankind tells us what the title of Sandburg's poem announces—the people will live on.

The fifth phase of comedy views human life from the vantage point of a mountain top or some other high place. This implies a certain detachment from the strife provoked by jealousy, ambition, hatred, and greed, all tragic emotions. And from the perspective of that height, our imaginations are free to envision the creation of a new and tolerant human society.

The perspective of the sixth phase of comedy is not so much vertical as horizontal. Time provides the great comic promise. For tragic man, caught in the chains of necessity, time always seems to be running out. But from the comic perspective, there is always "one more time." As Sandburg tells us, "man is a long time coming" and so "time is a great teacher."

If time is a great teacher, then memory can be a source of renewal. Many of the pieces in this last phase involve the recollection of a life lived through and understood. There is comfort in the knowledge that memory tends to be selective, and that it often brings back to life happy times with greater clarity and vividness than times of trial and tragedy. So Dylan Thomas's memory of an August holiday keeps later life green, even for someone who "might never be happy again," at least in terms of external events. So too the memory of the "fresh jasmines that filled my hands when I was a child" continually refreshes the spirit of the poet, on "gray mornings" as well as "festival nights." And if memory is a reservoir of survival power for the individual, that power is increased a thousandfold when the individual life is placed in the context of the history of the human race, where there really always has been "one more time."

So it is the power of men and women to endure hardships and come out on the other side that counts. As the narrator of the story "Just One More Time" tells us, we can be thankful for "the people who never got along and who never gave up" and who are "smart enough to know that summertime would come again." These are the same people whom Sandburg praises as "so peculiar in renewal and comeback." It is essentially the same sea of throbbing humanity that Thomas remembers on the holiday beach of his childhood. And it is the promise of people like this, the "millions" who will shelter a Professor Barnhouse, who save all our lives, just as the Beers saved the life of the narrator in "Just One More Time."

Looking back over all the phases of comedy, we see that comedy is a literary form that deals with the adventures of a human society in search for survival and renewal. In the first, or ironic, phase the hero suggests the infancy of such a society. Like a child he is still rather powerless. The dying generation he is to replace is still strong and influential, and he is pretty much at its mercy. In the second phase the hero has gained some strength and power, but he is still too innocent, too ignorant of the cruel ways of the world, to change society totally. In the third and fourth phases, however, his power of renewal increases. As he marries and starts a new generation, more and more people around the hero are influenced by the vitality of his creative life and imaginative vision. In the fifth and sixth phases we witness the vision of the redeemed and renewed society itself.

This, then, is what comedy is about—the power of the human spirit to renew itself, and of the human animal to adapt himself, to resist deadening in-

Drawing by Charles Addams, © 1954, The New Yorker Magazine, Inc.

fluences, to rejoice in the transformation of the commonplace through imagination and love, to reclaim the past through memory, and to accept the oneness of all things and all men. The happy ending that all comedy demands is often thought of as unrealistic. But that is a matter of just how broad and long-term a view one takes of humanity. By demanding for his very human people a happy ending, the comic artist is like the Beers. He is resisting with all his inventive and imaginative power the attempts of disaster and death to write a tragic ending to the human story.

Index of Authors and Titles

"All for a lady fair," 99
"All the Sweet Buttermilk . . . ," 101
"And I saw a new heaven and a new earth . . . ," 220
Arsenic and Old Lace, from, 68
Aucassin and Nicolette, 140
Autobiography of Malcolm X, The, from, 237

Ballad of a Clairvoyant Widow, 295
Beautiful Changes, The, 184
Black Skins, White Masks, from, 255
Blake, William, 114
Blessing, A, 192
Body in the Window-seat, The, from Arsenic and Old Lace, 68
Boor, The, 126
Busu, 92

Carry On, 262
Catbird Seat, The, 82
Catch-22, from, 9
Changes IV, 233
Chase, Richard, 58
Cheever, John, 263
Chekhov, Anton, 126
Childhood's End, from, 203
Clarke, Arthur C., 203
Cummings, E. E., 56, 294
Cupid and Psyche, 115

Day, Clarence, 44
Dhammapada, the, from, 232
Durrell, Gerald, 221

Fanon, Frantz, 255
First Jasmines, The, 275

Gertrude the Governess; or Simple Seventeen, 147
Goodbye to All Cats, 27
Greatest Man in the World, The, 2

Hamilton, Edith, 189
Happiness, from the Dhammapada, 232
Heller, Joseph, 9
Holiday Memory, 268
Human World, A, from Black Skins, White Masks, 255

Importance of Being Earnest, The, from, 14
Isaiah 11:6–9, 231

John B. Sails, The, 12
Just One More Time, 263

Keary, A. and E., 218
Keene, Donald, 92
Kesselring, Joseph, 68
Key, The, 193

Lane, Richard, 65
Leacock, Stephen, 147

MacDonagh, Donagh, 101
Macpherson, Jay, 115
Madame La Gimp, 171
Making the Right Connections, from The Importance of Being Earnest, 14
Malcolm X, 237
Mecca, from The Autobiography of Malcolm X, 237
Moore, Marianne, 252
Muller, F. Max, 232
Mutsmag, 58
My Family and Other Animals, from, 221
My Father Enters the Church, 44

New Life at Kyerefaso, 212
New Race, A, from Childhood's End, 203
Nobody loses all the time, 56

People Will Live On, The, 297
Picard, Barbara Leonie, 140
Pratt, E. J., 166
Putting Winter to Bed, 166
Pygmalion and Galatea, 189

Refusal to Mourn the Death, by Fire, of a Child in London, A, 276
Report on the Barnhouse Effect, 277
Revelation 21:1–5, 220
Roethke, Theodore, 295
Rose-Beetle Man, The, from My Family and Other Animals, 221
Runyon, Damon, 171

Saikaku, Ihara, 65
Sandburg, Carl, 297
Since feeling is first, 294
Singer, Isaac Bashevis, 193
Song, 114
Steeple-Jack, The, 252
Stevens, Cat, 233

Stills, Stephen, 262
Stone, Brian, 99
Sutherland, Eufa Theodora, 212

Tagore, Rabindranath, 275
"The wolf also shall dwell with the lamb . . . ," 231
There Goes the Bride, from *The Graduate,* 156
Thomas, Dylan, 268, 276
Thurber, James, 2, 82

Umbrella Oracle, The, 65

Vision of Odin, The, 218
Vonnegut, Kurt, Jr., 277

Webb, Charles, 156
Wilbur, Richard, 184
Wilde, Oscar, 14
Wodehouse, P. G., 27
Wright, James, 192

Yarmolinsky, Avrahm, 126

A 3
B 4
C 5
D 6
E 7
F 8
G 9
H 0
I 1
J 2

304